# A FEW OF THE FIRST

By the same author:

THE TECHNIQUE OF TELEVISION ANNOUNCING
(Focal Press, 1966)

FOUR MEN WENT TO WAR
(Leo Cooper, 1987)

AIRCREW
(Leo Cooper, 1991)

# A FEW OF
# THE FIRST

The True Stories of the Men who
Flew in and before
The First World War

by

BRUCE LEWIS

LEO COOPER
LONDON

To
Paul Herbert George Lewis
In Tribute to His Bravery

First published in the United Kingdom in 1997 by
LEO COOPER
an imprint of
Pen & Sword Ltd
47 Church Street
Barnsley, South Yorkshire S70 2AS

Copyright © Bruce Lewis, 1997

ISBN 0 85052 509 8

A CIP catalogue record for this book is
available from the British Library

Printed in England by Redwood Books, Wiltshire.

# CONTENTS

# INTRODUCTION

It was almost by chance that I learned of an annual luncheon held at RAF Lyneham in Wiltshire. The local television station transmitted a brief news item showing a dozen elderly gentlemen sitting at the table attended by serving members of the Royal Air Force. The commentator told us that they were surviving aircrew of the Royal Flying Corps and the Royal Naval Air Service, men who had flown flimsy flying machines in the First World War above the trenches of the Western Front, over the cold seas surrounding the British Isles or casting shadows along inhospitable deserts where all too frequent engine failure could almost guarantee a lonely and unpleasant death. The 'junior' in this group was ninety-four years old, the oldest one hundred and one.

During research for previous books I have interviewed quite a few Second World War veterans who are now in their seventies or eighties, yet it never occurred to me that even a small band of aviators could still be living from that earlier war of more than three-quarters of a century ago.

Motivated at once to write a book in tribute to these men in their own lifetime, I was most kindly pointed in the right direction by the RAF authorities at RAF Lyneham; by Idris Heavers, of the Bath branch of the RFC/RNAS Association, who has co-ordinated these meetings for a number of years; by Norman Gilham, National Secretary of the RFC/RNAS Association, whose knowledge of his subject leaves me breathless. His lifelong enthusiasm was sparked off when, as a boy, he lived opposite the family of Major J. T. B. McCudden, VC, DSO*, MC*, MM, one of the RFC's top scoring fighter pilots. It would be difficult to imagine any lad being inspired by a more exemplary hero. Mr Gilham has been a constant support throughout the project and has also provided some unique photographs. I am indeed grateful for his unflagging interest and quiet encouragement.

Some of these stalwarts, who fought in an age that seems almost like a page from ancient history, are now too weary to go over the same ground yet again. They have patiently related their stories so many times, particularly in recent years, that it is only right in these circumstances to respect their wishes and leave them in peace.

Fortunately Margaret Brooks, Keeper of the Department of Sound Records at the Imperial War Museum, offered an alternative source of first hand knowledge without which it would have been difficult, if not impossible, to build up an authentic work on individual flying experiences during those dangerous years. She, and her helpful team, particularly administrative officer Rosemary Tudge, have done much to make *A Few of the First* a practical undertaking. This wealth of recorded material, not least that extracted by the Fred Morton collection at the Imperial War Museum, was generously made available to me, opening the door to a variety of personal accounts of what it was like to be involved in air fighting during that era.

I am most grateful to Andrew Nahum, Senior Curator of the Department of Aeronautics at the Science Museum, London, who, although engaged in a major display project at the time, still took the trouble to study my manuscript and from his expert knowledge thoughtfully suggested several important amendments.

My thanks are due also to Nick Lee of the University of Bristol Library for seeking out and placing in my care a rare book. Without his help the story of the Australian aviator, Fred Haig, could never have been completed.

And a special word of gratitude to Christina Gregory of the Royal Air Force Museum, Hendon, for seeking out some much needed photographs at the very last moment before publication.

I have tried to cover as many aspects of these early days as possible through the narratives of those who were there; it was an era when man really was clawing his way upwards with outstanding courage 'through hardship to the stars' and, poignantly, as so often during periods of rapid technical progress, with the single-minded aim of destroying his fellow man who just happened, at that particular time, to be on the 'wrong side'.

I salute Leo Cooper of Pen & Sword who contracted me to write the book based on the 'idea' long before he saw even one page of manuscript. Such faith is heartwarming and as rare in the modern world of publishing as would be the presence today of a Bleriot flying machine on the runway at Heathrow.

My final acknowledgements go to those men who, when very young, bravely carried out their duties under the most hazardous conditions. I owe them a debt of gratitude for the privilege of being able to record some of their stories in this book.

Bruce Lewis,
1 January, 1996

# CHAPTER ONE

# IN THE BEGINNING

When God banished those pioneer partners from the Garden of Eden it is easy to imagine Adam staring with longing at the ridge of mountains and saying to an unhappy Eve, 'If only we might fly like birds we could soar over that distant barrier and return to our beloved home.' How many times in human history have our ancestors looked up at a sky alive with flying feathered creatures and murmured, 'If only . . .'?

Five thousand years ago, above the steep cliffs of Crete, Daedalus and his son, Icarus, fashioned wings from feathers embedded in wax and strapped them to their arms. With the spirit of faith and courage that characterizes all such men of enterprise they launched themselves into the warm airs high above the sea. Daedalus, we are told, survived, but his son, revelling in his new-found freedom, flew too close to the sun; the heat melted the wax and Icarus, surrounded by a cloud of feathers, tumbled to his watery grave. A legend? Of course. But undeniably this story fascinated generation after generation to such an extent that those waters of the Aegean into which he plunged are known as the Icarian Sea to this day.

Even before the birth of Christ there are at least half a dozen names of men who were alleged to have taken to the air without the aids of Gods or magic. Relegate them all to the realms of myth if you like, yet the stories still stand witness to man's insatiable longing to soar above the earth.

I cannot walk past the ancient abbey of my adopted town, Malmesbury, in Wiltshire, the oldest borough in England and the country's first capital, without raising my eyes heavenwards and thinking of an Anglo-Saxon Benedictine monk named Eilmer who performed a truly extraordinary feat around the year 1010 when he was in his early twenties. Let me quote William of Malmesbury, the best informed and most reliable historian of his time, writing on the spot and not many years after the event:

'[Eilmer] ... in his early youth had hazarded a deed of remarkable boldness. He had by some means, I scarcely know what, fastened wings to his hands and feet so that, mistaking fable for truth, he might fly like Daedalus, and, collecting the breeze on the summit of a tower, he flew for more than the distance of a furlong. But agitated by the violence of the wind and the swirling of air, as well as by awareness of his rashness, he fell, broke his legs, and was lame ever after. He himself used to say that the cause of his failure was his forgetting to put a tail on the back part.'

Several people, including Professor Lynn White of the University of California, have made careful observations on the feasibility of Eilmer's achievement. Position and height of the then existing tower, plus the way in which the ground falls away to the river valley, plus the characteristics of the prevailing winds all point to a fairly loose-wing glide from the top of the building, at a glide angle of around 4.3 to 1, to the point of impact 660 feet below, where poor Eilmer made heavy impact with the ground.

The flying monk was too seriously crippled to make any further attempts at emulating the resident jackdaws, (still flying to this day), who seem to delight in soaring from the abbey along the hill, uplifted by the considerable turbulence of wind around the building as it funnels up the valley from the West.

He survived to a wise old age, continuing to stare heavenwards. Then, on an auspicious occasion he saw a comet trailing its long and fiery tail across the sky; this was Halley's comet. Bowing down the sage cried out, 'Thou art come! A cause of grief to many a mother art thou come; I have seen thee before,' (when he was a very small boy), 'but now I behold thee much more terrible, threatening to hurl destruction on this land.' This was in 1066, a few months before the Normans invaded England.

There are a number of stories referring to flights by men living in the Arab world but none of these come from reports written at the time. In fact one of the most interesting, a flight supposed to have been achieved by Ibn Firnas in 875 AD, near Cordoba, in which he completed a circular flight and landed back at his place of take-off, was not recorded until 750 years after the event and so has to be discounted, unlike Eilmer's effort, from serious historical consideration.

Two and a half centuries later would-be aeronauts and dreamers were still on the wrong track, believing that in order to fly they only had to imitate the birds by flapping a pair of wings. It took many more years before the message sank in that human arm muscles have neither the strength nor the constitution to support wings large enough to perform this feat. Nor was man's shallow chest suitably constructed for the job. To glide, yes. To flap, never.

In 1260 Roger Bacon was insisting that 'flying machines can be constructed so that man sits in the midst of the machine revolving some engine by which artificial wings are made to beat the air like a bird ... Such devices have long since been made, as well as in our own day, and it is certain that there is a flying machine. I have not seen one, nor have I known anyone who has seen one. But I know a wise man who has designed one.'

In 1504 an Italian ecclesiastic named Giovanni Damiani garbed himself in wings made of feathers and flung himself from the walls of Stirling Castle, of all places. He was lucky to survive with a broken leg. Damiani's scientific observation was that he had made an error in including hen's feathers in his wings, since hens have more affinity for scratching in dung-hills than for soaring to the heavens!

Perhaps the greatest stimulus to understanding the theory of flight came from the development of the kite. Flying a kite enabled man to study its reaction to air currents and the effect of wind at different altitudes. This was a form of flight that had long been known in China. Marco Polo writes of it, and even refers briefly to a bizarre form of man-carrying kite flown by merchant seamen about to set off on a voyage as a form of augury:

'The men of the ship will have a wicker framework, that is a grate of switches, and to each corner and side of that framework will be tied a cord, so that there are eight cords and all of these are tied at the other end to a long rope. Next they will find some fool or drunkard and lash

3

him to the frame, since no one in his right mind or with his wits about him would expose himself to that peril. This is done when the wind is high; when they raise the framework into the teeth of the wind and the wind lifts up the framework and carries it aloft, and the men hold it up by the long rope. If, while it is up in the air, the frame tips in the direction of the gale, they haul in the rope a bit, and then the frame straightens up and they pay out the rope and the frame goes higher. And if again it tips once more they pull in the rope until the frame is upright and climbing, and then they yield rope again, so that by this means it might go up until it could no longer be seen, if only the rope were long enough.'

In the pioneering days at the beginning of our own century many uninformed people no doubt placed our early flyers in the same category as those unfortunate Chinese aviators.

It is hardly likely that any of these past enthusiasts thought much about the practical uses of flight, even less its application in times of war; admirals and generals even at the start of the 20th century took long enough to cotton on to its potential.

It took the genius of Leonardo da Vinci in the 15th and early 16th century to first understand the value of flying machines in the pursuit of war. This was a natural train of thought in a man who was employed by the government to improve the effectiveness of artillery and develop the art of fortification. It is acknowledged that a number of his aeronautical drawings could have been used to create practical heavier than air machines that would have worked, if, a big *if*, technology had been sufficiently advanced at that time to build them, *and* had the right materials been available.

There are no records that Leonardo's contemporaries were inspired to develop these ideas, or that they even understood them. During the years that followed his notebooks, full of original drawings, with explanatory texts neatly annotated in mirror writing, were ignored by the world. It was not until the 1930s that they were rediscovered, by which time many of his dreams had come true, and one of his machines, the helicopter, was about to be developed.

Around 1670 an Italian Jesuit priest, Father Francesco Lana de Terzi, yet another cleric, went off at a complete tangent. The air-pump had recently been invented in Germany, and he conceived the idea of constructing four large globes with skins of wafer-thin copper, pumping out the air so they floated in the atmosphere with a boat-shaped carriage attached to them carrying men and deadly missiles. With the addition of a mast and sail he was on the way to inventing the first flying boat. Unfortunately, theory was not born out in practice. The thin walls of the balls collapsed when a vacuum was created and increasing the thickness of the copper made them too heavy to rise in the air. It is not difficult to picture the good Father giving a sigh of relief as he wrote with a clear conscience:

> 'God would not suffer such an invention to take effect ... For who sees not that no City can be secure against attack, since our Ship may at any time be placed directly over it, and descending down may discharge Soldiers; the same would happen to private Houses, and ships on the Sea: for our Ship descending out of the Air to the Sails of Sea-Ships ... it may over-set them, kill their men, burn their Ships by artificial Fireworks and Fire-balls. And this they may do not only to Ships but to great Buildings, Castles, Cities, with such security that they which cast these things down from a height out of Gun-shot, cannot on the other side be offended by those from below.'

A vision of our own fearful times.

Just over a century later the Montgolfier brothers, Joseph and Jacques of Annonay, in France, carried things forward by noticing that, as professional paper makers, paper bags floated up when filled with hot air. They had no clue that this was due to lighter, less dense air rising upwards and carrying the bags with it. But they did realize how this could be applied in a practical way. After experimenting with a number of models they built a man-lifting balloon.

On 21 November, 1783, Pilâtre de Rozier who, the previous month had made a brief ascent to 85 feet in the Montgolfiers' tethered balloon, now, accompanied by the Marquis d'Arlandes, made the first free manned balloon flight. Despite strong winds they took off from the grounds of the Royal Château La Muette in the Bois de Boulogne, Paris, cheered on by an enthusiastic crowd. They stood either side of the gallery to balance the giant gold and blue sphere which was described as being 'as tall as a seven-storey building'. The altitude they attained is uncertain, who could estimate the height of a flying object accurately in those days? Judgement varied between 1500 feet and 3000 feet.

Soon they came lower and drifted across the Seine. The fire in the wire mesh basket started burning holes in the balloon fabric and threatened the ropes connecting the balloon to the gallery. The balloonists, who must have been prepared for this eventuality, used wet sponges to extinguish the flames. Coming perilously close to the rooftops they threw more straw on the brazier and rose again. Twenty-five minutes later they made a safe landing some 5 miles from where they had taken off.

Within weeks scientists in Paris had taken up the challenge and on 1 December of the same year J. A. C. Charles had taken off in a balloon filled with hydrogen, a light gas, rather than ordinary air, 'lightened' by heat. The use of hydrogen, although dangerously flammable, became standard in the development of balloons in the coming years.

In June, 1784, at Lyon, in France, Madame Elisabeth Thible achieved the first flight by a woman in an untethered balloon. It is reported that she became so excited she burst into song!

It was only eleven years after this important breakthrough that Captain Coutelle rose in a balloon above the Battle at Fleurus to observe the enemy, thus becoming the first aviator to be involved in war.

The use of balloons and kites in conflict will be looked at more closely in the next chapter when we follow the fascinating career of Sergeant Major Edward Bolt. Meanwhile, we return to winged flight.

The principle of the fixed wing was first established by an outstanding engineer born in Scarborough, England, in 1771. Sir George Cayley experimented with a series of models and developed an understanding of the essential requirements of mechanical flight. He appreciated the importance of making a flying machine that was stable and hit on the advantages of a dihedral configuration by attaching wings that pointed gently upwards towards their tips in a shallow vee.

He constructed and flew a glider with a wing area of 300 square feet, probably the first heavier-than-air machine. In 1853, when he was eighty-two, Cayley built the first man-carrying glider. If some form of lightweight mechanical propulsion had been available in his day it is almost certain he would have been hailed as the father of powered flight. And yet how many people living today have ever heard of Sir George Cayley?

Gliders were now capturing the imagination of forward-looking inventors. In 1884 there was a report from the New World that a Professor John Joseph Montgomery, at the University of Santa Clara, had built three gliders and made many flights. But the man who made the biggest stir was a German, Otto Lilienthal, born in Anklam in 1849. In 1889 he declared the balloon to be a blind alley, '*ein falsche Bahn*', on the road to human flight, and lamented that for so long attention had been distracted by aerostats from the real problems of aviation. Two years later he built his first glider, a wicker framework covered with waxed cotton cloth; it bore a close resemblance to the birdman designs that Leonardo da Vinci had sketched some two hundred years earlier.

Lilienthal made hundreds of successful flights, believing that the art of flying was similar to that of learning to ride a bicycle; he achieved a measure of control by shifting his weight relative to the wings which he had constructed with a slightly arched or cambered shape. He had learned that fashioning them in this way gave better results than a wing with a flat surface. Sadly, his experiments came to an end when he crashed to his death near Berlin in 1896 at the age of forty-seven. His brother, Gustav, who lived until 1933, continued his work of pushing forward the boundaries of aviation.

In America, at the same time, the Secretary of the Smithsonian Institute, S. P. Langley, was writing an article in the *Strand Magazine*, recounting the flight of his steam-driven 'aerodrome'. To modern ears this conjures up a somewhat startling apparition! In fact, the term 'aerodrome' was used by Langley to describe aeroplanes or aircraft. (It literally means 'air runner'.) In this case it was a large model powered by steam that had flown for a distance of about half a mile over the Potomac River.

So we come to our own century and the work of two American brothers, Wilbur and Orville Wright, directly motivated by the experiments of those other two brothers in Germany. However, unlike the Lilienthals, the Wrights had figured that the best way to gain experience of air currents was not with a free glider but with a glider flown like a kite. By 1900 they were flying a kite-glider with a pilot aboard. Then, with brilliant inspiration, they decided that the tug of the kite string should be replaced by the push of a tiny petrol engine driving propellers.

It is interesting that these men, like so many of the pioneers before them, were not scientists or men of profound learning; they were mechanics who ran a bicycle repair outfit. When flying they probably applied the bike-riding principles laid down by Otto Lilienthal, although by now they had devised a means of control by flexing the rear edge of the wings, a function later taken over by ailerons.

At Kitty Hawk, North Carolina, on 17 December, 1903, with Orville at the controls, the machine that he and his brother had built took off with the aid of a car. It was not a long flight – it only lasted 12 seconds – but it was the first powered flight in the history of mankind.

It was only eleven years after the successful flight of the Montgolfier brothers' balloon that Captain Coutelle rose above the battlefield at Fleurus. And it was to be only eleven years after the Wright brothers' remarkable achievement at Kitty Hawk that powered aircraft were to rise above far more dreadful battlefields in the most terrible war that man had ever known.

The rest of this book is the story of those who were there, men hovering precariously at first, but with ever growing technical competence, above those ghastly scenes of human destruction.

# CHAPTER TWO

# EDWARD BOLT

Edward Bolt was 17 years old when he joined the Royal Engineers. The life seemed to offer at least two important inducements to a spirited and physically fit young man. The army held out the promise of travel and adventure, while the engineering aspect guaranteed instruction in a useful trade at the expense of the War Office – a fine opportunity to acquire skills that were certain to stand him in good stead for the rest of his working life.

On 6 August, 1909, Ted reported to the army depot in Plymouth and was sent to Chatham the next day. Here he did his three months' basic training which turned him from a raw civilian into a promising soldier in embryo.

From there he was posted to the Balloon Section of the Royal Engineers at Farnborough in Hampshire and was billeted in Blenheim Barracks, about half a mile from the aerodrome. The Sappers lived in three rooms, the rest being occupied by the 1st Battalion of the Grenadier Guards.

His instruction probably bore little relation to what he had visualized when he volunteered to become an engineer. He was trained for two jobs, both vital in the smooth operation of flying balloons and man-lifting kites – one as a winchman, the second as a storeman. He could hardly have guessed in those early stages that these humble tasks would one day lead to his promotion to the highest non-commissioned rank in the Royal Flying Corps.

By the time Ted signed on the Royal Engineers had already been associated with the technique of flying balloons for a remarkably long time – over forty years – twice as long as the Royal Air Force had been in existence by the outbreak of the Second World War. In the earliest days a few stalwart individuals had attempted to convince those in authority of the valuable part balloons could play in war, including a British officer, Captain F. Beaumont, RE, who had attached himself to the Federal Army balloonists in the American Civil War and observed their usefulness on the battlefield at first hand.

But recognition by the British Army of how balloons could be put to good use in keeping an eye on what the enemy was up to was only really acknowledged in 1878, when authorization was given for the experimental production of balloons and field equipment at Woolwich Arsenal. The two army captains appointed to carry out this work were generously awarded a grant of £150 to assist them in their efforts.

One of these officers, Captain Templer, arguably the father of British army ballooning, was an intrepid aeronaut who owned his own balloon. His promising career was almost cut short when in December, 1881, (not an ideal month for ballooning) he rose above the city of Bath during an overcast afternoon in a balloon called the 'Saladin', filled with coal-gas. The exercise was mounted with the intention of carrying out meteorological observations. He was accompanied in the basket by a Mr Walter Powell, MP for Malmesbury, and a young lieutenant of the South Wales Borderers Militia. Soon the clouds became so dense that the ground disappeared from sight and the wind began to rise alarmingly as night closed in. It was, after all, not far from the shortest day of the year. Captain Templer shrewdly decided to land.

As they descended they could hear the sound of breaking waves beating on a nearby shore. Emerging beneath the cloud and hurriedly consulting the map they realised they were drifting fast towards the sea near Bridport. For a moment it looked as though they would tumble headlong into the middle of a village, but, hastily throwing out ballast, they just managed to skim over the rooftops of the cottages. Valving hard, to release gas, Templer brought the balloon down on the other side of the buildings, landing about 150 yards short of the cliff top.

Realizing that the grapnel hook was not holding as the balloon dragged along the ground in the strong wind he rolled out of the basket, calling on the others to follow him. The lieutenant jumped clear, breaking his leg, but Mr Powell, who may have become entangled in the rigging, remained aboard. The Captain, badly bruised, hung on to the valve line until his fingers were cut to the bone. The balloon, relieved of the weight of the two men, rose at great speed and disappeared over the sea carrying the Member for Malmesbury with it, never to be seen again.

After this tragic event Captain Templer gave up personal ballooning and concentrated instead on his valuable work of strengthening and improving the balloon establishment in the British army.

Apart from regular manoeuvres and exercises at home the balloon sections were employed in the Bechuanaland and Sudan expeditions. By this time steel cylinders containing hydrogen under compression had been introduced to fill the balloons while on active service. This replaced the cumbersome business of manufacturing gas for every inflation in the field.

In Britain a horse-drawn balloon wagon was used to carry the cable and winch, an empty balloon prior to inflation, and various accessories. Separate wagons transported the gas tubes and these were pulled by a traction engine or 'steam sapper'. Overseas it was a different matter; because of shortage of men and equipment in the Sudan, for example, the gas cylinders were humped by camels. It was noted with satisfaction that, although the Arabs normally put up stiff opposition, at the sight of balloons they dispersed in all directions.

At the turn of the century the British used balloons successfully in the South African War much to the chagrin of their enemies who had none themselves. The Boers made frequent efforts to destroy them by gunfire, but only succeeded in inflicting minor perforations that were easily repaired and, on one occasion only, they wounded an observer.

During the various campaigns observations from tethered balloons reported the Boer positions and movements, useful sketch maps were made, the enemy's big guns located and our own artillery accurately directed.

At the high ground levels encountered on the South African plateau, (up to 5,000 feet above sea level), the standard 10,000 cu. ft. capacity balloons had insufficient lift, and larger 13,000 cu. ft. balloons were used when necessary. Although greater lengths of cable were available the practical working altitude was normally restricted to 1,000 feet.

The army even sent a balloon section to Northern China. This was to join the British contingent of the international force occupying Peking to protect foreign interests menaced by the Boxer Rebellion. It arrived too late to join in the fighting, but practice balloon ascents were made and the equipment compared favourably with that of other nations.

Among the numerous innovations introduced by Templer, now Colonel Templer, had been the substitution of goldbeater's skin in place of all other balloon fabrics. Goldbeater's skin was manufactured from the membrane of the lower intestine of the ox and was so called because of its use in the process of making gold leaf. It had a high degree of imperviousness to hydrogen, was very tenacious and lighter, strength for strength, than any other material previously tried.

There was no secret about the preparation of this material, but the method of welding together the individual pieces was known only to one family, the Weinlings, who had immigrated from the Continent to the East End of London. Colonel Templer pressed them into government service to provide coverings for his balloons, which they and their descendants then continued to do over a period of more than thirty years. Some contract!

By the time Ted Bolt arrived in Farnborough in 1909 the camp was well established. Colonel Templer had recently retired after doing so much to foster recognition of the value of balloons and kites. In the last few years of his service he had concentrated on the construction of Britain's first military airship and, most importantly, the development of heavier-than-air machines. He had always shown dogged tenacity in the face of either official indifference or, on occasions, downright opposition. A fine example of the blind prejudice he sometimes had to counter was displayed by General Sir W. G. Nicholson, Chief of the Imperial General Staff, when he referred to activities connected with flying as 'A useless and expensive fad, advocated by a few individuals whose ideas are unworthy of attention'.

Ted found Farnborough a hive of activity, centred on the recently constructed factory. (The unit had moved from more cramped quarters in Aldershot three years previously.) This factory included an airship shed 160 feet in length and 72 feet high, a large hangar for those days, but small in comparison with what was needed later.

There was an electrolysis plant for the manufacture of hydrogen gas to fill the balloons. In other hangars experiments were under way with the building of power-driven aircraft. Foremost among the civilian pioneers at work here were the enterprising De Havilland brothers, two cheerful young men, full of optimism about the future success of flying machines. In all it must have been a stimulating environment.

Ted was attached to a balloon section, but was also involved in flying kites. Some years previously experiments had been carried out to find some way of getting observers into the air when winds were too strong for the use of balloons. The possibilities of kites for military purposes had been on the slate as far back as 1894 when Major B. F. S. Baden-Powell (brother of the great B P of boy scout fame) devised a system of man-lifting kites that succeeded in raising a man a hundred feet above the ground.

But it was a civilian named Cody, then working at Farnborough, who first developed a practical kite system, so efficient that it was adopted by the Royal Engineers as an addition to their existing balloon sections. With this combined equipment, and no extra manpower, they were able to provide static aerial reconnaissance at a normal altitude of 1500 feet from calm conditions up to winds of 50 mph.

This system proved much more successful than the elongated kite-balloon method originated in Germany and tried by several foreign armies. Apart from other advantages, Cody's invention needed only about one third of the personnel and half the transport that was required for a kite-balloon.

When Ted first came in contact with Samuel Franklin Cody, or 'Colonel' Cody as he was popularly known, he was busy construct-ing an aeroplane, helped by his two sons, as well as assisting in the completion of the pioneer airship in the big hangar.

Cody, a Texan, after living in England for a number of years, had become a naturalized British citizen in the year Ted arrived at Farnborough. In his early days he had been a cowboy, and later, assisted by his sons, had entertained the public in 'Wild West' shows with feats of horsemanship, shooting and lassoing. Oddly, although a friend, he had no family connection with Colonel Cody of 'Buffalo Bill' fame. When he first arrived in England he sported a large stetson above his shoulder-length hair and goatee beard, and clomped about in leather boots with silver spurs. Later, possibly influenced by Britain's more restrained conventions, he tended to dress more soberly. Yet he remained a rugged individualist to the end of his days.

A fervent advocate of flying, he had long been connected with ballooning, airships and the development of man-carrying kites. Because of his flamboyant personality he had probably done more to publicize flying in England than anyone else. Now he was deeply involved in the business of building and flying aeroplanes.

Ted underwent a thorough training in every aspect of the operation of Cody-kites: To send up a man-lifting kite the winch, equally suitable for balloons or kites, was removed from the balloon wagon and aligned in the direction of the wind. It was securely anchored to the ground. Then a lightweight pilot kite was sent up on a 1000-foot length of cord of piano wire. Lifted by this, a steel cable capable of withstanding a pull of 2 tons was let out. Along this was dispatched a series of winged box kites, any number between two and seven according to the strength of the wind – the stronger the wind the less the number of lifting kites. These gripped the cable at short intervals from the upper end by means of cleats.

When the necessary pull of one ton was exerted on the cable, indicated by a dynamometer on the winch, the large man-lifting kite or carrier, 19 ft in span between its principal wing tips, was hooked to the cable and sent up. This drew a balloon basket or car fitted with a telephone and three signalling lines, a tug on one of which by the observer indicated either 'up, 'stop' or 'down'. (The basket replaced a trapeze seat in the inventor's original version!) It was slung from a steel trolley on the cable to which the bridle of the kite was attached.

On one occasion Ted went aloft in a stiff breeze and achieved an altitude well above the normal. When he came down, Cody was standing by the wagon obviously well pleased with the performance of one of his kites. The big American, who was hardly built for lifting into the air himself, held out his hand. 'Well done me boy!' he said, 'You've just gone higher than I've ever been in a kite myself.'

The strain on the cable was much greater than with balloons, so the hauling-down pole could not be used. Instead, the flight of kites was brought to earth through bearing down the cable with a snatch block fastened to the equipment wagon, or by pulling the cable in, through a fixed snatch block, by moving the balloon-winch wagon.

As was the practice with balloons, with horse-drawn wagons hauling down could be rapidly done at the trot, or at the canter when the winch wagon was used. Over suitable country the kites could be readily towed against the wind; during the 1905 manoeuvres Colonel Capper, who succeeded Colonel Templer as Commanding Officer, was towed several miles in the air, observing and reporting the course of 'battle' and the 'enemy' positions and movements.

In his role as trainee storekeeper Ted had to make sure that every piece of equipment was on hand for the smooth completion of an exercise. He provided pupil observers with sketch pads to draw areas of Laffan's Plain and include any landmarks such as the airship shed, factory, chimney stack, roads, telegraph poles, water towers, copses and so forth as if they were surveying enemy territory. The officers were allowed twenty minutes to complete their sketches; then they were hauled down to have the accuracy of their work assessed.

Ted soon realized how much responsibility rested on his shoulders; men's lives were at stake every time he raised them by means of his winch. The petrol-driven version caused few anxieties, but the older, steam-driven machine harboured a potential danger. It sometimes emitted sparks and great care had to be taken to keep the balloon well clear, filled as it was with highly combustible hydrogen.

Ted never failed to be impressed by the downright bravery of some of the early pioneering officers. On one occasion he witnessed Captain Maitland, his CO of 1 Company (the balloon, kite and airship company) make the first parachute descent of all time. Maitland, he remembers, was a slight figure who walked with a limp from a previous flying accident. He was courteous to everyone, whatever their rank, and was always ready to discuss any matter connected with flying, and keen to offer whatever advice and guidance he could to men under his command.

On this particular day Ted was given the privilege of 'rolling' the captain's parachute. He carefully placed a sheet of newspaper between each fold to counter the effect of static electricity and prevent the silk clinging together. Then, as part of the airship crew, he ascended with his CO who was about to take this hair-raising plunge into history. Ted himself actually contributed to this event by fixing the parachute in place and making sure that everything was secure.

Maitland sat on a plank, for all the world like a swing, supported by two ropes attached to a hook on the underside of the airship. Unlike modern parachutists he wore no form of harness; he merely slipped his hands through a couple of wrist-straps and gripped a bar lashed between the ropes. The parachute itself was suspended above his head in its folded form, with the shroud lines attached to the ropes. It was secured by a string with a breaking strain of only four pounds, so that when it parted it released the chute as Maitland fell earthwards.

It is hard to imagine the emotions of the intrepid Maitland as he sat on his precarious perch beneath the great bulk of the supporting airship, looking down on Farnborough aerodrome far below, observing scattered groups of tiny white faces staring up in anxious anticipation. He was about to launch himself on a journey where no man had gone before, a journey that most reasonable men would conclude could only end in disaster.

But his courage was rewarded. He descended steadily and, caught in a gentle breeze, drifted away to land unharmed in a duckpond some two miles from the airfield. By making this drop into the unknown, and through a series of subsequent experiments, Maitland secured the lives of countless future aviators who would otherwise have died.

Sadly many more deaths could have been avoided if the authorities had shown a modicum of concern during the First World War. Balloon observers alone were equipped with parachutes as a means of escape from the very real danger of their balloons being destroyed by the enemy, but those who flew in aeroplanes were never issued with them.

One of the most renowned of airmen, Marshal of the Royal Air Force Lord Douglas of Kirtleside, writing many years after both World Wars, said, 'To put it mildly, it would have been a great comfort to us to have had such a means of escape to rely on in emergencies, and it would certainly have saved many men from horrible deaths. It was only a few months ago that I learned to my disgust that the reason we didn't have them was an astonishing policy during the First World War that denied us the use of parachutes – and the reason, "that pilots would have been encouraged to leave their machines", was insulting and its source has never been traced.'

Douglas, who had better right to speak on the matter than most, called it a 'contemptible decision'. It was certainly no fault of Maitland that the invention he pioneered was not accepted universally at an earlier date. German aircrew were issued with parachutes in the First World War, based on British designs.

Among his many enthusiasms Maitland remained a fanatical believer in airships throughout his life; even years later when all his contempories had transferred their allegiance to aeroplanes, he still maintained his faith in the lighter-than-air dirigible. As Air Commodore E. M. Maitland it was the final irony that he should lose his life during trials of the airship R.38 in August, 1921. While flying over the Humber, it broke in half, killing all those on board.

Ted never forgot his CO's sense of humour which often left the recipient wondering whether the officer was serious or not. One evening Ted and a few of his pals cycled into nearby Camberley for an evening on the town. They enjoyed themselves immensely and drank rather more than was good for them. Knowing they had to be back before midnight they mounted their bikes and pedalled furiously homeward. Unfortunately the road running alongside the aerodrome was a rough, unadopted route full of deep, muddy potholes. It would have been difficult enough to negotiate even when sober and in daylight. In pitch darkness, in a more than merry condition, and, unlike his companions, without a light on his cycle he was courting disaster. Inevitably disaster came. Plunging into a particularly deep hole, Ted flew over the handlebars and landed heavily in the mire. When his mates rushed up to examine the damage they realized he was suffering from more than a few cuts and bruises.

For the next two or three days he was in Camberley hospital under the stern gaze of a disapproving matron. As soon as he returned to camp he was hauled before an unusually grim looking Maitland. 'I am issuing you with an ultimatum,' barked his CO, 'either you throw away your bicycle, or you will be dismissed the service.' Ted assured the officer he would get rid of the bike immediately. The idea of leaving No. 1 Company and returning to civvy street appalled him. Yet as he left the room he thought he detected a faint twinkle in the CO's eye.

After a few weeks he pulled his bike out of its hiding place and resumed his trips into town. But he took care to imbibe rather less, and always rode in formation between his better illuminated companions on the way back to camp. Later he became convinced that Captain Maitland, who never missed a trick, was well aware that his recalcitrant pupil had again taken to the road. But not another word was said on the matter.

Ted spent a lot of his spare time exploring every nook and cranny of Farnborough where experimental work was going on. He was fascinated by the recently installed wind tunnel in which tests were being carried out on models to check air resistance and stability. Small, free-flying balloons were being used to measure wind velocity, temperature and pressure at great altitudes, using Dines anemometers. Instruments were being put together to enable bombs to be aimed from airships.

Photography was recognized for its importance in information gathering; wide aperture speed cameras and telephoto and panoramic lenses were all being tried, as was an apparatus for developing photographs in the field. By 1911 even the development of air-to-ground wireless apparatus was well under way. One of the problems concerned the trailing aerial fitted to one of the aircraft in which experiments were carried out.

Either the aerial, 100 yards in length and fitted with lead weights like a fishing line, endangered personnel and property when the machine was flying low or coming in to land or, losing its weights as it glanced off an object, the wire tended to whip round and ensnare the tail of the aeroplane.

Ted assisted a Captain McNeece in an attempt to overcome this difficulty. They constructed a pilot kite that was only one tenth the normal size and took it out to Frimley Heath where there was a long, straight road. They attached one end of the wire aerial to the kite and the other end to the Captain's motorbike. They thought that if they could devise a method of flying the aerial above the machine, well out of harm's way, then their troubles would be over.

The Captain kick-started his motorbike and roared off down the road. As soon as the slack was taken up the kite rose into the air towed by the speeding machine. Then, as if having a mind of its own, the kite tugged the Captain and his motor bike clean off the ground. McNeece remained airborne for some moments before he and his bike crashed ignominiously back to earth, landing in a gorse bush. Ruefully he said to Ted, 'I think we'll have to mark that one down as a failure. If it has that effect on a motorbike, what the hell could it do to an aeroplane?'

Still at Farnborough on 13 April, 1912, Ted, like all his mates in the Air Battalion, was absorbed into the newly formed Royal Flying Corps which, in the course of about a year, donned its own distinctive uniform. In spite of this official recognition of the air arm in elevating it to corps status, the daily routine of life around the aerodrome went on much as before except for a gradual increase in activity, especially in the growing numbers of aeroplanes to the point where kite flying had to be stopped for fear of accidents.

Some of the pilot kites were afterwards used for a new purpose. They were taken over to Lydd on the south-east coast where the winches were mounted on railway flat trucks. The kites, flown at a height and towed along the rails, afforded excellent target practice for the Dungeness garrison artillery.

Around this time Ted remembered an incident in which he was closely involved. A lad called Jimmy had joined the Sappers as a 15-year-old bugle boy in 1910. Now, three years later, he had arrived at Farnborough to begin his training as an engineer. On his first day he was detailed to report to the De Havilland's hangar to familiarize himself with a 70 hp Renault engine installed in a Maurice Farman. He was further ordered to practise propeller-swinging on a French Caudron machine which was also in the hangar.

After dutifully examining the engine, Jimmy went over the Caudron and put in some time exercising his muscles on the propeller. A morning well spent. After lunch the young 2nd Class Air Mechanic returned with instructions to rub the rust off the wires of the Maurice Farman. After a while he tired of this monotonous task and went back to the Caudron to practise a little more prop-swinging. Unknown to him someone had been fiddling with the controls during his absence and had left the machine switched on. As he swung the prop the engine burst into life and the aeroplane leapt forward. Jimmy threw himself to the ground, avoiding decapitation by a split second. The Caudron was brought to a halt when it crashed into the Maurice Farman destroying its tail booms and slicing off part of the wing. Jimmy struggled to his feet, leapt into the cockpit and switched off the motor.

Ted and his companions, who happened to be working near at hand, heard the noise and rushed into the hangar, grabbing fire extinguishers as they ran. It was thick with exhaust fumes and the heavy smell of castor oil. Order was soon restored and when the Sergeant Major arrived Jimmy was put under arrest. Ted was detailed to escort him to the guardroom. When the young air mechanic was brought before the CO, Captain Maitland spoke in his usual quiet manner. 'Not a good start is it? On the other hand you showed initiative in switching off promptly. In doing this you may have avoided a serious conflagration. I award you ten days CB and for God's sake be more careful in future'.

As far as Ted remembers, Jimmy never put a foot wrong after that. To use an expression then current, 'he was as keen as mustard'. Coming from a family of British Army Sappers he always appeared smartly turned out with immaculately polished boots, perfectly rolled puttees and well pressed uniform. Even in his overalls he contrived to look more of a real soldier than most of his contempories. Such was his enthusiasm for aeroplanes that he never missed an opportunity to cadge a flight whenever the chance came along.

He must have done well because, early the following year, he and Ted were promoted to corporal on the same day. Later, after war with Germany had broken out, Jimmy did even better by becoming Major Jimmy McCudden, VC, DSO and bar, MC and bar, MM, one of the most honoured fighter aces of the First World War.

Ted was to recall another event that took place in 1913. After nearly four years at Farnborough, he had become familiar with virtually everyone on the camp. He spent a great deal of time helping Cody and his sons, Leon and Vivian, in their hangar. They were great believers in the value of bamboo poles, as used in the kites, for the construction of the main spars and out-riggers of their aeroplane. Ted, who knew that everything they did was at their own expense, was only too happy to lend a hand in binding the poles and splicing wires.

He worked most closely with Leon, the younger son, who, under his father's supervision, concentrated on the construction of the airframe, while his brother, Vivian, specialized in looking after the engine and tuning it for maximum performance.

It took six men to wheel Cody's aeroplane out of the hangar but there was never any shortage of willing helpers among the Royal Engineers. On occasion they would space themselves out at various points along the aerodrome to act as markers while Cody tested his machine in a series of short hops.

One day Cody was assisted by twelve men in the charge of a Corporal Frank Ridd, who was shortly to become the first corporal pilot in the RFC. It was a perfect flying day with a clear sky and only the lightest of breezes. Cody, his latest plane still at the experimental stage, took off and completed a full circuit of the field before coming back to land. The Sappers rushed up and surrounded the plane as Cody fished in his pocket and produced a pound note. 'Corporal,' he said, 'here's a pound. Take the lads to the Queen's Hotel over there and buy them a drink. Its the only pound I've got, but they deserve it more than I do.'

Ted was full of praise for the 'Colonel'. Cody never failed to thank the boys for their efforts, and he used to say, 'As this aviation business takes off and we start to get somewhere, just remember this – if any of you, at any time, need any help, then always remember I'll be there.' Sadly, this courageous, inventive showman did not live to witness the First World War with its phenomenal development in aviation.

There is some doubt as to what went wrong on that day, 7 August, 1913, but Leon and Ted were standing on the aerodrome watching Cody flying sedately at about 1000 feet in fine weather. A man had turned up from Reading requesting a flight and was flying as a passenger behind Cody. Suddenly, it seemed to Ted and Vivian that the man panicked. They saw him frantically shaking the pilot's shoulders. The aeroplane side-slipped, went out of control and crashed to the ground killing both men. Cody was 52.

Although the RFC's airships were eventually handed over to the Naval Wing, soon to be renamed the Royal Naval Air Service, Ted had gained experience handling them as a member of the ground crew and also flying in them on various trial flights. HMA *Gamma* had been launched in February, 1910, with an envelope of 72,000 cubic foot capacity and incorporated a number of improvements over her contemporary, HMA *Beta*, a rather smaller airship. Instead of goldbeater's skin, her 152-feet-long shape was covered in rubber-proofed fabric. She was propelled by an 80–100 hp Green engine, the first all-British aero-engine, and fitted with swivelling propellers to facilitate ascents and landings, a system that worked well. She carried a crew of five in an open, fabric-sided gondola and achieved a speed of 32 mph. Most airship flying took place at night in the realization that these enormous, slow-moving dirigibles would be extremely vulnerable in time of war.

*Gamma* was involved in an incident that Ted Bolt believed to be 'a one off' in airship history. She had set off on a flight but before long her captain signalled that her engine had 'frozen' and they were drifting out of control. A very small airship, the *Willows*, (named after Ernest Willows who devised the swivelling propellers) was hastily launched and set off in pursuit. Overtaking the *Gamma* she flew above her big sister and dropped a tow rope to the helpless crew below. As soon as the line had been made fast the diminutive *Willows* began the long, slow journey back to Farnborough at no more than three or four miles per hour. Over the aerodrome the *Gamma* dropped her mooring rope and, after releasing the tow-line, she was hauled down by the ground crew in the normal fashion.

In its wisdom the British government decided to sanction the purchase of two French airships, the semi-rigid *Lebaudy* and the non-rigid *Clement Bayard*, for what was then a considerable sum of money. After many months' delay the *Clement Bayard* was the first to arrive over England. On both the French and English coasts she was guided by captive balloons and escorted across the channel by a British destroyer. She flew straight to Wormwood Scrubs where a shed provided by the *Daily Mail* had been waiting her presence for a year. It was discovered that she was leaking gas badly and was in a generally poor condition. After further prolonged inspection it was decided that she was not worth renovating and never flew again.

Ten days later the *Lebaudy*, enjoying the same navigational assistance, flew over the coast at Brighton and headed inland to Farnborough where she was destined to be housed in a new airship shed specially built for her. With a cubic capacity of 353,000 she was the biggest airship of the kind then built and carried a crew of nine. Her two 135 hp engines were geared so that either or both could drive the twin propellers. She arrived over the aerodrome as scheduled, and everyone, including 160 Sappers and Guardsmen detailed to haul her down, gaped in amazement at her size. As her mooring cable was lowered it swept across the roofs of nearby houses, knocking off chimney pots. Eventually it became entangled in the airfield's boundary fence. Within moments Ted and the others had grabbed it and began dragging the airship down towards the hangar entrance.

The wide-awake Air Battalion officer in charge of the landing party noticed that the shed opening was a little too low and ordered the men to stop hauling. Whether a high-ranking officer who was present was overcome by the excitement of the occasion will never be known, but, although he was only there as a spectator, he shouted to the men to 'carry on'. So the *Lebaudy* was hauled into the shed ripping a great gash in its fabric as it tore along the metal girder at the top of the entrance. As the gas escaped the whole collapsing envelope cascaded down on top of Ted and his companions. Within moments they were buried beneath the shroud. Fighting for breath, Ted worked his way out of the entanglement of metal tubes, broken wires and torn fabric. When he finally reached daylight he found himself staring up at a smartly dressed civilian who was standing beside Maitland, his CO.

Cut and bruised Ted put his hand to his face and realized it was bleeding. Leaning forward, the stranger said, 'Are you hurt?' At which Ted snapped back, 'Of course I'm hurt, you bloody fool. What does it look like?'

Maitland, with a face like thunder, said, 'Do you realize who you're talking to? This is Field-Marshal Lord Roberts. I'm putting you on an immediate charge for gross insubordination.'

Lord Roberts turned to the CO. 'Come, come, Maitland. There's no need for that. I asked this soldier a silly question – and I got the answer I deserved.'

Ted threw up a rapid salute, then hurried away to lick his wounds.

It transpired that the overall height of the *Lebaudy* was 10 feet more than the French manufacturers had specified. The height of the balloon shed was subsequently increased by 15 feet.

Soon after the outbreak of war in August, 1914, No 1 Squadron, as it was now called, was posted to France and landed at Boulogne with about 250 officers, NCOs and men, and a dozen lorries which included mobile repair shops, with a wireless and telephone outfit. One of the trucks also carried a couple of spare aero-engines. They made their way by a circuitous route to the outskirts of St Omer where they established the main Aircraft Park for the RFC.

Ted wondered what impression their outfit made on the French population as they marched through the countryside. Of the two officers in charge, Captain John Moore-Brabazon walked with a stick because of his pronounced limp, while Captain Carden only had one arm. Several of the men fell out along the way, including one who collapsed at the side of the road under the weight of a personal supply of 24 tins of bully beef.

The months that followed were among the most hectic they had ever experienced. Ted was now employed as a rigger, repairing shot-up and damaged aircraft. Struts, rigging and control wires had to be replaced, canvas patched and renewed. It was a treadmill. No sooner had refurbished machines been returned to the front line squadrons than more battered ones arrived for attention. Three test pilots, including Gordon Bell, gave each aeroplane a quick trial flight before passing them as fit for further service.

Working day and night at an impossible rate, it was a welcome moment when reinforcements arrived from England. The strain was only eased when it became possible to organize properly regulated shifts and periods of rest.

Lieutenant-Colonel Trenchard, then commanding the RFC's newly formed First Wing in France, paid regular visits to the Aircraft Repair Park. Ted remembers him as a stickler for discipline and fanatical about carrying out every job to perfection. Even in such a detail as splicing wire, the great man insisted on four tucks (a tuck being one wire placed under another wire and then drawn through) rather than the more usual three. This, of course, increased the strength and added to safety. It became known as the 'Trenchard tuck'. He seemed to know more about everything than anyone else around. Tall in stature and with a booming voice, he cut an imposing figure.

After some months Ted was posted back to England and joined 14

Squadron at Shoreham, under the command of Major, later Squadron Leader, Barry Martin. This officer was no respecter of individuals, however exalted. On one occasion, towards the end of the war, the Duke of York, who was a flight commander, had landed his Maurice Farman Longhorn on the wrong side of the aerodrome fence and strolled back across the field to his quarters. Unknown to him, his misdemeanour had been observed by Barry Martin. The verbal roasting that His Royal Highness received from his squadron commander for this infringement was the talk in every flying mess for many months to come.

In March, 1915, Ted, who was by now a sergeant, received a telegram to report to the War Office immediately. Here he was ordered by Colonel Boyle to accompany him to Farnborough to select eighty physically robust men to form a new unit. This was to be known as the No 1 Kite-Balloon Section of the RFC.

Taking his newly formed section to Roehampton, he instructed the men, who had no previous experience of the work, in the basics of balloon and kite handling. Realizing how green his unit was, he persuaded the Roehampton garrison to release an experienced balloon rigger, a winchman and a basket man to reinforce the section.

Within days they had reported for duty in France. Establishing themselves in well-camouflaged positions beneath overhanging trees, as near as possible to the front line, they began their important work of information gathering. Observers, on hourly shifts, were sent up with sketching pads and binoculars to spot enemy trench positions, gun emplacements and the general movement of troops – just as in the far-off days of the Boer War.

Two or three times a week visiting artillery and infantry officers accompanied the observers; they went aloft in the basket to get a bird's eye view of their own segment of the battle. The section moved positions constantly in order to confuse the enemy. As protection against attack from hostile aircraft each observer was provided with two loaded rifles.

In spite of the provision of parachutes, observing was still a perilous undertaking. Ted recalls one day on the Somme sector when thirty-five balloons were shot down. By good fortune No 1 Section was the only section never to loose a balloon.

In June, 1916, he was promoted Warrant Officer Edward Bolt, 1st Class, and sent home from France for two important purposes: first, to form a new kite balloon station in England, and, secondly, to marry his girlfriend who had waited patiently for his return.

CHAPTER THREE

# CHARLES GEORGE
# EDWARD TYE

To be living in London towards the end of the Edwardian era must have been no bad thing. Many of the stuffy restrictions imposed by the Victorians had been shrugged off in this new age of progress and individual freedom.

Charlie Tye was a contented man. Recently qualified as a coppersmith, he was now master of a good trade much in demand and, most importantly, he was doing work that he enjoyed. At weekends he was able to indulge his passion for football by playing for Barking Football Club's first team.

Each weekday Charlie made his way across London from his home in Barking to his employer's place in Chiswick by 6 o'clock in the morning. The company, situated on the banks of the Thames, was engaged in the business of building yachts and Charlie was an integral part of the workforce. They worked hard and put in long hours. On a good day he would be back in Barking by 7.30 in the evening. This gave him time to cram in some training indoors, or over at the football ground during the lighter evenings.

On Friday nights he invariably looked in on the club's head-quarters in Barking Broadway to find out where he and his mates were playing the next day and to confirm his position in the team. It was on one of these occasions that Charlie, having received his instructions for the next day, walked into the club bar and ordered a beer. As she pulled his pint the barmaid said, 'See that young gent over in the corner, Charlie?'

Charlie nodded.

'Well, he told me he's looking for a coppersmith and I told him about you. Hope you don't mind.'

He looked at the stranger. Charlie was twenty-one and he guessed this man was, perhaps, three or four years older. He was a big man and, in spite of his youth, had a certain air of authority. He, in turn, was staring at Charlie. Drink in hand, Charlie strolled over, introduced himself and sat down. 'The barmaid tells me you're looking for a coppersmith?'

'Yes, that's right.' said the man. 'I intend building a machine and I've just acquired Baden-Powell's old kite shed down in Movers Lane for the purpose. Do you know it?'

Charlie nodded. He knew it all right. It was where Major B. F. S. Baden-Powell of the Scots Guards had been experimenting with his man-lifting kites for the past dozen years. They had been taken up by the British army and used successfully in military manoeuvres on Salisbury Plain, either for artillery observation or for spotting the movements of opposing forces.

The shed was in front of some waste ground used for dumping asbestos and other rubbish near Barking Creek down by the docks. The area was easily identified by the clouds of choking dust that permeated the atmosphere on dry days. But Charlie was interested because the place was only minutes from his home, whereas the yacht-builders were miles away. Travelling to Chiswick each day cut into his free time, while getting there cost him quite a bit of money.

'I'm looking for a man who can use a blowlamp,' the big man continued. 'Can you handle a blowlamp?'

'It's part of my trade,' Charlie explained. 'You can't be a coppersmith unless you can braze bits of metal together.'

The stranger told him that he had recently sacked a man who turned out to be quite incapable of handling the work.

'Look,' he said, 'I'll give you a trial. Come down to my place tomorrow morning and show me what you can do. If I think you're suitable then I'll give you a job. By the way, my name is Handley Page.'

The name meant nothing to Charlie. He could hardly be expected to know that the man who was offering him the chance to work in his shed would one day become Sir Frederick Handley Page, acknowledged as one of the world's great manufacturers of military and civil aircraft. Within a year of this meeting he had founded Britain's first aircraft manufacturing company.

The next day being a Saturday, Charlie had plenty of time to report for his brazing test before his team kicked off. Handley Page handed him a blueprint, a copper plate, a copper tube and a blowlamp. The plan was straightforward – to cut out a flat disc, drill a hole in the middle with two projecting tags and then braze the tube on to it in an upright position.

Charlie completed his test with care and handed it to Mr Handley Page for inspection. The man studied it for several moments, holding it up to the light, checking it for flaws. Eventually he put it down on the bench. 'Excellent!' he said. 'You've got the job. How soon can you start?'

Charlie told him he would start as soon as possible, after giving the appropriate notice to his present employers.

He was still puzzled about the nature of the machine they were going to build and his curiosity increased when he arrived to start work. The workshop was enormous – almost as large as some of the balloon hangars he had seen in photographs. Its vastness was emphasized by its emptiness. Apart from a couple of work benches, a tiny coke brazier, some strips of timber, a wood plane, a hammer and chisels and the blow lamp there was little else in sight, although there was evidence that someone, possibly Handley Page himself, or the man he had sacked, had been making unsuccessful attempts to weld various bits of metal together. Beginning to wonder if he had made the right decision in throwing up his secure job with the yacht builders Charlie asked his new boss what sort of machine they were going to build.

'You and I, Charlie,' said Handley Page, 'are going to build an aeroplane.'

In the year 1909 this was hardly a commonplace statement. Nor was it one likely to inspire confidence. In fact, the number of heavier-than-air flying machines throughout the world could still be counted on the fingers of a very few hands. After the Wright brothers had made their historic first flight in an aeroplane at the end of 1903, at Kill Devil Hills, near Kitty Hawk, on the coast of North Carolina, no one flew in a powered, winged aircraft in England until 1908.

A man called A. V. Roe, who had started his working life as a railway apprentice, later becoming a marine engineer, had built an aeroplane powered with a French 24 h.p. Antoinette eight-cylinder water-cooled engine and flown it that year at Brooklands motor track on 8 June. At his first attempt he had covered sixty yards at a height of two or three feet above the ground.

His achievement had sent the establishment into a flurry of indignation. They were convinced that what he had done was either illegal or immoral, or both. He was immediately banned from using Brooklands for his unnatural experiments. When he appealed to the War Office for some land on which to fly his machine his request was turned down. When Roe later applied to be recognized as the first man to have flown a powered heavier than air machine in Britain his claim was disallowed on the grounds that he had not covered sufficient distance.

Alliott Verdon Roe, undaunted, flew successfully the following year over Lea Marshes. This time he piloted a new triplane with a British built 9 h.p. J.A. Prestwich motor-cycle engine, thus establishing two records; the first all-British aeroplane to fly, and also the lowest powered aircraft ever to get off the ground. All this activity was considered so improper that court proceedings were instituted against him.

Yet A. V. Roe, like Handley Page, was to become one of Britain's most important aircraft manufacturers. (Where would the RAF's Bomber Command have been in World War Two without the Avro Lancaster and the Handley Page Halifax?)

But in those early days when many people dismissed anyone engaged in attempts to fly as being 'dangerously deranged', Charlie Tye could have been forgiven at that moment if he had turned and run. Nevertheless, he set to with a will assisting his new boss.

Handley Page bought a number of additional tools on his new employee's advice. Then Charlie set about manufacturing a series of copper devices similar to the one he had made during his test. The tubes were designed to secure the longerons while the tags held the multitude of wires.

For some time the two men worked alone on the construction of their aeroplane. Then they were joined by Cyril, a singularly adroit carpenter who fashioned wing spars, ribs, struts, longerons, even the propeller, as though he had been doing this specialized kind of work all his life.

Later an enthusiastic young man called Edward Peter arrived, straight from university. Rumour soon spread that he was the son of an earl, but he mucked in with the others. He just wanted to be involved in all things to do with aviation and was quite happy to turn his hand to any task, however menial, without payment. Among other things Charlie taught his eager pupil how to braze metal.

Eventually the completed monoplane skeleton stood proudly in the middle of its spacious home. A band of women, recruited locally and armed with needles and thread, set about the task of stitching a cloth covering over the wings. The team carefully treated every inch of the fabric with yellow dope solution which, as it dried, drew the material as tight as a drum. They christened their suprisingly sleek new creation 'The Yellow Peril'.

Britain having no aero engine manufacturer of its own at that time, aviation pioneers had to look abroad for their requirements – almost exclusively to France. Handley Page visited the workshops of Laurent Seguin and his brother in France and ordered one of their newly developed 'Gnome' rotary engines of some 50 h.p. After this had been installed back at Barking the 'Yellow Peril' was considered ready to fly.

Some reports say the initial flight took place on the waste ground behind the workshop in Movers Lane, but the rubbish tip would have been the least suitable place imaginable for a take-off. In fact the machine was dismantled, the components placed on a horsedrawn cart and trundled the short distance up to Fairlop Park in Ilford where the authorities had given permission for the attempt to take place.

On arrival, the plane was re-assembled by Charlie, complete with all its flying wires, skids and twin pram-wheel undercarriage. The area was roped off to discourage curious members of the public from coming too close and possibly damaging the delicate machine. He covered it with a large tarpaulin and left it for the night.

Returning to the park early the following morning, a fine August Saturday, Charlie was accompanied by an engineer called Heath who had meticulously checked over the engine back at the workshop. After a further inspection on the spot he pronounced everything in good order. Soon after they were joined by Edward Peter.

Handley Page, who was expected to turn up with the pilot, a naval lieutenant called Wilfred Parke, had so far not put in an appearance.

But Charlie was not worried. He had learnt that his boss was invariably late, whatever the occasion.

It was around 10 o'clock when they removed the rope fence in readiness for the flight. Heath said, 'Let's start the engine, just to give it a bit of a warm up.' As he climbed into the cockpit he motioned to Edward to swing the prop. This was a drawn-out process as fuel had to be sucked into each of the five cylinders. With a final swing the rotary roared into life and the aeroplane started to creep forward over the grass. Quickly Charlie jammed two blocks of wood under the wheels, preventing any more forward motion. Heath, concluding that the engine was revving too hard, climbed down to investigate. As he did so, Edward Peter took his place in the cockpit. This was the first chance he had had of sitting in the machine of his dreams.

The two men then noticed that he was fiddling around with the controls, moving the joystick this way and that, trying out the rudder bar. They yelled at him to stop mucking about but he took no notice. Before they had time to think, the Gnome rotary gave an exultant roar as the wheels bounded clean over the wooden chocks.

'Come back! Come back you fool!' yelled Charlie and the engineer. But it was too late. The untested machine was already gathering speed across the park with Edward at the controls. After covering about two hundred yards the wheels left the ground as the 'Yellow Peril' lifted into the air for the first time.

At that moment Handley Page and Lieutenant Parke arrived. The look on the boss's face was difficult to interpret – a mixture of exultation, puzzlement and anxiety. But there was no doubt that the joy of seeing his creation actually flying took precedence over any other emotion in those first few seconds.

As everyone stared in wonder, Edward Peter brought the 'Yellow Peril' round in a graceful circuit above the park as if to wish his earthbound companions a fond farewell. Then, setting course in a south-westerly direction, he and the machine disappeared from sight over the chimney pots of suburban Ilford.

All day Charlie and the others were eaten up with anxiety, wondering what had happened to their impetuous colleague and the precious aeroplane, but at last news came through. At first Edward had headed towards the Thames which he could see over on his left.

Then, he flew up river as far as Weybridge. Spotting the race track at Brooklands he turned into the wind, throttled back and landed.

After the weekend Charlie had to travel over to Brooklands to collect the machine, take it to pieces and bring it back by road to the workshop at Movers Lane. To his relief 'Yellow Peril' was undamaged.

Edward rejoined him at the workbench where, at that time, they were assembling two aeroplanes ordered by Japanese enthusiasts to their own design. The young man told him he had received a rare roasting from the top brass at Brooklands for landing without permission, and, more seriously, piloting a machine without an authorized certificate. However, because he spent much of his spare time at the track, he had established quite a few contacts and knew men such as Martin and Handasyde, A. V. Roe and Major Fletcher, people of growing importance in aviation circles. The unimaginative authorities at Brooklands had been superseded by more forward-looking men, and there seemed little doubt that a few words were said on young Edward's behalf.

It was a pity that the matter had to be hushed up because of the clandestine nature of the event. The flight, in those pioneer days of aviation, had been remarkably successful in terms of height, endurance and distance attained.

Handley Page himself viewed the incident philosophically. After all 'The Yellow Peril' had proved itself superbly by flying diagonally across Greater London – and no damage had been done. On the quiet Charlie thought that the boss had a sneaking respect for Edward.

This regard was shared by others, including the company of Martin & Handasyde which undertook to give him flying lessons. Edward proved to be such a gifted aviator that he was eventually appointed as test pilot to the Martin-Handasyde aeroplane factory. Sadly (Charlie thinks it was on Christmas Day, 1911) Edward Peter took off on an attempt at a record-breaking long-distance flight. His intention was to fly in one of the company's machines from Brooklands to Glasgow. While passing over Thirsk in Yorkshire his wing broke off and he plunged to his death.

At Handley Page Ltd, in Movers Lane, business was expanding rapidly and the whole company was transferred to what had previously been a riding school in Cricklewood Lane. By now the workforce had increased to over twenty. Charlie had been made supervisor and was still the only metal worker in a team made up mostly of carpenters. After attending a course on the art of welding various other types of metal, he was given his own workshop, equipped with all the latest tools and appliances and separate from the main assembly area.

At this time he was living in comfortable digs across the road from the factory, sharing accommodation with two or three of Handley Page's draughtsmen. (His landlady's attractive daughter, Ethel, was married to George Robey of music hall fame.)

Charlie, like his boss, was not noted for punctuality, especially first thing in the morning, and he realized that the casual working practices at Movers Lane had gone for ever when H. P. installed a clocking-on machine. As a matter of principle Charlie hated the thing on sight. As a skilled craftsman he was offended by this unwelcome intrusion into his individualistic routine and his fertile brain immediately sought ways of outwitting the thing. All the workers were given a personal card which they had to insert in a slot beneath the clock on arrival at the factory. The time was automatically punched on the card thus displaying an accurate record of the workers' daily time-keeping. Within an hour Charlie had thought of a solution; it consisted of nothing more than a wafer thin piece of metal. Scheduled to arrive at 8.00 am the next morning, he strolled in at 8.55. Covering the *minute* section with his slip of metal he allowed the machine to record the 8 on the card. Then, when the time reached 9.00 he repeated the process, but this time covered up the *hour*. Result 8.00 a.m.!

This system worked successfully for nearly six months, until one day he arrived to find his card missing from the rack beside the clock. A young man called Dudley Barton (an amateur balloon pilot and son of a doctor) was his assistant welder. He told Charlie that the boss had taken the card and wanted to see him in his office without delay.

'You've been cheating me for months,' said Handley Page, holding the card in his hand. 'How the hell have you done it?'

Charlie protested weakly but his boss brushed his protestations aside. 'I know you too well, Charlie. You could never manage to get to work on time with such regularity. What's the trick?'

Charlie was at a loss for words. He felt sure he was about to be fired from the finest job he had ever dreamed of.

'Look!' said H. P. 'I'm not angry with you. I'm just intrigued to know how you did it.' He felt in his pocket. 'Here's a guinea if you tell me.'

With that Charlie took him to the machine and showed him.

'Ingenious!' exclaimed his boss. 'Come with me and bring that lousy contraption with you!'

Removing the clock from the wall and clutching it in his arms Charlie climbed into his master's open tourer. They drove down to Watling Street, home of the manufacturer. Handley Page asked the managing director to repeat the terms of the guarantee on his equipment – foolproof, tamper-proof, failsafe – virtues which the man was happy to re-affirm with confidence.

Charlie was waiting patiently outside the office. 'Come in Charlie,' yelled H. P. through the open door. 'Now, show this man how to beat the clock!'

As they climbed back into the car his boss patted him on the back. 'Well done Charlie,' he said. 'I'm proud of you.'

Charlie kept his job and was a guinea better off. Meanwhile Handley Page undoubtedly arranged a compensatory settlement with the clock machine manufacturers, a satisfactory outcome for a planemaker constantly in need of cash.

In an effort to ease the financial burden during those pioneering days Handley Page had installed 'The Yellow Peril' at Hendon aerodrome where members of the public were invited to fly as passengers. A pilot called Whitehead, working on a commission basis, took people on ten-minute flips as far as Hyde Park and back at a guinea a time.

Charlie occasionally gave up his Sundays to help out in Hendon for an extra five shillings a day. On one occasion business had been so bad that 'The Yellow Peril' had not taken off all day. They spotted Handley Page standing near one of the hangars. He was accompanied by Gladys Cooper, the well known actress, and two other female companions. Whitehead, who was bored by the lack of activity, suggested that Charlie should go over and ask H. P. if he himself would like a flip. When he had delivered the message his boss took him by the elbow and led him away from his guests. 'Listen,' he said when they were out of earshot, 'I build the bloody things, I don't fly them!' In this he was almost unique among his contemporaries.

Among other projects, Handley Page was constructing an aeroplane designed to compete in the Military Trials competition due to take place in August, 1912. The army had arranged for the trials to take place at Larkhill on Salisbury Plain. The object of the exercise was an attempt to find the most suitable reconnaissance aeroplane to serve in conjunction with an expeditionary force. Current military thinking on how aeroplanes could be used in time of war had not moved beyond this basic concept.

The constructional requirements that Handley Page and his rivals had to bear in mind were:

1. Accommodation for at least one passenger in addition to the pilot, both having the best possible view of the ground in a forward arc.
2. The aircraft should stand still on the ground with the engine running, without being held back; and the engine should be easy to start, preferably from the pilot's seat.
3. Dual controls to be fitted.
4. The occupants are to be sheltered from the wind and able to communicate with each other.
5. All similar parts of the airframe must be interchangeable, like parts with each other, and also with sample parts picked from stock.
6. Operating the machine should not impose an undue strain upon the pilot. A vital consideration on active service.
7. Each aeroplane has to be capable of being dismantled and transported by road, either by trolley or on its own wheels. The width, packed for road travel, must not exceed ten feet.
8. Each aeroplane is to be presented in a packing case suitable for rail transport. The case itself to be easily taken to pieces for storage in a small space.
9. The engine should be silenced effectively.

With these stipulations in mind Handley Page had again designed a monoplane. It had accommodation for two, in twin cockpits fitted with dual controls. It was really a slightly larger version of the original 'Yellow Peril' with a more powerful Gnome engine. But in Charlie's opinion it lacked the outstanding flying qualities of the former aeroplane.

When the time came, Charlie was again responsible for looking after the machine, this time on Salisbury Plain. Once more Lieutenant Parke, RN, was to fly, which, from Handley Page's point of view was an ideal arrangement; not only was Parke an excellent pilot out for experience on as many aircraft as possible, but, as a serving officer, he came free. The young officer was so much in demand that he had also agreed to pilot A. V. Roe's entry.

There were eighteen other competitors, including A. V. Roe, Vickers, Maurice Farman, British Deperdussin (which in the event came second), Martin-Handasyde, Tommy Sopwith, the Short Brothers and others. As a show of fairness the Royal Aircraft Factory at Farnborough was not entering its own aircraft as these were built at the expense of the State.

In the end it hardly made any difference because arrangements had already been made for Farnborough to provide large numbers of B.E.2 biplanes from its own factory to equip the newly formed Royal Flying Corps. Naturally, the owners of the privately financed aircraft knew nothing of this at the time of the trials.

On the first day of the test packing cases, like a row of immense match boxes, stretched out across the plain. On a signal from the judges each team had to break open their container and assemble the aeroplane. The time taken varied considerably. A. V. Roe's machine was completed and ready to fly in the commendably short time of fourteen and a half minutes. On the other hand five men laboured for nearly nine and a half hours to get their Maurice Farman into flying shape.

The rigorous tests that followed reduced the qualifying competitors to eleven. It had been necessary for them to fly for at least three hours carrying two people with a combined weight of not less than 350 lb. Sufficient fuel had to be carried for a four and a half hour flight. They had to attain a height of 4,500 feet at some stage during the flight and also maintain an altitude above 1500 feet for at least an hour.

Following this there were climbing, gliding, fuel consumption, calculated range, speed, speed range, landing distance, take-off and rough-weather tests. Of these speed range was considered most important and on this criterion an aeroplane built and flown by Cody left the others standing. His machine, the 'Cathedral', had a top speed of 72.4 mph but could remain airborne at only 48.5 mph giving a speed range of 23.9 mph, far beyond that achieved by anyone else.

Each entrant was allocated a space for his machine and Charlie found himself next to the 'Cathedral', so named, it was thought at the time, because of its immense size, but actually it was derived through a play on words – the aircraft was actually a 'kata-hedral', that is a machine where the angle between the wings inclined downwards towards the tips.

This large biplane, powered by a 120 h.p. Austro-Daimler engine, had been built by 'Colonel' Samuel Franklin Cody, himself a giant of a man and already a legendary figure in aviation circles as we learned in the previous chapter. Because it was a warm summer both he and Charlie slept next to each other at night under their respective machines.

Although Cody was more than holding his own in the trials he was worried about the trim of his aeroplane; he admitted to Charlie that it was not handling quite as well as it should. Charlie walked round the machine, testing the bracing wires, squinting along its length to see if everything was true. 'Would you like to come up with me?' asked Cody, 'just to check it out for yourself.'

Jumping at the chance, Charlie took his place behind the American. He perched precariously on a bicycle saddle with his hands clutching Cody's shoulders. Behind him, within a few precarious inches, whirled the great pusher propeller driven by the Austro-Daimler engine. The 'Cathedral' bounced across the rough grass and floated into the air after a surprisingly short run. Cody put his machine through its paces, climbing, diving and turning, and occasionally glancing round at his passenger to assess his reaction. Charlie realized almost at once what needed to be corrected. He appreciated that making a proper assessment of the problem was much simpler in flight than on the ground. When they landed he immediately sorted things out – a small adjustment to the wires here, an easing of tension there. He also concluded that 'Yellow Peril II' was a superior machine.

The final test was for each aeroplane to land in a ploughed field and then take off again. Not one machine, including the Handley Page, already penalized in other tests, had yet succeeded. Cody, who had been circling overhead, came in last. He made a perfect landing, paused, turned into wind and took off again to the astonishment of all those watching.

Charlie was convinced that things had been made easier for Cody by the previous aeroplanes. Their efforts to get off had had a steam-roller effect on the ploughed furrows, producing a flatter surface. Be that as it may, Cody was declared the winner and received a cash prize of £5000. With the money he built the new machine in which he was to die the following year in the crash witnessed, as we already know, by his son Leon and Ted Bolt.

Charlie continued to work at the factory in Cricklewood Lane for the next two years until the outbreak of war. The workforce grew steadily until it passed the hundred mark. The skilled craftsmen, employed at 9 pence an hour, asked Charlie, in view of his special relationship and his long service, if he would approach the boss and request an extra halfpenny an hour. He was glad to comply as he only received the same pay as the others in spite of his extra responsibilities. All he got for his pains was a lecture from Handley Page pointing out how grateful his men should be, and how much less he himself had received when he once worked as an electrician before being unfairly sacked.

Before he left, Charlie saw the start of the company's greatest project up to that time, the building of the prototype 0/100, a huge twin-engined biplane specifically designed to bomb Germany and known as the 'Bloody Paralyser'. (See Chapter Nine) Studying the plans, he was convinced that certain aspects of its construction were based on the concepts of the great Russian aircraft designer Igor Sikorsky.

Charlie had become friendly with John Alcock, a mechanic who had travelled south from his home in Manchester to work at Brooklands with Martin-Handasyde. He was most enthusiastic about cars and aeroplanes. On one occasion he worked on a racing car, but not being skilled in metalwork like Charlie, he fashioned the external exhaust leaving pronounced kinks in the bends. The burnt gases, impeded by these kinks, produced loud bangs. Colin Bell, the owner, had a stutter and it was through a combination of this and the noises emitted by the exhaust that they thought of the original name for the car. They called it 'Chitty Chitty Bang Bang'.

Brooklands was an exciting place in those days. On a sunny afternoon they watched the French pilot, Adolphe Pégoud, execute a seemingly impossible manoeuvre by looping the loop.

One evening Charlie and John were drinking in the Bluebird Inn near the track. John told him he had asked Martin-Handasyde to reduce his pay from 6 to 3 pence an hour on the understanding that he was taught to fly at the company's expense. They had shaken hands on it and, after a short period of instruction, John received his pilot's certificate. When war broke out Charlie volunteered as an artificer in the Royal Naval Air Service and at the depot he bumped into Alcock, now commissioned as an officer pilot in the RNAS. He was on his way to Eastchurch to train new cadets as pilots.

After that Charlie lost touch with his friend. In those days promotion came quickly to skilled men and Charlie ended up as a Chief Petty Officer. It was not until June, 1919, that he opened his newspaper to read that Captain John Alcock with his companion, Lieutenant Arthur Whitten-Brown, had achieved the first non-stop transatlantic flight, 1,890 miles from St. John's, Newfoundland, to Clifden, Northern Ireland, in a converted Vickers Vimy bomber.

## CHAPTER FOUR

# GEORGE WORTH EDDINGTON

In 1913 twenty-three-year-old George Worth Eddington had a good job which offered plenty of freedom and not much interference from head office. He enjoyed being out on the road in his big six-cylinder car. At that time not many young men had even been in a motor vehicle, let alone driven one. He was employed by the Marconi Company as a demonstrator of wireless sets. The day of the transistor was decades away and George towed an enormous sample of his company's product on a trailer.

It is not hard to understand his disappointment when the job came to an end. The company expressed its regrets and gave George a glowing testimonial. For a time he toyed with the idea of returning to his parents' home in London. He was a single man and free to move where he liked. But, as he said, 'I had many faults but laziness was not one of them.' He wanted to move on as quickly as possible.

With money running low, he decided to apply for the new Royal Flying Corps, inaugurated only a year before. The requirements for the job seemed to be more challenging than those expected from recruits for other regiments in the army, or for that matter the police force. Instead of mere physical size and robustness, the emphasis was placed on personal initiative, the ability to absorb technical detail and good mental and bodily co-ordination.

While he was neither large nor robust, he had plenty of initiative; moreover he understood the technicalities of wireless, *and* he could drive a car, not achieved without co-ordination. In early November, 1913, he marched into the nearest army recruiting office and applied to join the RFC. After a few questions from the recruiting sergeant, he was given a railway warrant and sent to a nearby army barracks for possible enlistment. He was further questioned by an officer who, presumably satisfied by his answers, passed him on to the MO who gave him a thorough examination.

George's only worry was a slight deafness in his right ear. When it came to the hearing test the doctor plugged up this inferior ear with cotton wool and then whispered from the other side of the room, 'What is the name of your brother?' Receiving this with his good ear he had no problem in replying. With his left ear plugged up and his less receptive ear exposed, George made a good guess and said, 'I do not have a sister, sir.'

The doctor said, 'No problem there. I can pass you fit for service.' George was already learning that initiative did count in the RFC.

As with every other recruit who signed on in those days he was handed the 'King's Shilling' by an officer. This shilling was the forerunner of the amount he was to receive each day, plus food and uniform, but not always accommodation, until he became qualified and later promoted.

Issued with another travel warrant he was ordered to report to Farnborough for training. Accommodated in Blenheim Barracks, George was a little shaken by the stark sleeping arrangements. Each recruit was given some rough blankets and three 'biscuits' – square canvas containers stuffed with horse-hair which, when placed end to end, formed what was euphemistically called a matress.

With the minimum space between each iron bedstead it was possible to house thirty recruits per barrack room. All the men were provided with a knife, fork, spoon and tin mug, a combination known as 'irons', a mess tin, a cut-throat razor and a 'housewife' – a little cloth pouch containing needles and thread and a few buttons for running repairs to one's uniform.

Square-bashing was of the highest order; George's particular squad was drilled under the stern eye of Sergeant Kemper of the Grenadier Guards. Keeping formation was difficult in those days because it was traditional to 'form fours', rather than the later introduction of marching in columns of three, a more manageable arrangement for controlling men.

Among so many soldiers from long-established regiments, these few RFC types felt very much in the minority. They certainly had no special privileges. On the contrary there was a tendency, especially among some of the long serving NCOs, to look down on them as being something without form or substance, neither fish nor fowl.

During the three months that George spent at Farnborough he almost forgot that he was anything to do with an air corps. No opportunity was missed to impress on him and his companions that they were nothing more than an inferior kind of soldier. They were shouted at, punished for the slightest misdemeanour and cursed in the foulest language. George took it very hard. He had come from a good home and had modelled his standards of politeness and good manners on those of his father, a public school man. So it was with a sense of relief that he completed his final days at Farnborough and started on the long train journey to Scotland to join No 2 Squadron of the RFC, then situated at Montrose, on the east coast, about thirty miles north of Dundee.

Not surprisingly, because of his previous experience, George was attached to the motor transport depot. Very few of the men or NCOs could drive a motor vehicle and he never saw an officer behind the wheel. Even if the Commanding Officer himself could handle a car it would be beneath his dignity to be seen doing a chauffeur's job.

The squadron's complement of aeroplanes consisted of about a dozen B.E.2cs, powered by Renault engines. The original B.E. was designed and built at the Royal Aircraft Factory in Farnborough under the supervision of Geoffrey De Havilland who, by now, had been made a captain in the RFC.

The designation B.E. then stood for 'Bleriot Experimental', M. Bleriot having originated the 'tractor' type machine, that is with a front-mounted engine and a propeller 'pulling' as opposed to 'pushing' the aircraft through the air. Later B.E. came to stand for *British Experimental*'.

The M.T. section had two Crossley tenders used to ferry fitters and riggers out to the aircraft. A stately Crossley touring car was reserved for the CO. Apart from the routine cleaning and polishing of the vehicles and regular transporting of technicians and aircrew, George and his fellow drivers were sometimes called out to collect pilots who had forced-landed in remote areas of the country.

George retained clear memories of his Commanding Officer, Major Burke, an Irishman of considerable girth who had great difficulty in squeezing himself into the restricted cockpit of his B.E.2c. Blessed with massive fists, it was not easy for him to apply the light touch required to control such a small and delicate machine. But he was always a gentleman. George and his mates had to remain in uniform at all times, even when off duty. While wandering the streets of Montrose, waiting, perhaps, for the cinema to open, they would often encounter one or two of their officers and be obliged to salute them even though *they* were invariably in civvies. Frequently their salutes would go unacknowledged. But if they chanced to meet Major Burke he would immediately raise his hat and wish them good evening. George remembered this small act of thoughtfulness all his life when more dramatic events were long forgotten.

War was declared against Germany on 4 August, 1914, and within days all 2 Squadron aircraft had headed south, eventually crossing to France via Dover. These tiny aeroplanes, with their 70 hp Renault engines, could just about manage the weight of their pilots and observers, but without the slightest hope of carrying any of the squadron's equipment. Workshop paraphernalia, spare engines, fitters' tool kits, stores, emergency rations, officers' and mens' essential gear, and all other squadron items were moved by motor transport. When all the other officers were winging their way to France, one remained to supervise the road convoy.

It became essential to commandeer extra vehicles for the journey and George found himself in charge of a brightly painted baker's van, a rugged and reliable Albion built in Glasgow. And it was to Glasgow that the convoy of about a dozen lorries headed on the first leg of their journey. Much of the men's personal gear had to be left behind for lack of space. Packed into spare kit bags, it was assigned to the squadron store and none of it was ever seen again. Because of this, it was George's bad luck to be parted from a much prized camera.

They drove into Glasgow docks in good order, but the ship assigned to transport them had not arrived. For 72 hours they were given the freedom of the city. If George, a Londoner, had any prejudices about Scottish meanness, these were swept away when he encountered the generosity of the citizens. Even the doors of the city's cinemas were thrown open free to RFC personnel. But this pleasant interlude came to an end when the ship docked and the vehicles were hoisted on board.

No one had troubled to tell George or the others where they were going, but after sailing south round the coast of Britain and joining ships at Southampton carrying the road transport for 3, 4 and 5 Squadrons, they headed across the English Channel and finished up in the port of Boulogne.

The Aircraft Park, with Ted Bolt and his mates, had arrived there a short time before, having sailed from Avonmouth, ready to set up a depot to supply, maintain and provide repair facilities for all the other squadrons. But in 1914 such an enterprise was completely new and a puzzled landing officer had sent a wire to GHQ which read: 'An unnumbered unit without aeroplanes which calls itself an Aircraft Park has arrived. What do we do with it?'

The whole convoy, now considerably swollen by the addition of the other three squadrons' lorries and cars, made their way from Boulogne inland to Maubeuge, a distance of around 110 miles. It was more like a triumphal procession than an attempt to prepare for war. Every time they paused the men were beseiged by back-slapping French men, women and children who plied them with food and drink. The RFC flashes on their shoulders worked wonders. 'Aviateurs Anglais!', the people cried.

Reaching Maubeuge they were reunited with their various squadron aeroplanes that had flown from England between 13 and 15 August, not without some accidents, a few of them fatal. These were very early days, and, disregarding any interference from the enemy, flying itself was still a hazardous and only half-understood occupation.

The honour of being the first to land in France fell to a member of 2 Squadron. At 8.20 am on 13 August Lieutenant H. D. Harvey-Kelly put down an Amiens. He was one of the RFC's best young pilots and was later to die of wounds after more than two and a half years' active service.

The aerodrome was covered in a motley display of machines. Apart from the B.E.2cs of George's squadron, there were the Bleriots and Henry Farmans of 3 Squadron, the B.E.2cs from 4 Squadron and 5 Squadron's Henry Farmans, Avros and B.E.8s. No 6 Squadron was still being formed in England.

The four flying squadrons in France were supported by 105 officers, 755 other ranks, sixty-three aircraft and ninety-five vehicles. A nucleus of airmen had remained in England along with a further 116 machines of which, apart from twenty at the Central Flying School, Upavon, were only fit for the scrap-heap. Not much of an airforce by later standards!

First priority was to protect the aeroplanes, and all hands were employed in erecting two large portable canvas sheds with wooden frames, known as Bessoneaux hangars. Within days the machines were under cover. Such care was not afforded the drivers. The number one drivers slept at night in their *open* cabs, while the number two drivers, which included George, did the best they could by crawling under the lorries and sleeping on the bare ground. It was not possible to climb inside the vehicles as these remained packed with aero engines, cans of petrol and other equipment.

George could never understand why the lower half of their uniform had to consist of pantaloons and puttees. Such equestrian attire seemed highly inappropriate for a newly formed service manned by technicians. The puttee, a strip of khaki ribbon wound spirally round the leg from ankle to knee, was originally designed as protection from thorns while operating in the African bush! This hated piece of gear had to be wound with meticulous care with no gaps showing. Often, from necessity, the men remained in their uniforms, day and night, for two or three weeks at a stretch. If it rained, as it frequently did, the waterlogged puttees became appallingly uncomfortable. George, and many of his companions, attributed their subsequent varicose veins to wearing these senseless pieces of apparel.

George was kept busy ferrying pilots and observers out to the aircraft. The RFC was in action without delay carrying out reconnaissance and observing the enemy's activities. Within days it had made a major contribution in saving the British Expeditionary Force from the advancing German armies. By 22 August reports from the air showed that the whole Second Corps of General von Kluck's First Army was marching westward on the Brussels – Ninove road, while General von Bulow's Second Army was advancing through Charleroi. The British Army was in danger of being trapped in a pincer movement.

On 25 August three machines of 2 Squadron chased an enemy monoplane and forced it to land. Lieutenant Harvey-Kelly and his observer landed near it and continued the chase on foot but the German pilot escaped into a wood.

Thanks to the keen eyes of the RFC the British forces were always capable, in retreat, of keeping one step ahead of the oncoming Germans. Early in September von Kluck found he had marched into a salient at the Marne between the Fifth and newly formed Sixth French Armies. By 9 September the Battle of the Marne had been won and the German First Army retired to prepared positions on the Aisne. Trench warfare had begun.

The British took up new defensive positions guarding the Channel ports. The German line was eventually fixed after a series of fierce engagements, ending in the First Battle of Ypres, where, in spite of poor weather, the RFC was able to forecast the impending attack in which the Germans outnumbered the British by three or four to one. With the holding of this attack there came a lull in the fighting which continued through the first winter of the war.

After these encounters the earlier cynicism with which so many military authorities had regarded the use of aeroplanes in war had progressed from disbelief in the reconnaissance reports to grateful acceptance and, in the end, downright admiration. In his first despatch to Field Marshal Lord Kitchener, the British War Minister, Sir John French, commanding the British Expeditionary Force, wrote:

'I wish particularly to bring to your Lordship's notice the admirable work done by the Royal Flying Corps ... Their skill, energy, and perseverance have been beyond all praise. They have furnished me with the most complete and accurate information, which has been of incalculable value in the conduct of operations. Fired at constantly both by friend and foe, and not hesitating to fly in every kind of weather, they have remained undaunted throughout.'

And all this was achieved by sixty-three flimsy little machines, flown by a handful of pilots and observers, developing as they went along the new skills essential in aerial warfare.

Sir John French's point about 'friendly fire' was real enough.

British and French ground forces were without a clue when it came to 'aircraft recognition'. Anything that flew was to be shot at on the grounds that it was better to be safe than sorry. The Union Jacks that the RFC then painted on the underside of their aeroplanes were only partly successful. It was only when they adopted the red, white and blue roundels on the wings and sides of the fuselage, still in use to this day, that they at last achieved a degree of immunity from Allied bullets.

During the general withdrawal the four squadrons had to keep back-pedalling, finding fresh landing fields ahead of the German advance. Again, George and the others had little idea why all this was happening, only that they were constantly on the move. Sometimes they barely had time for the fatigue parties to dig latrines before they were ordered to up sticks and were on the way again.

Their machines frequently returned to the base from which they had earlier taken off only to find it had been overrun by the enemy. The fact that much of their transport consisted of brightly coloured civilian vehicles aided Allied pilots in spotting their new temporary homes further down the road.

Rations were at their most basic, consisting of tins of bully beef and almost unbreakable army biscuits. The people of the districts through which they passed no longer hailed them as conquering heroes, nor, any longer, did they have food to spare. They too had taken to the roads and were heading away from the approaching Germans.

When the enemy was finally halted the squadrons became separated. 2 Squadron finished up at Merville, a small town about fifteen miles south-east of St Omer.

George and the other drivers were billeted in a barn attached to a farmhouse. The hay was dry and warm and the roof kept out the rain. This was a new-found luxury. He really thought his luck had changed for the better when the sergeant in charge of transport told him he was to report for fresh duties. He was to become the Commanding Officer's driver. This held out the prospect of a proper billet, clean uniform, regular baths and, biggest bonus of all, better food in the kitchen of the officer's mess. Promise of a higher standard of living was summed up by his mates who referred to him as a 'jammy bastard'!

The situation would have been perfect if only the admirable Major Burke had still been the CO. Unfortunately the Major, a regular soldier, had grown homesick for his old regiment, the Royal Irish, and had volunteered to return to fighting at ground level. Sadly, he lost his life in battle shortly afterwards.

His replacement, a Major Dawes, was a different type. Overbearing and impulsive, he had no time for the men in his charge. They were there to do his bidding without question – and woe betide anyone who crossed him. On one occasion he ordered George to drive him to the scene of a forced landing. The machine stood at the edge of a heavily ploughed field. It was out of fuel, but quite undamaged. Major Dawes summed up the situation, 'No B.E.2 is going to take-off with the bloody field in this state.' His solution was to round up a company of infantrymen, ordering them to march up and down the furrows until two hundred heavy boots had flattened out a temporary runway enabling the aeroplane to fly out. Not a word of thanks was given to the mud-bespattered soldiers.

One of George's duties was to drive his CO to Wing HQ at St Omer. On one occasion Dawes was more than usually impatient. 'Get a move on, man! What's the matter with you?' George accelerated and the lumbering Crossley responded sluggishly. It was almost worn out and its heavy steering was badly out of alignment. Apart from that, the road was full of deep potholes, but Major Dawes kept urging him to go faster. In the end George could take no more: 'If you're not satisfied, sir, perhaps *you* would like to drive?' Not an unreasonable suggestion, but it was a remark that nearly landed him in extremely hot water.

His face flushed with anger, the Major slumped back in his seat and said nothing more for the rest of the journey; nor did he break the silence on the drive back to base at Merville. But as soon as the car drew up at the orderly office, Dawes yelled for the Sergeant Major: 'Put this man under arrest and march him to my office in ten minutes.'

Standing stiffly to attention, George was told by his Commanding Officer, 'I would sentence you to seven day's field punishment for insolence, except that I need you as a driver. Instead you are confined to camp for fourteen days.'

This meant, in effect, that he had got off scot free. By the very nature of his duties he was unable to leave camp anyway, being constantly on call. On the other hand the field punishment would have been most unpleasant – tied to a wagon wheel in all weathers for a stipulated number of hours per day.

But relief was at hand, for within days Major Dawes was posted and a new Commanding Officer, Major Webb-Bowen, took his place. By contrast, Webb-Bowen turned out to be the most approachable officer that George ever met.

For more than two years he continued driving a succession of COs back and forth, back and forth, on the ever-deteriorating road to St. Omer. Once Major Webb-Bowen asked him what he would most like to do if he had the chance. Half-jokingly George replied, 'I would like to become a pilot, sir.' It was almost like a road sweeper asking for a job as a cabinet minister.

By early 1917 he had had enough. On duty twenty-four hours a day, always at the beck and call of the CO, currently a Major George Beck, George was thoroughly fed up and asked to return to driving lorries. He thought Beck looked a little put out by his request. 'Permission refused, Eddington. However, I'm going to post you back to England.' To George his words were like music, He had not seen his home country since August, 1914. Without the slightest idea why he should have been sent there, he finished up in Thetford, Norfolk, within a week.

He was then whisked away to Northolt Flying Training School, to the west of Wembley. Here, to his astonishment, he was kitted out with helmet, goggles and all the other items of flying clothing designed to withstand the rigours of operating from an open cockpit. It was like a miracle! The following day a cheerful Canadian Lieutenant took him up in a Maurice Farman for a familiarization flight. The S.7, a French-manufactured machine, was powered by a 70 hp Renault engine. The 'Longhorn', as it was known because of its long curved outriggers protruding in front of the undercarriage, had flown operationally during the early days of the war, but had soon been relegated to training duties.

Sitting in the small two-seat cupola about nine feet long, with the pusher propeller whirling behind his head, George was fascinated by the experience. Watching pilots on his squadron vaulting into their machines and taking off, he had often wondered what it was like to fly. Now he knew. And to him, as the Canadian instructor explained the controls, the whole business seemed far less mysterious than he had imagined. Soon he was handling those controls himself and within three hours he had soloed! After this he was instructed to undergo several tests including a forced landing exercise. It was straightforward enough – to land successfully within a circle painted on the aerodrome.

Similarly, as a test of his bombing skill, he was obliged to drop a flare within a marked area – not too difficult, flying at 60 mph on a calm day, only a few feet above the ground.

By now he had graduated from the Farman 'Longhorn' on to the B.E.2c, as flown by his old squadron. This, it seemed to him, was a more sophisticated aeroplane, more suitable for navigational exercises. After plotting his own course for his test, he had to fly from his training school at Northolt to an airfield near Potters Bar, a distance over the ground of some 15 miles. Here he had to land, obtain the duty officer's signature as proof of arrival, and fly back to base.

A trip by road to Hounslow completed his examinations. Here, on a very small aerodrome, he had to take over an aircraft and fly it at night. Completing two circuits he came into land between two lines of flaring tins stuffed with rags soaked in paraffin.

Now a fully qualified pilot, with his log book recording nearly four and a half hours flying, he received his RFC Flying Badge and was promoted to sergeant. His stay at Northolt had been the happiest of his career. He loved flying, his results were above average and he was convinced that, at last, he was in his right element. The fact that he was the only 'other rank' among so many officer trainees worried him not a bit.

Posted to South Carlton, on the northern outskirts of Lincoln, he converted onto R.E.8s (R.E. standing for reconnaissance experimental). These aircraft, derived from the B.E. types, were only slightly bigger, but much more robust, and faster, thanks to a more powerful 130 hp RAF (Royal Aircraft Factory) engine. It was a new type only brought into service towards the end of the previous year.

George was told that the R.E.8 was tricky to fly compared with the ladylike B.E.2c, but after a few circuits and landings he was convinced he had the better of it. His officers must have felt the same because almost the next day he was given the job of instructing some of the newcomers.

After two or three hours flying at South Carlton, both as pupil and instructor, George was posted back to France and spent a few hours at the all-too-familiar St Omer before being sent just over the Belgian frontier in late February, 1917, to join 6 Squadron at Abeele, eight miles west of Ypres.

Such was the reputation of the R.E.8 as a man-killer (something which George, being perfectly comfortable with the machine, could never understand) that the squadron sent all its new pilots up with the rear cockpit loaded with sandbags until they had properly mastered all its idiosyncrasies; in this way they avoided risking the precious lives of their observers who, previously, had to sit behind every cackhanded novice who joined the squadron.

6 Squadron's operational duties were to carry out reconnaissance flights behind the enemy lines to observe German activities. Sometimes this was achieved by reports based on the observer's sightings, sometimes by photography, and sometimes by wireless – usually when co-operating with artillery.

Radio messages could be transmitted from the aircraft to the guns on the ground. No signals could be received in return. A simple clock code enabled the observer to indicate the position of the enemy battery and direct the fire on to it, sometimes a long and perilous process, as the R.E.8s flew steadily in one direction, before retracing their course over and over again, fulfilling their spotting role and braving the anti-aircraft shells bursting all around them.

Weather permitting, this was normally a twice daily task, a dawn patrol and a dusk patrol. Losses among reconnaissance aircraft were frighteningly high. Apart from the ever-present menace of 'Archie' (fire from the ground), enemy fighters were constantly lurking at greater heights ready to swoop on the slow, poorly armed information gatherers as they plodded about their business, often trying to maintain a steady line of flight while taking photographs thousands of feet below their predators.

Fortunately, they had protectors in the form of S.E.5s, superb fighter planes with a phenomenal top speed for those days of 138 mph. They too had been released into service only a few months previously. Numbers of these twin gun fighters were detailed to look after the reconnaissance squadrons such as George's No 6, by chasing the Fokkers and Albatroses away and destroying as many of the enemy as possible in the process.

It was not always possible to synchronize their presence with that of the reconnaissance patrols. When the R.E.8s flew unescorted they were in constant peril of being shot down. As they went about their routine work day after day, they were the unsung heroes who, unlike the fighter aces, received little acknowledgment of how courageously they were fulfilling their vital duties.

George was soon recognized by the squadron as a skilled and conscientious pilot. In the air he was accepted as a reliable member of the team. On the ground, however, he lived in a kind of limbo, dwelling in a strange, rather lonely no-man's-land. Often he was struck by the thought that he had exchanged one chauffeur's job for another. He never attended any of the briefings but waited by his plane until the observer, invariably an officer, arrived with the details of their mission. It was always 'Good morning, sir,' from George and 'Good morning, sergeant,' from his observer. So different from the free and easy attitude enjoyed by the mixed rank aircrew of the Second World War, where informality between crew members, no matter what their service status, was accepted procedure.

Landing back at base after an operational flight, whatever dangers had been shared above the trenches, the officers would depart to their quarters, while George made his way to the sergeants' mess. Here he tended to be on his own. As a flyer he was not involved in any of the squadron's routine duties such as orderly sergeant; nor was he responsible for any men or equipment. There was little ground for mutual conversation; his experiences in the air were not shared by the earthbound men around him. He sensed resentment among some of the NCOs who probably considered him a lucky, jumped-up oddity, best left to his own devices.

By early November George was a veteran pilot of many months operational flying and had outlived all but a few of his more senior colleagues. He took off on a routine 'shoot' – spotting enemy guns by their tell-tale flashes. He was accompanied on this occasion by a Lieutenant as observer, a young, self-opinionated officer who had not made much of an impression during his short time with the squadron.

It was a clear day and, flying at 6,000 feet as they neared the target, George noticed eight tiny dots high in the sky over to their right. 'Keep an eye on them,' he warned his observer. 'They look ominous to me.'

'Don't worry about them,' the Lieutenant replied. 'They look like British Nieuport fighters. Concentrate on getting closer to the guns.'

George, who had considerably more experience than the man in the cockpit behind him, again said, 'Keep an eye on those characters all the same.'

His observer, who was radioing instructions back to the British gun batteries asked sarcastically, 'Got cold feet, Sergeant?'

Next moment there was the sound of a sharp crack, crack of gunfire. The eight 'Nieuports' had, as George suspected, turned out to be eight German Albatroses, each armed with deadly twin Spandau 7.92 mm machine guns. The enemy fighters had circled astern of the R.E.8 and were coming in fast, each eager to finish off the sitting duck.

Turning his head to see if his observer was returning fire from his single Lewis gun, George was alarmed to find him slumped on the floor of the cockpit, knocked out by the first burst of enemy fire. From long experience he knew that there was no chance of fighting back in these circumstances. He had worked out a number of tactics designed to make things as difficult as possible for the Hun. Executing a series of flat turns at quite low speed he was able to deflect the aim of his attackers. Flying much faster, they were unable to draw a bead on him as they overshot their target time after time. The German pilots had to exercise great care as they well knew their biplane's inherent weakness. The Albatros had an alarming tendency for the lower wing to break away in highly stressed manoeuvres. If only a handful of British S.E.5s had come along at that moment George would soon have been left in peace.

But he knew they would get him in the end. There were too many of them. Gradually losing height, he edged south towards his own lines no more than half a dozen miles away. Suddenly, as he glanced round, he spotted one of the brightly painted Albatroses coming in fast, directly behind him. He recalled his instructor's warning: 'Never, never stunt an R.E.8.' It was not designed for that sort of thing and would undoubtedly break up if involved in any form of aerobatics.

1. 'Colonel' Samuel Franklin Cody was born in Texas, but became a British citizen in 1909. He won the Military Trials competition on Salisbury Plain in 1912 but was killed in an air crash the following year. *(RAF Museum)*

2. 'Walking' an airship like the 152-foot-long 'Gamma' back into its hanger was extremely labour-intensive. On calm days it was no problem, but in high winds the struggle could be herculean. Note the Willows swivelling propellers. Docking was one of the many duties that fell to Ted Bolt when he joined the Royal Engineers at Farnborough.

3. 'Yellow Peril The Second'. A remarkably 'modern' looking monoplane for 1912, though it was not successful in the Military Trials of that year.

4. Charlie Tye, who, as a young civilian artificer, helped Handley Page build his first aeroplane - The Yellow Peril - before joining the Royal Naval Air Service. *(Imperial War Museum)*

5. A rarity in the Royal
   Flying Corps, George
   Eddington was a sergeant
   pilot in a service where
   virtually all pilots and
   observers were officers.
   *(Imperial War Museum)*

6. Cody's 'Cathedral', winner of the Military Trials of 1912. Its performance was
   enhanced by its 120hp Austro-Daimler engine, far more powerful than any
   other competitor's. *(Imperial War Museum)*

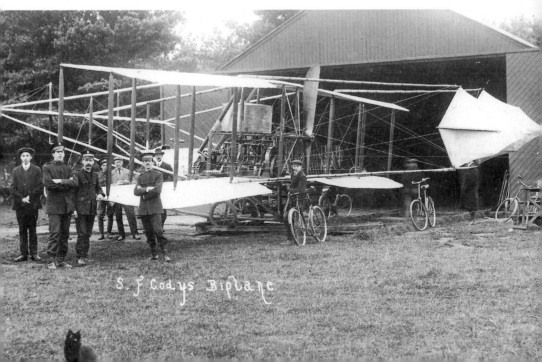

7. Used in large numbers by the RFC in the early part of the war on the Western Front for spotting and reconnaissance, the B.E.2 series suffered heavy losses. This one was the first RFC aircraft to land in France on 13 August, 1914. The pilot, Lieutenant H.D. Harvey-Kelly, can be seen lying by the hayrick (bottom right-hand corner) studying a map. *(Imperial War Museum)*

8. The R.E.8, affectionately known as the 'Harry Tate', was the replacement for the B.E.2c. Better armoured, but almost as slow and unmanoeuvrable as its predecessor. More R.E.8s were used on the Western Front than any other 2-seater. *(Imperial War Museum)*

This was the moment to break the rules. He decided to imitate a tactic of the well known German air ace of the earlier war years and execute an 'Immelmann Turn'. He pulled the stick right back, stood the R.E.8 up on her tail, kicked left rudder and, just as she started to stall, over she went and well away in a frantic spin. It was the quickest way to get down provided she didn't disintegrate on the way.

During those moments George felt quite calm. He was far too busy trying to remember how to get out of a spin. 'Centre all the controls,' the instructor had said. With the earth rushing up to meet him, he did just that. Juddering in protest, the staid reconnaissance machine pulled out of her giddy descent and began to fly straight and level once again.

Suddenly George heard two sharp cracks, not gunfire this time. Both the upper wing extensions had broken off, right up to the struts, reducing the span of the upper wings by half. The ailerons had been carried away with the outer parts of the wings, leaving George with no lateral control and precious little lift. The ground ahead looked reasonably clear of obstructions. When he judged that they were about thirty feet above it, he pulled back the stick with all his strength, hoping that the elevators were still functioning. The machine hit the earth with a resounding crash. George rarely did up his safety belt, hating the way it restricted his movements, but on this occasion he happened to be wearing it. The webbing snapped like an elastic band and he was pitched forward against the instrument panel. He remembered switching off the petrol tap before blacking out.

They had landed just over the British forward lines, in front of an area known, appropriately, as Sanctuary Wood, sheltering a number of field guns. An artillery officer and some soldiers rushed to the scene of the accident. George remembers a voice saying, 'Are you all right, old man?'

By some miracle, apart from cuts and bruises, he *was* all right and was told that the observer, although wounded, would recover after treatment. 'We saw it all, we saw it all,' they kept saying, 'You did damn well. It was a first class effort.' Later he proudly wrote their remarks in his log book.

When the ambulance arrived George had regained his wits sufficiently to cast an appreciative eye over the vehicle that had come to collect him. It was a Model T Ford, the only motor transport, apart from a tank, capable of negotiating the deep mud ruts and shell holes of the battlefield.

He spent about four days recovering in a casualty clearing station. Still suffering from shock, he returned to his squadron to resume his duties. He was told to take it easy for a week or so, but after this short break, Major Archibald James, his CO (and the subject of our final chapter) gave him a long, hard look. 'My boy,' he said, 'you've already done more than your bit. I'm sending you home for a well-deserved rest.'

After an extended leave George Eddington was posted to a small RFC air station at Dymchurch, on the south-east coast of England. Here he flew Avros, helping to train observers in the skills of air gunnery. He was still there when the war ended in November of the following year.

CHAPTER FIVE

# THOMAS BLENHEIM WILLIAMS

Thomas Blenheim Williams' father was a mercantile sea captain with a good weather eye for business. Along with his partner, another sea captain, he had purchased two cargo steamers which plied for trade between Great Britain and South Africa. Thomas had been apprenticed as a junior to the managerial department of the Union Castle Shipping Line in the City of London. The idea was that when he had learned his trade he would join his father in the family business.

It was an exciting life and by no means office-bound. He looked forward to Saturdays when he often sat down with his father on board one of the vessels in dock for a slap-up lunch. Another of his weekend activities took him to the aerodrome at Hendon where he was fascinated by the new-fangled flying machines that, for the most part, hopped into the air, did a circuit or two and then landed. He made himself useful lugging cans of engine oil from the hangars; it was sufficient reward to be in the company of aviators like De Havilland and other pioneers. His head was filled with dreams of aeroplanes and ships.

Then war broke out. Actively engaged in the process of importing essential merchandise Thomas was exempt from service in the armed forces. But, like so many high-spirited young men of that time, he was determined to enlist. In the end, after more than a year of badgering, his exasperated father, who had strongly advised him to stay where he was, gave in and took him to see an old friend, an admiral in the Royal Navy. 'We are building some small airships to help defeat the U-Boat menace,' he told the boy. 'How would you like to command one of them?'

Thomas was overwhelmed. 'Very much, sir. Yes, I would!'

The Admiral went on to explain that these airships were to be classed as naval vessels of war in charge of naval officers. Thomas had been offered a combined role as a sailor/aviator that opened the door to all his wildest ambitions.

Reporting to the Naval College at Greenwich in November, 1915, he was subjected to a series of stringent medical examinations, followed by aptitude tests and a number of written papers. He later admitted that he was so excited at the time he could hardly recall anything about the place afterwards!

He had read about airships, seen photographs and marvelled at the enormous sheds built to house them, but had never actually encountered one. Overnight, as a naval officer in waiting, he transferred his loyalty from heavier than air machines, more the concern of the army anyway, to the Navy's 'superior' ships of the air.

Sitting at breakfast soon after his visit to Greenwich his mother handed him an official-looking envelope addressed to Probationary Flight Sub-Lieutenant T. B. Williams RN. The letter announced that he had been accepted for training and was posted to HMS *President*, which he subsequently discovered to be a hulk lying in the Thames (still there at the time of writing). This was in effect a 'ship of convenience' as every naval officer had to be attached to a vessel of some description. He never set foot on this vessel, but finished up at Wormwood Scrubs, the Navy's main airship station. His arrival in brand new uniform caused a stir that was not soon forgotten. It is easy to imagine the looks of horror in the mess when the fledgling sprog walked in wearing a navy blue tie instead of a black one.

The complement of the station was no more than a hundred, including administration, landing parties, engineers and aircrew. Thomas was one of only four airship pilots under training. The small airships were kept in the giant shed built under the patronage of the *Daily Mail*, originally to house the huge French dirigible *Clement Bayard* (see Chapter Two). Four of the newly constructed diminutive navy airships could be accommodated in this hangar.

A gas-producing plant had been constructed on site beside the hangar. Over the years Wormwood Scrubs grew in importance as a centre for the construction of more sophisticated airships. Later in his career, as a fully qualified airship captain, Thomas, during his operational rest periods, was occasionally called on to deliver newly manufactured models from this centre to active service stations around the country.

In the early part of training the probationary sub-lieutenants were instructed in aeronautics, navigation and engineering when it was overcast, windy or raining. On fine days they travelled by road to the balloon training centre at Hurlingham, to the south-west of London, conveniently situated next to a coal gas plant whose output was piped into the balloons as needed.

Under the supervision of warrant officers they were shown how to lay out the 'envelopes', enclosed by net coverings, to which a circle of sandbags was attached by individual hooks. Then, connecting the pipe from the balloons to the gas-holder, the bag was steadily inflated. More sandbags were added as necessary to prevent the balloon rising into the air prematurely.

When the balloon was fully inflated and a basket toggled into place the pupils clambered aboard accompanied by an instructor, one of whom was C. F. Pollack, the holder of Aeronaut's Certificate Number One. Pollack and Thomas were to work closely over the years.

The importance of acquiring balloon-handling skills was its relationship to commanding an airship if the engines failed, a not uncommon occurrence in those early days. At the mercy of the elements, it was essential to learn the art of executing a successful emergency landing under adverse weather conditions.

Urged on by the prevailing wind, the cadets often flew over London. On one occasion the breeze died away and they hung almost motionless a couple of hundred feet above Marble Arch. One of the cadets, bored by the lack of progress, took his supply of currant buns and began to 'bomb' passengers sitting on the open top decks of buses passing underneath them. The instructor soon brought this enterprise to a stop. A more useful task was scattering leaflets over the metropolis urging people to buy war bonds.

Normally they would land in open countryside beyond the city. The procedure was then to find a man with a horse and cart to convey their parcelled-up balloon to the nearest railway station. With a label attached, it would eventually arrive back at Hurlingham. In those days the pace of life was measured by different standards.

By April, 1916, Thomas had successfully soloed both by day and night. On his daytime solo he had the misfortune to be caught in a thunderstorm which rocketed him up through five layers of cloud until he reached a height of 13,000 feet. He was so affected by the cold that he fainted. Fortunately, recovering his wits, he was able to descend through each stratum of cloud, feeling, as he glanced up and down, like the filling in a cotton wool sandwich. At 1000 feet he at last broke through the lowest layer and saw the ground below him. Assessing that he was descending too fast, he threw out some ballast, a huge clod of earth; this bounced against the side of a cottage dislodging a zinc bath hanging on the wall. The bath landed on the concrete path with a resounding clang that brought an alarmed old lady to the door.

The examiner looked stern as he examined Thomas's report. 'You know the cardinal rule of ballooning, surely?'

'Yes, sir. Of course. Never fly out of sight of land.'

'Exactly. So what were you doing at 13,000 feet above umpteen layers of cloud?'

'I had no option, sir. The thunderstorm took over and whisked me straight up.'

A grin spread over the examiner's face. 'Fully understood, Thomas. You did very well under the circumstances and were lucky to get down alive.' He was awarded his Aeronaut's Certificate.

Towards the end of the five months' training he and the others also received instruction on the miniature two-man SS Submarine Scout type airships that the Admiral had told him about at his initial interview.

When the cadets flew from their air station at Wormwood Scrubs the flight path went directly over the prison. Thomas felt some pity for the prisoners, slowly shambling round the exercise yard, while he and his companions flew through the skies above them.

Posted to the airship station of Kingsnorth on the Medway, Thomas discovered for the first time that he had entered the world of the Royal Navy. The language used was full of strange nautical terms. The members of the 'crew' even had to ask permission to 'go ashore' when they left the camp.

Apart from two SS airships, SS 14A and SS 31, the type with which he was already familiar, there was also a larger Coastal C1 Type dirigible. Being naval craft they each flew the White Ensign. He remembers his instructors at Kingsnorth with respect. They included such aeronauts as George Herbert Scott who came to be acknowledged as the leading airship pilot of the time, sadly to meet his fate, along with many other notable men, in the R101 disaster of 1930. It was this tragedy that finally killed Britain's interest in further construction of rigid airships.

Thomas was a natural flyer who described his mood at that time as one of jubilation. Exhilarated by every flight his spirits soared and he felt at one with the birds. There is no doubt that his instructors sensed his enthusiasm and recognized his innate ability. It was hardly necessary, but they encouraged him to work hard also at his theoretical studies, meteorology, aeronautics and the rest. The result was that he passed out high on the course and was given command of SS 31, one of only two cadets to be so honoured, the other cadet, Taylor, taking over SS 14A.

The SS Types had only been under development since the previous year and were still, to some extent, experimental. They consisted of a gas bag with a wingless aeroplane fuselage slung underneath. The SS 14A (the 'A' indicated that it had been rebuilt at some time in its history) had the fuselage of a B.E.2c with its 'tractor' motor, while his own SS 31 supported the 'pusher' engined fuselage of a Maurice Farman.

SS 31 was nicknamed the 'Flying Bedstead' because of its tendency to fly sideways. The two star pupils, now airship commanders in their own right, were given the task of flight testing their craft in order to improve performance. Thomas soon found, for instance, that he could reduce the sideways drift by fitting a large rudder.

It was never forgotten that the purpose of the SS airships was eventually to seek out and destroy submarines. With this in mind experiments were carried out to lighten Thomas's craft in order to accommodate the maximum weight in bombs. In one ill-advised experiment all the heavy-gauge control wires and the cables supporting the fuselage were removed and replaced with thinner wire. The result was that he had hardly become airborne when vital wires, including those designed to control the airship, began to snap. Then the cables on the starboard side broke, pitching the fuselage and its occupant sideways. A flaying elevator wire whipped across the propeller tearing off its blades. Thomas quickly closed the throttles and the whole contraption came down in a heap, straddling the aerodrome hedge. Miraculously, he walked away unhurt.

On one occasion the Renault motor of Taylor's SS 14A was removed and replaced with a more powerful American Curtiss water-cooled engine. Thomas was asked to accompany his companion on the test flight. At first the two pilots were well pleased with the improved performance. The airship moved faster through the air in level flight and later proved that it could also climb more rapidly with this new source of power. Disappointingly the engine conked out at 8000 feet. The two took it in turns to climb out of their cockpits, stand on the skids and attempt to get it going again by swinging the prop with one hand while precariously holding on with the other, an extremely perilous manoeuvre in those pre-parachute days. Unable to fire up the engine, their crafts drifted down until they managed to land undamaged on the edge of a field adjacent to the village of Hoo, near Chatham, by coincidence the birthplace of Thomas's mother. They secured the mooring rope to a substantial tree and then, leaping over the boundary wall into a graveyard, made fast another line to some of the upright gravestones. Followed by a group of admiring youngsters, they made their way to the local sweetshop to buy some chewing gum. This proved effective in stopping up the holes in the engine's burst radiator and, when they had refilled it with water from the village pump, they were successful in restarting the motor. During their descent they had lost a quantity of gas and there was only enough buoyancy left to lift one person. So, while Taylor flew his airship back to base, Thomas returned on foot.

Apart from their experimental work, he and Taylor were employed as instructors, passing on their newly acquired knowledge to the fresh intake of cadets. Also they in turn were taught to fly the larger Coastal C1 Type airship. Thomas, who had a passionate fondness for the single-engine SS Types, was unable to generate the same affection for the more cumbersome twin-engined Coastals. He lived in fear of being posted to an operational airship station flying Coastals rather than one equipped with Submarine Scouts. He need not have worried.

In November, 1916, he was posted to the Royal Naval Air Station in Anglesey and immediately given command of SS 25, another airship fitted with a B.E.2c fuselage. To his delight he discovered that his commanding officer was his old instructor George Herbert Scott, who had preceded him by a few months. Thomas's duties involved flying out over the Irish Sea to meet incoming convoys and escort them into Liverpool docks, the 'backdoor' to Britain.

These convoys were made up of large numbers of merchant ships led either by a battleship or a cruiser and flanked by destroyers. Coming up via the southern route, the Anglesey flights would take over from other escorting airships out of Pembroke. Those approaching round northern Ireland were handed over by protecting airships operating from Stranraer. The operations were directed by the naval Commander in Chief stationed at Holyhead.

Some of these flights were of long duration under adverse weather conditions. Exposed in an open cockpit, the wind and rain buffeted the pilot who was protected only by his helmet and leather flying coat. Under such circumstances it was a problem to sort out a practical way of answering the call of nature, always a pressing problem in such chilling conditions. Some carried a tin, others a bottle to be emptied over the side. Thomas devised his own sanitary arrangements by drilling a small hole in the floor of his cockpit, inserting a tube and attaching a petrol filler funnel to the top end where it nestled conveniently in his lap.

Returning after braving a particularly stormy passage, Thomas had to be lifted, soaking wet, from a cockpit half-filled with rain water. He developed sciatica and was forced to spend a period in the sick bay.

Armament at this time was, of course, rudimentary. A few 20 lb bombs rolled about on the floor at the pilot's feet ready to be slung over the side attached to a piece of string. A penknife was kept handy to cut the string when the bomb had to be dropped. The 'bombsight' consisted of two crossed nails. In those days Thomas's defensive armament was a Webley Scott pistol hanging on a hook in the cockpit.

The station at Anglesey had a complement of 250/300 personnel, of whom only about half a dozen were airship pilots. On calm days a similar number of ground crew would be sufficient to haul in and make fast an SS airship, but on blustery occasions every available man was needed to ensure a safe docking in the large single shed which housed the station's four SS airships.

The navy had recently established a mooring-out airfield to the north of Dublin in the grounds of Lord Talbot's estate at Malahide Castle. This was an ideal position to fly from when making contact with convoys steaming through the Irish Sea. On various occasions Thomas made use of this facility and once stayed a night in the castle. Unfortunately his sleep was interrupted when armed Sinn Feiners attempted to storm the castellated walls in an attempt to oust the hated English. The intruders were successfully repelled after a sharp exchange of rifle fire.

Once Thomas was bound for Malahide while watching over a convoy made up of four troopships, the Irish mail packet and four destroyers, all led by the cruiser, HMS *Patrol*, commanded by Captain Gordon Campbell VC, the most highly decorated officer in the Royal Navy. In this instance the convoy was heading west out of Liverpool to Ireland bringing reinforcements to help in quelling 'The Troubles'. He was flying ahead of the convoy at his normal cruising speed of 25 mph, eyes peeled for signs of enemy activity. All of a sudden he spotted a dark object on the surface of the water, but, coming lower, he was unable to identify it. Flashing his Aldis lamp he sent a message to HMS *Patrol*: 'Suspicious object directly ahead of you'. *Patrol* relayed the message to the rest of the ships who immediately scattered. Thomas was momentarily overcome by a sense of power – to see a whole fleet of vessels scatter at his word was an experience to be savoured. A destroyer dashed up and began circling the spot. Then he saw the ship's cutter rowing over to investigate. As he watched, the object was hauled on board. In no time HMS *Patrol* was relaying a message to him: 'Your "suspicious object" is a fisherman's float'.

Later Thomas happened to meet the commander of HMS *Patrol* in the mess. In some trepidation he apologized for scattering the great man's fleet. Gordon Campbell looked at him kindly. 'On the contrary, my boy, we were glad to know your sharp eyes were watching out on our behalf. It could so easily have been something much more dangerous.'

Thomas remained in Anglesey for over a year and became the senior flying officer on the station. During this period, thanks to his efforts and those of his fellow pilots, the four SS Type airships on the station's strength were modified and improved. Meanwhile, both Kingsnorth and Wormwood Scrubs were building a replacement model known as an SS P Type. (The 'P' stood for pusher.) Six of these were constructed with a larger gas capacity and a purpose-built gondola replacing the original aircraft fuselage.

With high hopes Thomas went down to collect SS P No 1 and later also delivered SS P Nos 5 and 6 safely back to Anglesey. He must have been both lucky and exceptionally skilled as a pilot because the remaining three SS Ps allocated to other stations all came to grief on their delivery flights and never took to the air again. There was nothing wrong with the design, but the newly fitted 100 hp water-cooled Green engines let it down badly – unreliable, difficult to maintain and hated by the engineers who had the job of trying to service it. There were so many breakdowns that operational efficiency was impaired and flying hours seriously reduced.

But relief was at hand. A more advanced SS had been developed that proved to be the ultimate model that Thomas and his companions had always dreamed of. This was the SS Zero powered by a 100 hp water-cooled, 6-cylinder Rolls Royce Hawk engine. The machine was flown by a crew of three sitting in a boat-shaped fuselage.

The wireless operator, stationed in the bow, received and transmitted morse signals and also acted as gunner, firing the forward-facing machine-gun. The engineer, in the stern, kept an eye on the pusher engine. The captain sat between them. His right hand took care of the elevation on the wheel. He steered with his feet, adjusted the throttle with his left hand and from time to time freed one or other hand to attend to the gas controls and pressures.

The gondola, or nacelle, was rigged closer to the gas envelope than previously and the twin fuel tanks, containing a mixture of 80% petrol and 20% benzol, were mounted on the underside of this gas container – an efficient arrangement allowing the fuel to be gravity fed to the motor. It was a surprisingly economical unit, demanding no more than 6.5 gallons per hour with an oil consumption of only half a gallon over the same period.

Because the motor only had a single carburettor it was remarkably easy to start and could be throttled down for slow running without fear of cutting out, often an anxiety with other engines. The motor could also be stopped in flight with every assurance that it would re-start on demand, something by no means certain with previous power units. The Rolls Royce was so reliable that the engineer in Thomas's crew developed the confidence to snatch an occasional sleep – a welcome luxury on flights that sometimes lasted more than 24 hours!

Once, when he was commanding SS Z 35, Thomas and his crew were flying low over Liverpool Bay after receiving a report that a U-Boat had been spotted heading north out of the bay. Their immediate intention of setting off in pursuit was frustrated when the motor packed in – a very rare occurrence with a Rolls Royce engine. Ballooning some feet above the sea they let out their sea anchor in the form of a drogue on the end of the trail-rope. The wireless operator sent a message to base which was intercepted by a Liverpool patrol boat, soon on the scene accompanied by an armed trawler. The trawler took up SS Z 35's rope and Thomas shouted orders to tow them to Red Wharf Bay on the north-east coast of Anglesey. After a time the seas became choppier and the wind increased; they then received a signal from the air station that they should proceed instead round the Great Ormes Head to Llandudno where a party of soldiers was waiting to assist them.

Being buffeted about above and behind the trawler, and losing gas, Thomas decided to lighten ship. He defused their 100 lb bomb and dropped it into the sea just astern of their rescuers. Eventually they arrived off Llandudno pier where the waiting soldiers took over the trail rope from the trawlermen, 'walked' the airship floating no more than 50 feet above their heads, along the pier, across the promenade and hauled it steadily down to ground level where it nestled between two hotels. One of the soldiers bent down and handed Thomas a small object. 'This has just fallen off the bomb rack, sir,' he said. Thomas looked at his crew with a wry smile as he realized that this was the fuse wire that should have de-activated their bomb. 'Good thing I sent you over the side to "safety pin" all our bombs and depth charges before we started the tow, Jim,' he said to the engineer. 'Otherwise none of us would be sitting here now!'

Over a period of eighteen months Thomas and his crew sighted and attacked six U-Boats of which they felt certain they had destroyed at least two. One submarine on average every three months may not seem a high score, but when seen in relation to the deterrent effect of the overall SS operation it underlines the value of using airships as escorts. Thousands of ships carrying food, arms, raw materials and troops from overseas got through home waters unscathed. The combination of the convoy system, escorting destroyers, aided by the eyes of the fleet overhead, paid dividends in cutting losses to a minimum off Britain's coasts.

Thomas had a hunch that what U-Boat attacks were being made followed a regular pattern. He sensed that this was conditioned by the submarines' need to return to base for refuelling, repairs, and for the crews to rest after enduring unpleasantly cramped quarters beneath the sea. He talked to the junior officer in charge of the small intelligence department and asked him to compile a record of sightings, attacks, times, dates and locations. It emerged that a definite pattern *did* exist. One of the U-Boats' favourite hunting grounds was in the vicinity of Bardsey Island, off the North Wales Lleyn Peninsula, where the steamer track altered course. And Thomas had been right. These attacks took place with methodical regularity on certain dates and always at dawn.

When the appropriate day arrived three small airships, engines throttled back, hovered in line-ahead formation above the seas round Bardsey Island. Thomas's SS Z 35 was in the rear. Just as dawn broke they received an urgent message from a ship to say it was being fired on by a surfaced submarine. Simultaneously Thomas and his crew picked up a signal from the SS airship immediately ahead telling them they had spotted the U-Boat and were diving to attack. As soon as the bombs were dropped SS Z 35 followed suit and released her bombs. The leading airship, by then ahead of the action, swung about, dived and did likewise.

Meanwhile Thomas's wireless operator had called up all destroyers patrolling the area. Within moments the aeronauts' favourite destroyer, D.O.I, with whom they shared the closest co-operation, arrived on the scene. She was followed by three large American-built destroyers. These four ships raced back and forth dropping depth charge after depth charge. Between them they literally 'blew the bottom out of the sea'. That was one U-Boat that never returned to base – and the airships were given the credit for it.

In May, 1918, right out of the blue, Thomas was ordered to report to Wormwood Scrubs. He was now a full naval lieutenant, the equivalent of a flight lieutenant in the newly formed Royal Air Force. On arrival he was instructed to proceed to Ciampino, in Italy, via cross channel ferry to Le Havre and then on to Rome by train, to help in the collection of airship SR 1, an acquisition by the British Admiralty, and fly it back to England. The SR 1, unlike the SSs and other operational airships during the war, was of a 'semi-rigid' structure consisting of a long keel which enabled the envelope to retain its shape at lower pressure.

Apart from Thomas, the acceptance party consisted of an engineering officer and a group of eight other ranks made up of wireless operators, engineers, riggers and mechanics. Flight Lieutenant Ralph Cochrane (who was to become the Air Officer Commanding No 5 Bomber Group in the Second World War) and Captain George Meegan, as first pilot, joined the group at a later date.

Billeted in a comfortable hotel in Rome, Thomas was driven out on the first morning by an officer of the Italian Air Force to have a look at their new charge at Ciampino, to the south of the city. He was surprised to discover that it was by no means ready to fly. In fact, it took another five months to complete its construction. So while the war raged on elsewhere Thomas and the others had to put up with an extended holiday in Italy!

Several times the Commanding Officer of the Italian Air Force establishment at Ciampino took Thomas up in another semi-rigid airship to familiarize him with this type of dirigible. He found very little difference in the handling characteristics compared with those of the non-rigid airships he had previously flown. At least these flights gave him a head start over his fellow pilot, George Meegan, who had not yet arrived from England.

When at last SR 1 was ready for test flights Thomas was impressed with the workmanship that had gone into building this huge airship. It had a capacity of half a million cubic feet of hydrogen, seven or eight times greater than that required to support the SS Types. It was propelled, ironically enough, by two large 300 hp German-designed Maybach engines built under licence in Italy. In addition the Italian engineers had fitted a subsidiary S.P.A. engine (made in Turin by the Societa Piemonese Automobili) above the cupola with the idea of assisting its forward motion.

The Admiralty had ordered this particular airship because of its bomb-carrying capacity, its range and its operational altitude – all far in access of anything an aeroplane could match at that time. The airship was fitted with variable pitch propellers so she could be reversed, thus setting up a braking effect. When Thomas first saw the Italians in action he was amazed at the speed with which they came in to land. In fact, there was an emergency medical ward on the edge of the aerodrome ready to treat injured members of the landing party, often brushed off their feet by fast-moving trail-ropes. He sensed that the ground crew appreciated the traditionally cautious approach of the British when they brought in SR 1 after her test flights.

After his experience on the diminutive SSs, Thomas now really felt in command of a ship with a full crew: a 'height' coxswain had charge of the elevators, a 'rudder' coxswain was responsible for port and starboard motion, each motor had its attendant team of engineers, while riggers kept an eye on the condition of the airship in flight. The pilots were in overall command and took over the controls themselves from time to time.

In October, 1918, when weather conditions were considered suitable, the SR 1 took off for England, the first ever flight from Italy to the United Kingdom. Thomas was to remember it as a nightmare. Before dawn they passed over a brilliantly lit Rome and flew up the west coast of Italy. Turning out to sea, they crossed over Cape Corse, on the northern tip of Corsica, arriving at Marseilles, their first destination, after a 10-hour flight.

Here, in spite of previous assurances, they found the airship shed was not big enough to dock the SR 1. They moored up as best they could between the hangar's 'windscreens', tying down the dirigible with the aid of 'screw pickets' inserted into the ground, and also securing lines to a number of heavy lorries.

Fortunately there was plenty of petrol and hydrogen on hand to top up their supply, but the process took the whole night. To add to their discomfort the S.P.A. engine immediately above their heads had sprayed them with oil throughout the flight.

They set off again before dawn and flew up the Rhone Valley. They were buffeted head-on by the *mistral* and made hardly any forward progress. At one time a convoy of French army lorries on the road below easily overtook them. It was fortunate they had three engines, not for the power that these provided but because more than two were rarely running at any one time. The engineers were constantly battling to keep them going, especially the little oil-leaking terror above their heads. 'What wouldn't we give for a couple of Rolls Royces?' they grumbled.

Finally they came down on an emergency landing ground near Lyon, realizing they were never going to make Paris that day as they had hoped. Again they spent the night refuelling.

An early start next day saw them climbing through heavy fog, a normal phenomenon in that area at that time of the year. They were soaking wet and chilled to the bone from the vapour. The dampness weighed heavily on the airship, preventing it from climbing. They threw quantities of ballast overboard in a desperate attempt to stay airborne. Branches of a tree lodged in the front of the control car taking away the windscreen. Both an Italian and a French airship pilot were on board as observers. By this stage they must have wished they had stayed at home. The French pilot's contribution was to remind the crew that there was a war on and there was every possibility they could be mistaken for a German Zeppelin and shot down. After being threatened with a raised spanner, he lapsed into silence.

Thomas was working the elevators when the S.P.A. engine decided to disintegrate. It threw its oil pump directly at him, catching him on the head. Fortunately he was wearing his leather flying helmet or he would have been badly injured. But, like the others, he was deluged in black oil.

To his horror he noticed that the engine's white-hot exhaust pipe had fallen on top of one of the fuel tanks. This was below the envelope containing highly combustible hydrogen. He yelled to an engineer called Harry Leech, 'Quick, follow me!' Hooking on a portable ladder they shinned up onto the top of the tank. Using nothing but their hands, they scraped off every piece of sizzling metal. Clambering down again, Thomas said to Harry, 'We really shouldn't be alive, you know.' His companion most certainly continued to lead a charmed life. At a later date he was one of only six to survive the ghastly R 101 airship disaster in 1930.

Still in thick fog, by dead reckoning and the use of the compass, they eventually arrived in the vicinity of Paris. By now the crew was in an extreme state of discomfort. Landing at the designated airfield they suffered the final straw when the French authorities told them they were not expected. Apparently a radio message had been sent instructing them to proceed to Le Havre as the shed at the Paris field was again too small to accommodate them. They had received no such message.

Once again mooring in the open as best they could, the bedraggled party retired to the French Air Force mess for a clean-up and a much needed meal. On the way back Thomas tripped over a railway line and split open an old shin wound previously sustained in a balloon crash. He used his handkerchief as a makeshift bandage. Hobbling about in agony, he sustained the stiff upper lip then expected of an officer and a gentleman, making light of it to the others. But every time he put any weight on the injured foot he nearly fainted.

Warned by the French authorities of an impending gale, they took off in darkness, passing so close to the Eiffel Tower they could have thrown a biscuit onto its top balcony. Again they proceeded in thick fog, Thomas controlling the elevators. After a while he sought Captain Meegan's permission to descend through the gloom to see if they had reached the coast. The Captain agreed. Cautiously decreasing altitude SR 1 broke through the fog layer and Thomas found himself staring into the eyes of a cow! He hauled back on the controls, forcing the nose sharply upwards. In spite of the cold fog, sweat broke out all over his body. They had been inches from disaster. Would this nightmare of a flight never end?

At last they crossed the French coast at Dieppe and as they flew out to sea the fog cleared. As if to welcome them home it seemed that every wireless station in Britain made contact with them simultaneously. In contrast to the total radio silence that had accompanied them across the Continent, the airwaves were now alive with messages of concern about their welfare and questions as to where they had been.

Establishing strong wireless communication with the air station at Capel le Ferne, between Folkestone and Dover, messages were relayed back and forth between the airship and the Admiralty. As they crossed the English coast at Rye Bay they were instructed to proceed to Kingsnorth where the shed was being prepared for their arrival.

Flying steadily across south-east England they soon arrived at their destination. A huge landing party was waiting to greet them after their epic voyage. In true Italian fashion the SR 1 came in fast, which must have concerned those watching her approach, but at the last minute the engines were reversed to slow her down, trail lines were lowered and dozens of willing hands drew her gently into the great hangar.

A dozen oil-soaked figures, red-eyed, unshaven and weary, literally fell out of the nacelle and lay on the ground, totally exhausted. Such was their physical state that they were unrecognized by the many friends who had come to greet them.

On 11 November the Armistice was signed and arrangements were made to deprive Germany of all naval power. The enemy surface fleet, the second largest force of battleships, cruisers and destroyers in the world, was to be escorted by Britain's Grand Fleet, the world's mightiest navy, into Rosyth before eventual internment at Scapa Flow in the Orkney Islands.

The situation aboard the German ships was chaotic; for a year mutiny had prevailed throughout the navy and it was now in the hands of the sailors themselves under the Soviet of Workers, Soldiers and Sailors. The Red Flag flew from every vessel. It was only the submarine crews who remained loyal to their officers and the crown.

The Allies made separate arrangements for these U-Boats which were to be escorted across the North Sea into Harwich. Some of their commanders refused to strike the German Ensign and interned their vessels in Baltic ports rather than surrender. Most of the submarines on their way back from the Mediterranean when the Armistice was signed followed their lead.

Of the 150 U-Boats to be given up nearly 100 were ready by 20-November and at 7.00 am the first batch was reported by wireless to be approaching the rendezvous point with the Royal Navy's escort fleet some 35 miles off the east coast of England. The light cruiser HMS *Curaçao*, the flagship of Admiral Tyrwhitt, four other cruisers and a number of destroyers were at action stations ready for any last-ditch action by the enemy submarines. As the U-Boats hove into sight only one was flying the German ensign and all of them had removed their numbers. The British ships formed round them and led them towards Harwich.

As a special privilege, flying overhead was the SR 1. Looking down at his old foes sat a pensive Lieutenant Thomas Blenheim Williams and, appropriately enough, a number of other aeronauts who had endured the long hard years in their little Submarine Scouts.

# CHAPTER SIX

# F. ADAM COLLINS

It was early in 1915. Young Adam Collins had avidly followed the progress of the war, daily scanning the optimistic newspaper reports of battles in Belgium and France, soaking up every detail of anti-German propaganda, hoping in the innocence of his sixteen years that hostilities would not end before he had a chance to join in the 'fun'. Then it was reported that two of his older chums had been killed while fighting in Kitchener's Army and his mood changed from eager enthusiasm to grim determination. He now saw the war as a serious business. He must get into the army immediately and avenge the death of his friends.

Hurrying to the nearest recruiting office in his home town of Portsmouth, Adam asked to be enrolled at once. The sergeant looked at him. 'Go home and wait for your whiskers to grow, son,' he advised.

Instead Adam counted up the change in his pocket, then, in a local tobacconist, he bought a pipe, a pouch and some tobacco. There was already a blossoming instinct on how things could be made to work in the army. Returning to the recruiting office he placed them on the sergeant's desk. 'I noticed you are a smoker, sir. These are for you. Now will you please sign me up?'

The NCO glanced up at him and said, 'I don't know what your father's going to say, but if you can pass the medical then we'll let you in.'

The MO gave him a clean bill of health, but when he returned waving his chit from the doctor the sergeant had a surprise for him: 'I'm signing you up in the Royal Flying Corps. Its full of bright young lads like you and the pay is better.'

He had never even thought of the RFC and had taken it for

granted that he would be enlisted in one of the old-established regiments. Remuneration must have improved since the time when George Eddington joined up, because Adam was told he would receive two shillings a day as an Air Mechanic, a rank rather than a specific trade.

He had told the sergeant that he was able to ride a motorcycle. The legal age for driving a bike was only fourteen in those days. So the NCO put him down for Despatch Rider's duties, a triumph of logic almost unheard of in an establishment well known for hammering square pegs into round holes and where bakers were likely to finish up as blacksmiths.

Adam's first motorbike had been a two-cylinder Douglas 350cc. It had no kick start and no clutch; gear-changing was effected by raising the decompressor and letting it in again. To start the machine it was necessary to push like blazes running alongside the bike. When the engine fired the rider vaulted into the saddle and roared away in a cloud of fumes. If he failed to make the saddle, the bike still roared away in a cloud of fumes while he remained spreadeagled in the middle of the road.

Of course there was no test in those days. Adam first learned to ride with the assistance of a friend who gave him a shove to get him going. This initial spin turned out to be rather longer than he expected as his friend had forgotten to tell him how to stop, so he kept going until he ran out of petrol.

He was posted to Pinehurst Barracks in Aldershot and straight into the care of a sadistic sergeant. He acknowledged that the man was a good instructor who made sure than no recruit every forgot what he was taught – a case of 'mind over misery'. But the misery didn't last too long; after only ten days the hell came to an end and Adam was packed off to France.

Kitted out as a soldier (the RFC was then a corps within the British Army) Adam shouldered his kitbag and a crude form of gasmask – a P.H. respirator, no more than a flannel bag impregnated with the chemicals Phenate, Hyposulphite of soda and Hexamine. In addition he was given an enormous .45 revolver. As he came down the troopship's gangplank at Calais he looked cautiously at the warehouses and cranes, wondering if they were concealing any marauding German soldiers he could take a pot shot at!

He was soon moved up to the Ypres Salient. The Germans had foiled a combined French and British offensive by releasing clouds of chlorine and phosgene gas, causing horrific casualties. Although the enemy had broken through the Allied lines, they were unable to exploit their success through lack of reserves. Counter-attacking, the British Second Army finally stemmed the German advance after bitter fighting. The British lost 60,000 men during this period – the Second Battle of Ypres, while the French lost about 10,000 and the Germans some 35,000.

Adam was thrust into a terrifying world of carnage and destruction. His fellow despatch riders on the squadron wasted no time in telling him why he had arrived so precipitately. So many of their comrades had been killed or wounded that replacements were desperately needed.

Attached to 1 Squadron, now equipped mainly with Morane parasols and biplanes, and Nieuports, both the scout and two seater varieties, Adam was to remain with this unit for the whole of his four years on the Western Front.

The duties of the squadron in the air at that time were reconnaissance, observing and photographing enemy activities, pinpointing German artillery positions and directing allied fire on to those positions. Maintaining a liaison between the squadron and British artillery batteries at the front was the job of the despatch riders on the ground. The despatches normally contained codes and cyphers; these were used in the transmission of morse signals between the batteries and base, and also from air to ground when the aircraft was directing fire. As these codes were altered frequently to ensure secrecy, so the despatch riders rode back and forth across dangerous territory. In Adam's case this was the area from Poperinghe south to Armentières.

Called to his first assignment, he enthusiastically saluted everyone in sight, took careful note of where he had to go and roared off on his single cylinder P & M (Phelon & Moore) 500cc, determined to complete his mission in record time. Unfortunately, when he arrived at his destination, he realized that his journey had been pointless. He had left his bag, containing all the secret information, back in the office. A fellow despatch rider arrived with it ten minutes later and taught him some words he had never heard before.

The batteries at the front, mostly 18 pounders, were arranged at strategic distances from each other. On arrival the rider had to deliver his despatches to each gun emplacement individually. If the guns themselves were under fire at the time, this could be a perilous undertaking. More than once soldiers in dugouts shouted up at Adam as he slithered his machine round muddy shell craters, 'Rather you than me, mate. At least we're in a soddin' trench!'

Sometimes, during intense enemy bombardment, he was ordered to take shelter with the artillerymen. On one occasion during extended shelling he was holed up for nearly three days, snatching what little rest he could as he lay on a muddy duckboard at the bottom of a trench.

Later in the war, near Arras, he found himself in similar circumstances, but in this event called on to man a machine gun against advancing Germans. As the situation became crucial he realized he was on his own. His 'comrades' from some 'Latin' detachment had decided that retreat was the better part of valour. When a shell landed nearby, his trench collapsed and he was buried under a pile of mud and sandbags. Unable to extricate himself, he resigned himself to his fate. But within moments he was dragged free from the debris. He was more than relieved to find that his rescuers were a detachment of Australians who had arrived in the nick of time.

He was not alone in his fear of being caught in a gas attack. He had seen the awful effects of this dreadful weapon. A not unpleasant smell of pineapple warned of its arrival. Any soldier slow in donning his mask, which, in the earliest days was nothing more than a cloth soaked in urine (until the issue of P.H. respirators similar to Adam's) was condemned to an agonizing death as the gas mixed with his blood, creating a deadly compound. The Germans experimented first with chlorine, then developed phosgene, fired from shells, and finally employed mustard gas. This was sprayed out of shells in liquid form. At night, if a hand came in contact with the chemical and that hand rubbed weary eyes, by morning the man would be blind. As he lay sightless in the mud his skin peeled off as foam poured from his mouth and he gasped for breath. Gas had an effect, not unlike pneumonia, of drowning its victims as their lungs filled with fluid.

Adam often rode for miles wearing his mask, glad to put up with eye-pieces that misted over, rather than fall foul of those yellow-green clouds of death. The effect lingered long after the gas attack had passed. Phosgene left a deposit of green slime on sandbags; infantry-men, lousy with filth from the trenches, would sometimes try to wash themselves in puddles of water at the bottom of shell-holes. If this water was contaminated by gas they would suffer painful blisters that often left scars for the rest of their lives.

Time was set aside for Adam and his comrades to be taught the technique of starting an aeroplane by swinging the prop. If one of their machines was forced to land behind friendly lines and was not badly damaged an economical way of recovering the pilot and his aircraft was to send a despatch rider, complete with his normal kit of tools, a can of petrol and some clean spark plugs. Once the pilot was ready to take off Adam would swing the propeller and the machine, after climbing out of the field, made its short hop back to the aerodrome. He found that starting 'pusher' aircraft was more tricky than the 'tractor' variety. With the former it was necessary to climb between the longerons, give the necessary swing – the propeller was often situated quite high above the ground on these types – then, when it fired, leap back and crawl out near the tail section before the machine started to move.

He had only been on the squadron a short time when a terrifying incident occurred. He was sitting on a pile of sandbags with some companions, eating stew from his mess tin. Suddenly he was flung into the air as a stray shell exploded nearby. How long he lay unconscious he had no idea. All he remembered was grasping hands trying to raise him to his feet. His legs felt like lead. 'Don't pull me,' he pleaded. 'My legs have gone.' But his rescuers assured him there was nothing wrong with him. As he sat up he saw the dead weight that was pinning him down. It was the headless, armless and legless torso of a man who had been talking to him only a moment before. As he struggled to his feet he saw carnage all around him. How he had escaped the fate of so many of his companions he would never know. Then he saw a dog devouring the torn bits of flesh that littered the ground and, overcome with horror, was sick on the spot.

D/Rs had strict orders not to stop on their delivery run. If anyone tried to impede their progress the rule was 'Shoot first, ask questions afterwards'. It was clearly understood that if any man lost his despatches such a 'crime' was considered so serious he might just as well shoot himself. In such an event, or if it was suspected that despatches had fallen into the wrong hands, the current codes and cyphers were immediately scrapped.

Adam and his comrades always had to be on the look-out for booby-traps laid by enemy agents. Extreme caution was needed, particularly at night, when a motorcyclist could so easily suffer decapitation from a length of piano-wire strung across the road. Large nails, tacks or broken bottles scattered in the path of the machine causing an immediate puncture were not uncommon. There were instances where a D/R, having been halted by such means, was caught on his knees busily repairing a tyre. The enemy, having stealthily crept up behind him, would slip a length of cheese-wire over his head, pull hard and slit open his throat.

The possibility of such an occurrence must have been in the mind of Adam, when, one night, he suffered a puncture near Gouzeaucourt. Dismounting, he turned up the wick of his acetylene headlamp to examine the damage. Getting down to the repair as quickly as possible he had hardly been at work for a couple of minutes when his blood froze. He heard heavy breathing behind him. He could imagine the wire tightening round his throat as he drew his .45 revolver from its holster. Whirling round, he fired three bullets between the eyes of his assailant. There was a moment of silence. Then a pitiful, expiring 'moo'. He had shot a cow! He wished he had kept the details of the incident to himself. For ever after he was known to his companions as 'The Lone Ranger'.

His nickname could have applied to all despatch riders. Theirs was a solitary life, fraught with danger, and calling for a high degree of personal initiative. They maintained their Triumphs and Phelon & Moores themselves, taking pride in keeping their machines at peak performance under the most adverse conditions. Apart from tools, they carried what spares they could – plugs, a replacement chain and a puncture repair outfit.

The strain of their work at times took them to the limit. Only experience and a highly developed sixth sense gave them any chance of survival. At well-known danger spots like 'Hell Fire Corner' or 'Happy Valley' on the Ypres Salient it was a case of waiting for a shell to whine overhead, fall to the ground and explode. They knew another would arrive in a given number of minutes – regular as clockwork. Making full use of those precious intervals, they charged for their designated batteries.

Sometimes, when the weather was foul, this was enough in itself to bring on weariness and aching bones. The high-pressure tyres slipped and slid on the greasy *pavé* roads and the luckless rider often finished up in the ditch. Soaked through, bruised and shaking with cold at the end of a spell of duty, it was then that the despatch riders met to draw some comfort from each other's company.

They might go for long spells between meals, but they never went short of rations. It was a recognized rule that these men, whose work was so vital, should be supplied with a meal at any time of the day or night, whenever or wherever they requested it. Adam soon built up a mental list of the more hospitable stopping places along the various routes that he traversed behind the lines.

Like his comrades, he always had warm feelings for one particular institution centred in Talbot House at Poperinghe, recognized by symbols based on the morse code as Toc H. It was run by a remarkable army padre in his early thirties called Philip Clayton, better known to all ranks as 'Tubby' Clayton. This haven of spiritual and physical recreation was in a large house only a few miles from the front and in line of fire from all three sides of the salient. The French owner had rented it to the British Army for the duration of the war while he judiciously took up temporary residence on the Riviera. Enemy shells frequently criss-crossed its roof and craters appeared in the garden, but after four years of operation in which hundreds of thousands of servicemen visited the hostel only one casualty was sustained within its walls.

The padre established a chapel on the top floor with a carpenter's bench as an altar. The floor was rickety to say the least, yet, almost miraculously, it sustained the weight of up to a hundred and fifty men at a time during the innumerable services held there.

Tubby Clayton, a man of boundless energy and infectious good humour, enjoyed the help of an inseparable companion – an old Cockney soldier, Private Arthur Pettifer of the Buffs, with the regimental number of 239. He had enlisted in 1885, the same year that Tubby was born. Long before the current war he received an award for outstanding bravery. Apart from running the place, along with a gallant band of nurses like Miss A. B. S. Macfie, he had endeared himself to the remaining civilians, especially the children, in Poperinghe. He looked after everyone's needs as best he could under almost impossible circumstances – arranging repairs to homes damaged by shellfire and guiding people to shelter in times of bombardment. With his spare figure, narrow face and walrus moustache, the French nicknamed him 'le Général'. To his own people he was known simply as 'Gen'.

Tubby and Gen, never confined to headquarters, were a familiar sight ploughing through mud, laden down with hymn books and a portable harmonium visiting the most dangerous parts of their 'parish' – the trenches in the front line.

Whenever possible, the RFC despatch riders did their best to arrive at Clayton's place at the same time. It was a chance to enjoy a wash and brush-up and a chat over a hot drink. Occasionally, there was even a moment for a quiet read. The padre had managed to build up an extensive library for the benefit of the troops. It was a real place of rest where all ranks were equal and men could relax and try to forget the horror of their daily lives.

Adam also admired the efforts made by the Salvation Army and the YMCA to make life a little more bearable for men in the services. Yet he always looked on Clayton and Toc H as uniquely something special.

Another heroic figure who remained in his memory was a feisty little Irish priest, Geoffrey Studdert Kennedy, also in his early thirties, and known to all as 'Woodbine Willie' because of his ready hand-outs of Woodbine cigarettes that he always carried in his shoulder pack alongside his Bible. He would stand on an upturned ammunition box and announce in his Irish brogue that he was going to sing first: 'Mother Machree' for the sons; then 'Little Grey Home in the West' for the husbands; and finally 'The Sunshine of Your Smile' for the lovers. After that the men in the trenches were more than ready to listen to his brief but powerful spiritual message.

He was continually surrounded by lads handing him names and addresses scribbled on dirty pieces of paper imploring him to write home for them. They wanted him to tell their folks that he had met them and that they were in good spirits. Often he was handed a crumpled ten shilling note to accompany the letter.

In spite of suffering from chronic asthma, which brought about his early death, he was with the 137th Brigade of the 46th Division during the Somme offensive in June, 1916, with the 17th Brigade of the 24th Division at the attack on Messines Ridge in 1917, and was present with the 42nd Division during the Final Advance in 1918.

Far from physically strong, he always showed great courage in the most dangerous circumstances and often tended the wounded under heavy fire. In 1917 he was awarded the Military Cross. As the official citation said: 'He searched shell holes for our own, and enemy wounded, assisting them to the Dressing Station, and his cheerfulness and endurance had a splendid effect upon all ranks in the front line trenches, which he constantly visited.'

He also wrote simple, moving lines of poetry:

'There are many kinds of sorrow
In this world of love and hate,
But there's not a sterner sorrow
Than a soldier's for his mate.'

Adam and the others were also befriended by a kind-hearted French lady, Madame De Burgh. With only limited resources, she did her best to make life a little more comfortable for the lads who were fighting so bravely for her country. She washed and repaired their clothes, gave them apples from her orchard and occasionally an egg or two.

When the Germans broke through at Epéhy, Madame Deburgh's cottage came under fire and her most cherished possession, a sewing machine, was destroyed. The despatch riders clubbed together, and much to the old lady's delight, managed to present her with a replacement.

When her cottage was shelled a second time she had to be moved to the house of a relative who lived well behind the British lines. She now mourned the loss of her second sewing machine. Her 'boys' considered the possibility of recovering it, or what was left of it, from the ruined building now in no-man's-land. Adam volunteered for the job, but because he was on duty that night he had to do it during the day. Reaching his destination without mishap on his trusty Phelham & Moore, he crawled through the rubble. He recovered the sewing machine, damaged but probably repairable.

Strapping it on the back of his bike, he roared off towards the safety of his own lines. Then the enemy spotted him. Shells started to rain down all round. Suddenly there was a terrific explosion immediately in front of him and he was hurled in one direction, while his motorbike plunged into a crater, a shattered wreck.

He lay in the mud, shaken and dazed. Fortunately help was at hand and medical orderlies rushed to his aid and brought him back behind the lines. Apart from slight concussion and a few bruises he was none the worse for his adventure. This is all the more remarkable when it is realized that the idea of despatch riders wearing crash helmets had never been considered. They *were* issued with goggles, but Adam never wore them because the lenses quickly became splattered with mud and restricted his vision.

This experience, along with many others, including the time he was buried for hours under a ruined house where he had taken cover from shellfire, had a cumulative effect on his nervous system. When he was eventually dragged free he was quite unable to speak. In the end his voice came back, but he was left with a nervous speech impediment that remained with him until late middle age.

The infant Flying Corps made no bones about employing its personnel in any capacity for which it had need at the time and, to Adam's amazement, he found himself serving as an air gunner/ observer. During his years in France he flew with a number of different pilots and in a variety of machines, including Avros, Morane Parasols, Morane biplanes, Nieuport two seaters, B.E.2cs and R.E.8s.

His most alarming moment in the air occurred when he was flying in the rear seat of an old Avro 504 piloted by Captain P. F. Fullard, later to become one of the ten top-scoring British aces. A mile or two over hostile territory they were attacked by a German Albatros which fired a short burst at them as it closed in. By good fortune the bullets missed them. It all happened so quickly that Adam never had a chance to fire back. A moment later the red-painted machine with its black crosses was flying alongside them, so close that they could clearly distinguish the enemy's face. The German raised his gloved hand and gestured to them to return in the direction of their own lines. The 'sitting duck' needed no second bidding as it dived in hasty retreat over the trenches.

'That', said his pilot after they landed, 'was the most miraculous escape of all time!' Neither had any idea why they had been spared. Maybe the German had used up his ammunition or his guns had jammed or perhaps it was his birthday!

When the Armistice was declared on 11 November, 1918, Adam was a patient in a casualty clearing station at Tincourt receiving attention to a wound. He was also in isolation having picked up an infectious bug. In four years of continuous service he had had only three 10-day periods of leave with his mother and father at home in Portsmouth.

Earlier that year he had seen the Royal Flying Corps become the Royal Air Force – the first independent military air force in the world. As he lay in his hospital bed he had already decided that his future lay with this new force. When he eventually completed forty years service he never regretted that decision. Over the years of peace, punctuated by minor wars in Afghanistan and Iraq, he visited many places and met many people. In Baghdad he helped Gertrude Bell, the well-known writer, in an emergency. Between them they successfully delivered a baby born to the wife of an Arab chieftain. Near the North-west frontier he worked side by side with Aircraftman Shaw, the legendary Colonel T. E. Lawrence of Arabia. They got on well; both were 'loners' and both passionately fond of motorbikes.

In the Second World War Adam was again in France, now a Flight Lieutenant, in charge of three squadrons of vehicles. When the Germans broke through the Low Countries in the Spring of 1940 he was unable to evacuate his men and trucks via Dunkirk. With the enemy breathing down his neck he managed to keep just ahead of them, often traversing territory he had got to know well in the previous conflict, eventually bringing all three squadrons intact to the Cherbourg Peninsula. From there his precious cargo of airmen and their equipment was safely shipped back to Southampton.

*Note on motorcycles*: The Phelon & Moore was manufactured by a small South Yorkshire firm at Cleckheaton. During War Office summer manoeuvres in 1913 a 'P & M' had undergone evaluation with the fledgling Royal Flying Corps. When the RFC was put on a wartime footing the following year, the 500cc Phelon & Moore 'two speeder' was adopted by the corps as its standard motorcycle. When peace returned the machine became widely known as the 'Panther'. This rugged bike was always exceptional value for money – in the early '30s a 250cc Red Panther model could be bought for £29.75. Less if the purchaser was prepared to forego the electric lighting system!

Adam Collins' replacement machine, after his 'P & M' was blown up, was a Triumph. Equipped with a three-speed Sturmey-Archer gearbox, it would have been the legendary Model H with a chain primary and belt final drive. 30,000 were supplied for war use.

# CHAPTER SEVEN

# ERIC JOHN FURLONG

In the early summer of 1914, before the world plunged into a maelstrom of death and destruction, a delightful place to spend a sunny weekend must have been the grass airfield at Hendon in north London. It was not only a rendezvous for aficionados of flight, that growing band of enthusiasts absorbed in the development of heavier than air flying machines, but also a meeting place where food and drink could be bought and picnics enjoyed while, with a minimum of intrusion, tiny aero engines whirled and hiccupped in the air above.

On the south side of the field there was a row of hangars occupied by various flying schools including the Hall School of Aviation, the Ruffy-Baumann School, the Beatty Wright School, the Claude Graham-White School and others. A number of gaily coloured pylons stood at intervals marking a circuit round the field. Aeroplanes flew within inches of these structures on public show days, racing against each other in a spectacular display of flying, their wing tips only feet from the ground.

Not yet seventeen, Eric John Furlong, who lived only a few miles away, spent all his free moments at Hendon airfield. He examined every detail of the odd collection of aeroplanes owned by the various schools, and by private owners like the well known Clarence Winchester. Eric studied the performances of the different machines in the air, comparing individual flying characteristics.

It was a great thrill when he witnessed an early parachute jump. The intrepid man was taken up to around 2000 feet, seated precariously on the axle of the aeroplane's undercarriage. In his arms he clutched a great bundle of silk. Then, as he threw himself away from the machine, an umbrella-like canopy billowed out above his head, checking his downward plunge, and he began to float gently towards

9. Thomas Blenheim Williams spent all his wartime career in airships, mostly the small SS submarine scouts. *(Imperial War Museum)*

10. Airship SS Z 37 out of Royal Naval Air Station, Anglesey, flying alongside a coaster. Williams' airship was SS Z 35 carrying a crew of three; engineer, wireless operator and himself as captain. *(Imperial War Museum)*

11. Airship SR1. This 'semi-rigid' airship of enormous capacity was flown from Italy to England by Williams and his crew under nightmare conditions. *(Norman Gilham)*

12. The RFC version of this civilian Phelon & Moore motorcycle was ridden by Adam Collins in Flanders when he volunteered to help fill a gap for much needed despatch riders.

13. A row of training machines at the Central Flying School, Upavon, in Wiltshire. The line-up consists of two Henry Farman 'Shorthorns', one Maurice Farman 'Longhorn' and a couple of B.E.2a's. Many pilots gained their wings at Upavon even before the war, including Hugh Trenchard, who later became Commandant of the school. (*Imperial War Museum*)

14. Eric John Furlong is seen here as a very privileged schoolboy. His father paid out the considerable sum of £75 so that he could take flying lessons at Hendon. When he joined the RFC Eric flew giant Caproni bombers in Italy and also fought against the Bolsheviks in northern Russia. (*Imperial War Museum*)

15. The extraordinary Caudron II on which Furlong and many others learned
their trade as pilots by hopping across the airfield, 'blipping' like mad and
inhaling quantities of glycol. *(Imperial War Museum)*

16. The sturdy Airco D.H.4 day bomber flown by Furlong in northern Russia.
When introduced early in 1917 and fitted with a variety of engine types,
including the 250hp Rolls Royce Eagle III, it could outpace and out-climb
any German fighter of the time. *(RAF Museum)*

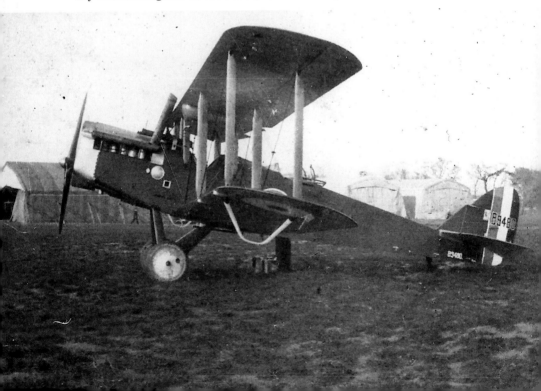

the ground. He missed the aerodrome and came to land several fields away, none the worse for his experience.

Soon after this Eric approached his father and asked his permission to take flying lessons. His father, who had been involved in motoring since its infancy and was interested in all things mechanical, gave his son a non-committal but hopeful answer. 'Go and make some enquiries. Find out what these courses actually entail.' Eric went to find out. For no particular reason, possibly because it was the first one he reached, he went into the hangar used by the Hall School. From Mr Hall, a man in his mid-twenties, he learned that the complete flying course, leading to his pilot's certificate, would set him back £75. The lessons would take place only on those days when the weather was suitable, roughly when smoke from the neighbouring chimneys went straight up. The best times would be early in the morning and late in the evening when the air was still. Hall pointed out that these restrictions, given the vagaries of the English climate, might string the course out a bit and entail some frustrating hanging about.

To test his potential pupil's reaction Hall took Eric on a brief flight, circling the airfield in one of his primitive Caudron Glls, nominally a single-seat nacelle and tailboom tractor machine, with its little 3 cylinder, 35 hp Anzani engine. The boy landed back on earth more besotted than ever with the idea of flying as a career and rushed back to tell his father about it. Furlong Snr, after brief reflection, signed the necessary forms and handed over the money.

When Eric went to arrange for his first lesson and pay for the course the financially hard-pressed Mr Hall generously gave him a discount in appreciation of his coming up with the full amount in advance.

Strapped into the Caudron, in the early part of his training, Eric had to content himself with bumping towards the boundary fence over to a spot marked out in whitewash, taking care not to get too close to the fence, so allowing room to swing round and repeat the exercise on the return journey. The trick was to learn to control the aeroplane and its motor while the machine was still on the ground. There was no question of taking off at this stage. The tiny engine ran at full throttle the whole time and could only be regulated by 'blipping', that is by manipulating the on/off switch to control the power. No one could hope to fly a Caudron without mastering this technique. It was also a particularly difficult machine to keep in a straight line, liable to swerve off in any direction without warning. So this initial 'ground training' to get the feel of the thing was essential.

With growing confidence Eric soon discovered that his runs back and forth across the airfield were becoming straighter, and there were occasions when he was actually rising into the air by two or three feet. Observing this, his instructor shook his head in mock severity, but it was really all part of the training technique.

Later, when he became properly airborne, he was affected by the constant spray of castor oil from the engine. This induced a compulsion to pay more than average visits to the lavatory. One young man who previously suffered from constipation used to run along behind the aircraft breathing in the fumes and shouting, 'Wonderful! Wonderful!'

At an altitude of approximately 50 feet left and right hand turns were practised above the airfield. In those days the instructors knew nothing of aerodynamics and, in blissful ignorance, taught manoeuvres that were later considered suicidal. Instead of banking to effect a turn, pupils were instructed to fly absolutely straight and then kick either left or right rudder when they wanted to change direction. This upset the aerodynamics of the aircraft, the nose dipped and the machine skidded round in the air until it faced in the direction from which it had come. The pupil then came in to land, taking off again immediately and repeating the process at the other end of the field. The same technique, but with a more gentle application of the rudder, was used in completing a circuit.

Arriving at dawn and perhaps hanging around all day waiting for his next half-hour session hardly fitted in with his school curriculum. The crunch came when he attended one of his school's OTC parades. They were inspected by some big noise from the army who then proudly announced, 'I don't know whether you realize this, but one of your cadets, Eric Furlong, is showing great initiative by actually taking *flying lessons*.' So the pupils and staff learned his secret.

After another discussion, his father, who had no illusions about the extent of his son's obsession, agreed that he should leave school in order to concentrate full-time on becoming a flyer.

To be nearer the airfield, Eric moved into digs run by a Mrs Curtis, a jovial landlady who looked after him like a mother, along with three or four apprentices from local factories. Being at the aerodrome all the time was a more satisfactory arrangement, and he became fully occupied assisting anyone who needed help in repairing their crumpled machines or servicing his own motorbike.

There were always plenty of diversions to keep him and his fellow pupils amused during the long waiting hours between lessons. Clarence Winchester, for instance, earned a living by giving brief 'flips' to joy riders. It was noticed that he always treated his passengers to a stern warning before starting up: 'Whatever you do, don't touch this, never lean on that. If you so much as breathe on the wire above you we're both finished!' By the time they left the ground the poor passenger was a quivering mass of nerves. Questioned about this, Winchester replied, 'I always aim to frighten them to death. Then, afterwards, they feel they've had their money's worth.'

Many of the early aviators displayed an enthusiastic fondness for the ladies and Graham White, who had his own school, was no exception. Because of the glamour associated with their trade, flyers had no difficulty in attracting large numbers of females. On one occasion White was seen arriving in a taxi accompanied by an attractive young girl. They hurried into his small office alongside the hangar slamming the door behind them. After a short interval another taxi drew up and Ethel Levy, the most famous musical comedy actress of the day, stepped out. She went to the office, flung open the door and disappeared inside. This was followed by total uproar clearly heard across the airfield. Following this, the first lady was seen to emerge, jump into Ethel Levy's taxi and depart.

A succession of inventors provided another source of interest. The brain child of one in particular caused an unexpected sensation. He turned up with a propeller on which the tips of the blades were bent sharply back at an angle of 90 degrees. Persuading the people at the Ruffy-Baumann School that this 'modification' would lead to increased efficiency they agreed to try it out on one of their machines powered by a Gnome rotary engine. The method of testing an engine was to tether the rear of the aeroplane to a stake in the ground. Tied to the rope was a spring balance fitted with a scale from which the pull of the motor could be measured. The revolutionary propeller was bolted in place, swung by hand in the customary manner and the engine burst into life. A mechanic sat in the cockpit operating the controls. Eric and the other pupils from the school next door were standing watching the proceedings with interest. To their surprise, as the engine revolutions were increased and the rotating cylinders whirled round ever faster, the backward facing tips on the blades began to straighten up. There was an excruciating sound of disintegrating metal. The engine and its entrails parted company from the aeroplane and shot up in a graceful curve, coming to rest some distance from where the onlookers were standing. It hit the ground with such force that the motor, and what was left of the offending propeller, bounced at least a hundred feet into the air. When it finally came to rest on a concrete path alongside the hangar the tangled mass bore no resemblance to anything connected with engineering.

Ruffy-Baumann had lost a perfectly good engine and the front end of an aircraft. All that could be seen of the inventor was a fast-receding figure legging it for the boundary fence.

Eric was much impressed by a young man who was to become a byword in aviation history – the unassuming Geoffrey de Havilland. He not only designed and built his own aircraft with meticulous care, but then tested them himself, showing true faith in his own products.

On the other hand some of the early manufacturers like, for instance, Handley Page who, as we learned from Charlie Tye, (see Chapter 3), preferred to concentrate on planning and construction while keeping his feet firmly on the ground. Handley Page was remembered by Eric as a man with natural presentation skills. He attended several of his lectures and came away recalling everything he had said. This was not surprising as the talk was couched in phrases designed to appeal to a young male audience. A mundane fact of physics would be explained as, 'When the centre of pressure gets near to the centre of attraction then, wow, things begin to happen!'

This builder of bigger than average aircraft had a sharp wit. Eric was at a social gathering at which H. P. was present. A pretty girl approached the great man wearing a brooch fashioned in the shape of an aeroplane. 'Do you like my aeroplane?' she asked. He replied,

'I didn't really notice the aeroplane. I was too busy looking at the landing ground.'

Oddly, there was a reluctance on the part of pupils to complete their training because, on receipt of their certificate of competence, the school had fulfilled its obligation and the newly qualified pilot had received his money's worth. From then on there was no valid reason for him to continue flying at the school's expense. Eric dreaded the day when he would take his final test and be left with no excuse to carry on at the school. But that day inevitably arrived. He executed the stipulated number of figures of eight above the airfield and then demonstrated that he could successfully bring off an emergency landing with a dead engine. That was it. He was handed his cherished 'ticket'.

It was now the autumn of 1915, the war had been on for a little over a year and Eric was just old enough to apply for service in the Royal Flying Corps. The interview at the War Office with a major who gave the impression he had never seen an aircraft in his life was a disaster. 'You cannot fly in the RFC if you weigh more than 10 stone, 11 lbs, and according to your report you weigh just over 11 stone.'

Eric tried to explain that he was already a qualified pilot who had learned to fly on one of the lightest aircraft ever built, but it was to no avail. The man had been given his instructions and was determined to stick to the rule book.

In disgust, Eric made use of his previous OTC training at school and joined the Royal Inniskilling Fusiliers as a junior officer. Soon he found himself in Salonika where he contracted dysentery and was hospitalized back to England. On recovery he was posted to France, became involved in a motor accident and again found himself in hospital followed by a period of convalescence.

Throughout his time as a soldier Eric had made repeated applications to join the RFC, but was turned down on each occasion by his colonel. The CO considered it an insult that one of his officers should wish to forego the honour of being in his regiment in order to join a crackpot outfit like the Flying Corps. Yet in the end, by the summer of 1917, the man relented, probably on the grounds that such a hairbrained idiot was not worth retaining anyway.

This time, the war in the air having moved into a harsher phase and countless more men and machines been lost, he was accepted with open arms by the RFC. After an initial ground course at Reading, he finished up at a flying training station at Harlaxton, Lincolnshire. For the first time he experienced the benefits of dual control instruction in a twin-seater Maurice Farman MF 7 'Longhorn', so nicknamed, as mentioned earlier, by the RFC because of its long curved outriggers protruding in front of the undercarriage.

In order to learn as much as possible he decided not to mention his previous training and subsequent qualification. But he was soon rumbled. 'You've flown before,' said his instructor. 'Only thing I can't understand is why you try to do flat turns when you want to go round corners. Highly dangerous procedure, if I may say so.'

When Eric explained, the instructor demonstrated the much better banking technique. At each turn the officer took over to show how easily it could be accomplished. On the final turn he again grabbed the controls and said, 'There you are. Nothing to it.' By this time they were lined up with the field and were gliding in to land. Eric relaxed in his cockpit happy in the thought that next time they flew he would be allowed to practice banking left and right turns to his heart's content. The following moment their aeroplane had nose-dived into the ground, smashed to smithereens, with the two occupants sitting miraculously unhurt amid the debris.

'I say, old man, what exactly were you playing at?' asked his instructor.

'What was I playing at?' exploded Eric. 'I thought you had the controls and were bringing us in to land.'

'By Jove,' exclaimed the instructor. 'And there was I thinking *you* had the controls!'

It was after that, Eric believed, that the phrase, 'You've got it – it's all yours,' was inserted into the training manual.

As he progressed he again flew solo, this time in a Martinsyde Scout powered by an 80 hp Gnome engine. Although it had established a good reputation on the Western Front early in the war, he did not include it among his favourite flying machines. To him it was somewhat heavy to handle and not really fit to be classified as a 'scout', a term superseded by the word 'fighter' in later years. He also piloted Geoffrey De Havilland's Airco DH 4s designed as light day bombers with 250 hp Rolls Royce Eagle V1s. In contrast these were a delight to fly, responding to the lightest touch, climbing like birds and with a good turn of speed. In its ultimate development, and fitted with an even more powerful 375 hp Eagle V111, the DH 4 became the fastest and most successful single-engined bomber of the war.

Once Eric safely forced landed a DH4 in a small ploughed field between Lincoln and Nottingham. He spent the night with a hospitable farmer and his family. Attempting to take off in the undamaged aeroplane the following day he only succeeded in wrapping it round the nearest hedge and completely writing it off.

On completion of his training he was posted to Italy, along with five other pilots who had successfully passed the course at Harlaxton. After a long train journey across France and into Italy, the party of half a dozen RFC flyers, who had now been joined by six RNAS pilots, arrived at an outpost of the RNAS stationed in Milan. They were interviewed by a naval commander who told them they were there to undergo a familiarization course on multi-engined bombers of the Corpo Aeronautica Militare. First they would fly the Caproni Ca 33 (Ca 3) biplanes powered by 3 Isotta-Fraschini engines of 150 hp each. These large bombers had been engaged on long-range raids against Austro-Hungarian targets long before Britain's Handley Page 0/100, or the giant German Gothas, had even been built.

In these war-proven aircraft two pilots sat side by side in the centre of the nacelle, with a gunner/observer in the open front cockpit armed with a Revelli machine gun or cannon. The rear gunner stood, in what can only be described as an elongated bird cage, behind the trailing edge of the top wing and directly above the pusher propeller of the central engine. Two substantial booms stretched back to support the tailplane and triple rudders.

Later, the commander told them, the British pilots would be taught to handle the even bigger Caproni C 42 triplanes with three 270 hp Isotta-Fraschini engines, or even more powerful Fiat motors, a veritable giant of an aircraft. In these the rear gunner's cage was replaced by positions for two gunners, one in each of the fuselage booms.

He stressed the importance of being on their best behaviour at all times. Their attachment to an Italian combat *squadriglia* was as much a diplomatic mission as anything else. An RFC squadron previously stationed in the vicinity had achieved an admirable reputation. Nothing must be done to lower the respect for the British currently held by the Italian Air Force.

On arrival at Galliate air station north-west of Milan, Eric's group were struck by the high standard and keeness of the instructors, but this did not apply to the pupils who appeared lethargic and generally uninterested in flying. Whether they were disgruntled at being posted to fly bombers rather than the more glamorous single-seat scouts never became clear.

The British were treated with the utmost courtesy by their hosts. They were invariably served first in the mess and treated to the best that was available. A rigid formality was upheld by the Italian officers. They dressed immaculately for dinner, always bowing to the commanding officer's chair on entry, whether it was occupied or not. Eric and his friends did their best to obey the rules, but it was difficult to match the sartorial excellence of their allies.

The intention was to form a squadron of six Caproni Ca 42s flown exclusively by the British. Healthy rivalry between RNAS and RFC pilots became a little strained when it was understood that the naval flyers would captain each of the bombers. After heated argument it was agreed that command should be evenly divided with three aeroplanes going to each branch of the service.

In practice the arrangement failed to work and it later became apparent that this was essentially a naval affair. After the crews had been trained, six of the huge Caproni triplanes were handed over to the Royal Naval Air Service and flown back to England. At a later date some were fitted with the mighty American Liberty motors of 400 hp. None of these bombers was ever engaged in combat and they were returned to Italy after the war.

When Eric and the others first started training on these monsters it came as quite a shock. Staring up at the massive bulk of the machines rearing nearly 21 feet above them, it was hard to believe they could actually get off the ground. To men whose flying experience had been confined to light, single-engined aeroplanes it was a daunting prospect.

The triplane was a real weightlifter, 3,197 lbs of bombs, carried in a metal tray fixed between the under-carriage, represented a phenomenal load in those days. Even the biplanes could carry twenty bombs weighing 110 lbs each.

In flight Eric found the biplane unusually heavy to handle and it rarely felt comfortably balanced. As there was no trimming mechanism it required considerable strength to hold the stick in the forward position in order to achieve a reasonable flying angle. The technique was to grip the column with one hand, elbow tucked into the stomach for support, while the other hand operated a wheel on the top of the column to control the ailerons.

Unable to speak English, the instructors made do with gestures or by placing their hands over the hands of the British pilots in order to shove the controls into the correct position. They demonstrated how to correct for lopsidedness if a port or starboard engine failed.

Accustomed only to low horsepower motors in the nose of the aeroplane, the effect of big engines roaring a few feet on either side and another behind the head, all in the open air, was absolutely shattering. The British pilots' admiration knew no bounds for the Italian airmen who flew on long, cold, perilous journeys over the Alps to attack targets in Austria.

Although of no consequence to Eric, who had never been used to such luxuries, the Capronis were singularly lacking in instruments. The airspeed was indicated by what the British pilots dubbed 'a penny on a spring'. A small round disc, spring-loaded, was mounted on one of the struts outboard of the fuselage. The angle of this disc was governed by the air pressure set up by the forward motion of the aeroplane. On a metal quadrant, situated at right angles to the disc, were etched the words 'Minima' at one end and 'Maxima' at the other. It was impressed on them that they must keep the bomber flying at a speed between these two extremes. Should the edge of the disc fall below 'Minima' then it was inviting an irrecoverable stall; if it rose above 'Maxima' the wings would probably fall off! Officially the cruising speed was around 70 mph, but how this was gauged with no airspeed indicator fitted no one was able to explain.

For each engine there was a rev counter and an oil gauge, but beyond that nothing, not even an altimeter. Presumably the Italians made a rough guess at their altitude by knowing the height of the mountains through which they were flying.

When they moved on to the triplane, the British pilots considered this larger aircraft to be a distinct improvement over its predecessor and easier to manage. After several abortive attempts Eric flew his CA 42 up into the snow-covered Alps and through a high pass. He was without a crew and had no bombs on board and could not begin to comprehend how the Italians accomplished such flights with a full load.

Returning to England, he spent a short period as an instructor before being called to the Cecil Hotel, then housing the Air Ministry in London. There he learned that he possessed certain qualifications essential for pilots and observers who were to take part in an undisclosed operation. These qualifications were threefold; experience on DH 4s, previous service in the infantry and a knowledge of machine guns.

After spending a night in the Tower of London with a cluster of similarly experienced aircrew, Eric and his companions were issued with a mountain of kit, some of it ideal for the hottest summer, the rest consisting of heavy fur garments suitable only for severe arctic conditions. This added to their perplexity and gave no clue as to where they were going.

They were posted to a camp in Blandford, south-west of Salisbury. This was a place for 'washouts' – those who had volunteered to fly in the RFC, but who had subsequently failed their course. Some had undoubtedly tried their best but were unable to make the grade, others were 'leadswingers' who had never had any intention of making a success of flying but had put themselves forward simply to get themselves a commission.

The régime, overseen by Guards drill sergeants, was physically harsh, starting with morning parade at an unearthly hour and continuing through the day with route marches, physical training and assault courses. No free time, no leave. The reward at the end of it all – reduced to the ranks.

To their astonishment, Eric and his group were immediately pitched into this routine. The ultimate humiliation came when he found himself sitting next to one of his former failed pupils; the young man emphasized how delighted he was to see his old instructor sharing the same predicament. With mutiny in their hearts Eric and the rest demanded to see the Commanding Officer. They insisted that a phone call be made to a certain officer at the Air Ministry. The call was made, apologies were offered, and for the rest of their short stay at Blandford they were treated with the utmost respect.

Officially it was only after they had boarded ship at Newcastle upon Tyne and were actually at sea that they learned their destination. But Eric had received advance information from a Geordie taxi driver taking him to the docks when the man had said, 'Why aye, are you going to Russia, too, sir?'

In times of war junior officers and other ranks are rarely told *why* the missions in which they may be expected to lay down their lives are planned. So, apart from being told they were on their way to Murmansk to teach the Bolsheviks a lesson, the flyers remained in the dark. The plan was euphemistically referred to as an Allied Invasion of North Russia. It involved small numbers of British, French and American forces under British command. The idea was to seize Murmansk and Archangel and then recapture arms and ammunition originally contributed by the Allies to the Czarists before their government was overthrown.

A quick 'in and out' operation of this nature before the onset of the Russian winter was within the bounds of reason. But what was not explained to the men were the grandiose plans to move east and south in the hope of joining up with the Czech Legion in the Urals, thus inspiring a White Russian counter-revolution to topple the Bolsheviks. The outcome was an undeclared war that went on for over a year and achieved nothing.

The passengers on board ship were made up of a disproportionate number of senior officers and very few other ranks apart from a contingent of veteran sergeants. The twenty or so aircrew, all lieutenants, were confined to the steerage area at the stern. It was rumoured that the pilots and observers would be employed instructing Russians opposed to the Bolshevik régime.

During the voyage the flyers were allocated machine-gun posts around the ship to repel attack. After all, they were all experienced in using these weapons in combat.

Sailing into Murmansk they moved to the largest quay and tied up without opposition from anyone. They were now in a dirty, unprepossessing timber-exporting seaport full of ragged civilians. The only spick-and-span object in sight was the British battleship HMS *Glory*, anchored in the bay and in gleaming contrast to a rusting Russian warship moored nearby. This filth-ingrained rust-bucket was crewed by the Bolsheviks and immediately nicknamed the 'Packet of Woodbines' because of its five slim cigarette-like funnels.

The British contingent set to work fortifying the area round the quay with barbed-wire and machine-gun emplacements at strategic points while supplies of food and ammunition were unloaded from the ship. So far the British appeared to be taking part in the most peaceful of invasions, so Eric and his observer decided to explore the locality and take a walk to a village three miles inland. Strolling through a dense forest they heard the sharp crack of small arms fire ahead of them. Retreating behind some trees, they saw a group of fierce-looking horsemen galloping furiously along the track firing in all directions at nothing in particular.

Concluding that war may have started, they made their way back to the dock area where they found their tiny enclave fully manned and ready for action. They were immediately ordered to take over a machine-gun post facing the bay. Anything resembling a boat that attempted to leave the Russian battleship was to be fired on at once.

After a while they saw a longboat full of armed men pulling away from the 'Packet of Woodbines'. Without hesitation Eric and his observer, both ex-infantry officers used to aiming straight and true, opened fire with their twin machine guns and sank the boat. They were relieved to see that HMS *Glory* had swung her guns round to point directly at the Russian warship. Although there was a good deal of sniping from the interior and from warehouses in the vicinity, fortunately for those ashore the big seagoing guns were not brought into play by either battleship.

A British colonel had been busy contacting a number of Russian officers opposed to the Bolsheviks. Some had travelled great distances to join the Allies. They were currently camping in railway carriages parked in nearby sidings. Delighted to become part of the 'invasion' force they were bundled into British uniforms and fed on Allied rations.

In August, 1918, orders arrived for a contingent, dubbed 'The Elope Force' to re-embark and sail to Archangel. As they reached the mouth of the Severnyy Dvina river they expected to be delayed by two sunken minesweepers left by retreating Bolsheviks to impede their progress. Fortunately, advanced Allied troops had enlisted the help of local tug masters who had managed to pull the vessels far enough apart to create a narrow channel to the pool of Archangel itself and their ship just succeeded in squeezing through. The seaport was virtually deserted. They had been instructed to set up camp at Bakaritsa, a commercial area on the opposite bank from Archangel, but, with no one ashore to help them, mooring was difficult. They lowered one of their own men by rope on to the quay to tie up the ship.

On board everyone had been organized into parties, some into armed units to keep the enemy at bay and hopefully chase them out of the area, others to look for transport – railway engines, trucks and motor lorries. Eric, in company with a sergeant, was given the job of finding a place to establish an airfield. They found a field to the north of Bakaritsa, just big enough for the purpose, with the advantage of a railway track alongside. The river bordered the opposite side and the ground fell away into a shallow quarry at the far end. It was not perfect but it was by far the best of the limited choices available.

The cargo was unloaded into railway trucks and crates containing aeroplane kits, aero engines and general stores were transported by rail to the field. In addition a passenger train was commandeered and parked alongside the airfield. With its dining car and kitchen, bunks and bathrooms, it served as the living quarters. Other sections of the train were converted into stores and workshops.

Portable hangars were erected and within a matter of hours the place took on the appearance of a well established air station. But the operation continued to be centred round the train. A locomotive was on constant stand-by ready to shift the whole affair to a new location if and when the need arose. Meanwhile they lived well as their cook happened to be an ex-Savoy Hotel chef.

Assembling the DH 4s was an interesting exercise. In true service fashion no manual of instruction had been included. So building the aeroplanes was very much a matter of trial and error. One of the more tricky jobs was lining up the twin Vickers machine guns in conjunction with the Constantinescu interrupter gear allowing the bullets to be fired forward between the propeller blades without hitting them.

When they thought they had got it right, Eric took off the first machine to test the apparatus. He flew to a safe patch of sky over the bay. Pressing the trigger he promptly shot off one of his propeller blades. With some difficulty and considerable vibration he limped back to the airfield. On landing he was besieged by a group of back-slapping comrades congratulating him on bringing down the first Bolshevik aeroplane. Having experienced nothing of an aggressive nature during his flight he was a little surprised. Apparently a Bolshevik pilot noticing an unidentified object flying over the water had taken off to investigate. Unseen, he had flown close beneath the DH 4. When Eric opened up with his machine guns the Russian pilot must have panicked and, immediately peeling away at a steep angle, had nosedived into the water.

Then there was trouble with the bombs. Apart from no written guidance about setting the fuses, neither the 112 lb H.E. nor the 40lb H.E. or even the 20 lb Cooper Phosphor bombs fitted the racks on the aircraft. Miraculously, no one was blown up while experimenting with this lot. They used the quarry at the far end of the airfield for their tests.

The 112 pounder was fitted with two fuses, one inserted at the rear of the bomb to allow for a delay of a few seconds after it hit the target, say a building, when it would pass through the roof and reach the lower floor before exploding. This was straightforward. But they puzzled long and hard over a second fuse in the shape of a tiny wind vane which screwed into the nose. Eventually they arrived at the conclusion that it was a safety device that only allowed the bomb to become activated when it had dropped to perhaps 2000 feet, well away from the aeroplane.

As a precaution they exploded the bombs by means of a long piece of string while they lay on their stomachs above the lip of the quarry. If an explosion took place that was fine; the train and the parked planes were protected from flying shrapnel by the sides of the quarry. If, however, the bomb failed to go off, that *was* a worry. It meant that someone had to go down and try to find out what had gone wrong.

The phosphor bomb, pre-set before take-off, had been designed for blowing up observation balloons on the Western Front. It was declared illegal for any other purpose; but not knowing this, and as there were no balloons in northern Russia, they used it to bomb other targets anyway.

The bombs did not fit the racks provided, but after a deal of hammering and drilling they fashioned new racks which held the largest and smallest bombs satisfactorily. The 40 pounders continued to fox them, so in the time-honoured manner, the aircrew carried them at their feet on the floor of the cockpit and chucked them over the side in the approximate direction of the target.

Eric returned from one bombing mission to see the ground crew frantically waving him to taxi away to a remote part of the airfield. On inspection he found a stray bomb hanging under the fuselage supported only by the string that was supposed to trigger off the fuse.

The British ground forces, a medley of naval seamen and infantry soldiers, harried the Bolsheviks, gradually driving them south along the railway. The track ran through dense forest, cleared to about two hundred yards on either side of the rails. From the air it looked like a broad ribbon stretching to eternity between the never-ending trees. Two further allied advances were being made in parallel along river banks to the east and west but at some distance from the track.

The Royal Air Force, as the RFC had become on 1 April, 1918, co-operated as closely as possible with the men on the ground. The aircrew flew ahead of the army and navy forces seeking out the enemy, assessing his strength, taking photographs, dropping messages to each group in canvas bags made more visible by long streamers, and reporting on supplies being brought up to aid the Bolsheviks.

The Bolsheviks became adept at concealing themselves on the edge of the forest bordering the line, but then they invariably gave themselves away by opening fire on the DH4s who promptly bombed and strafed them.

At intervals of some miles bigger areas had been cleared to accommodate staging posts stacked high with cut logs to fuel the locomotives. These depots made excellent targets. Eric and the others soon realized when they approached these clearings at tree-top height that, because of some strange echo effect, the enemy on the ground thought the RAF were coming from the opposite direction and were always looking the wrong way when attacked.

As time went on the Bolsheviks began to erect crude lookout posts to watch for approaching aircraft. They chose the tallest tree in the locality and so were easily spotted and dealt with.

The Allied ground forces captured a large naval gun mounted on a railway flat truck. With aircraft acting as spotters to direct fire there were high hopes of bringing considerable discomfort to the enemy.

Eric's companion in the air was a veteran observer who had been well used to guiding accurately-directed artillery fire on to the Germans on the Western Front. Yet to their chagrin, although they could see the intended target clearly enough, they were quite unable to spot any bursts from their own shells as they plopped down into the forest. There was just no way they could direct fire that was invisible. It was a mystery they never solved.

A war machine the aviators came to know well was a giant armoured train, usually stationed in one of the clearings and surrounded by protective machine-gun posts. They noticed that the powerful locomotive, unlike the woodburners, was fired by coal and had to go back down the line to some distant depot to be refuelled from time to time. One day Eric and his companion caught it out in the open, belching black smoke and heading south with a string of box cars in tow. They flew in low over the train, only a few feet above the roofs of the carriages, so close it was impossible for the Bolshevik riflemen to get a bead on their machine. They dropped their two bombs directly on top of the train. No results. Flying the length of the trucks Eric emptied the magazines of his twin Vickers machine guns into the engine's cab. Again no results as the train roared onwards. Opening up the throttles, he flew on beyond the train, executed a sharp turn and came back alongside the enemy giving his observer the chance to rake the train from end to end with his Scarff ring-mounted Lewis machine-guns. *Still* no visible results. Frustrated, they returned to base out of bombs and bullets.

A few weeks later some prisoners were brought back to base and interrogated. A handful had actually been on the train when it was attacked. Everything had been in uproar, they said, a number of their comrades, including the chief machine-gunner, had been killed and the side of one of the box cars had been blown out.

The airmen took every possible precaution to avoid being taken prisoner themselves by the Bolsheviks. The chances of living long were remote. There was plenty of evidence as to how captives were treated. It was not uncommon to come across a horribly mutilated body strung from a tree on the edge of the forest.

Eric and his observer carried iron rations and sidearms to help them evade the enemy should they be unlucky enough to force land in hostile territory. If capture seemed inevitable they were resigned to shooting themselves rather than fall into the hands of such ruthless foes.

As time went on and the Bolsheviks retreated further and further south along the railway line, the RAF were flying over greater distances until, in the end, they were covering 100 miles in each direction in order to reach the front. With a duration of only 3½ hours flying time, the DH 4s were able to spend ever less time in the actual war zone.

Suitable landing fields in that area of forest and marsh did not exist. The problem was eventually overcome when they commandeered a stretch of road with a hard-baked mud surface. Recruiting a gang of strong-armed peasant girls, they set them to work levelling the ground on either side of the improvised landing strip. Accompanied by their indispensable train the RAF flew in to take possession of their new base, much nearer to the fighting.

It was now November, yet it was still no colder than the onset of winter in England. On the 11th the Armistice was declared and 'the war to end all wars' was over. But Eric and his friends knew nothing about this until some Russian prisoners told them that there had been rumours from Moscow that the fighting was over. Confirmation came when a contingent of French troops, who happened to be at the front at that time, came hurrying back down the line. 'The war is over!' they shouted. 'We're all going home!'

Soon the Russian winter gripped them in earnest. Snow fell, the temperature dropped and dropped, oil froze, engines refused to start, frost-bitten fingers made slow work of repairs and maintenance. When an aeroplane did manage to stagger into the freezing air, aircrew had to sit stiffly upright in their open cockpits. Any leaning to left or right, away from the meagre protection of the windscreen, would result in a head being turned to a block of ice in an instant. Operations on the ground and in the air came to a standstill. And yet, as far as possible, engines were kept running in readiness for immediate take-off. Who could know when the Bolsheviks might return now there was no one to stop them?

It seemed impossible, but after Christmas it became even colder. Then in January they were pulled out of what must have been one of the most ill-judged campaigns in the history of war.

Eric John Furlong and his fellow flyers were lucky to return to England when they did. The Allies continued their forlorn efforts to overcome the Bolshevik menace through to the following autumn of 1919, before finally giving up the lost cause.

# CHAPTER EIGHT

# HENRY ROBERT STUBBINGTON

Like Adam Collins, who became an RFC despatch rider on the Western Front, Henry Robert Stubbington also grew up in the great seaport of Portsmouth, home of the mightiest navy the world had ever seen. So it was natural that, from about the age of ten, he should spend his leisure time sailing in the waters of the Solent. As the youngest member of the Melton Locks Sailing Club he learned to handle 14 and 16 foot sailing boats as expertly as men twice his age. He took part in yacht races, acquitting himself well. He learned to respect the sea, to read its infinite moods, to understand the currents, the winds and the squalls and not be afraid. He used his growing knowledge to handle any situation with increasing confidence. He became adept in the use of the compass and how to interpret charts; even when lost in a blanket of fog he never doubted his ability to find his way home.

Henry could not know how important this apprenticeship in boat handling would be to him in the years ahead, even to the point where this early training in seamanship would save his life and those of his comrades.

After leaving school, he took up an apprenticeship with Harry Philips & Co, a reputable firm of lighting engineers, who, among other contracts, had replaced the oil lamps at Waterloo Station with the latest gas lighting system. They were pleased to pay Henry the equivalent of 18p per week for the privilege of learning his trade.

Later, as the use of electricity progressed, he became involved in installing 100 volt DC generators in large country houses whose owners could afford this new form of lighting. All the time he was acquiring the engineering and mechanical skills that were to play a prominent part in his future life.

Some months after war broke out he decided to volunteer for the armed forces before conscription caught up with him. Having no desire to finish up in the mud and horror of the trenches he applied to join the RFC. After waiting three weeks for a reply, he came to the conclusion that this new service was not interested in anyone who had left school when only fourteen.

In the Royal Navy recruiting office just outside the dock gates he enquired about the possibility of joining the Royal Naval Air Service. He was given a medical and accepted immediately. Sent to Hendon, he was put through a series of tests which caused him no trouble. After all, he already had his indentures which marked him out as a qualified tradesman. To his delight he was classified straightway as an Air Mechanic 1st Class on what was then the substantial pay scale of 4 shillings per day. (Air Mechanics 2nd Class only received half that amount.)

Sent briefly to Wormwood Scrubs, he and his fellow recruits were kitted out and then posted to Sheerness on the Thames estuary for a couple of weeks under canvas. Here they endured the usual 'knocking into shape' through parade ground drill, PT and rifle training. Henry already owned two .22 air rifles and considered himself a fair shot.

After this they were sent north, finishing up at Thurso on the extremes of the Scottish mainland. From here they sailed across the Pentland Firth to the southern shores of Scapa Flow, the widespread northern anchorage of the Royal Navy's Home Fleet. The presence of this mighty fleet provided considerable employment for the locals, not least for the civilian skippers and crews who manned the scores of drifters that abounded in those sheltered waters. Each naval vessel was attended by its own particular drifter charged with ferrying personnel back and forth from ship to shore. In addition, these small boats brought supplies to the warships anchored in the Flow – including food, equipment and the regular delivery of mail.

'Stubby', as Henry was to be known for the rest of his naval career, and his mates were assigned to HMS *Campania*, originally built in 1893 by the Cunard Company as a fast passenger liner. Because of her turn of speed it was hoped at that time that she would win the Atlantic Blue Riband, but she was robbed of it by her sister ship, the *Lucania*. She was bought by the navy for the knock-down price of £10,000 and her conversion was authorized in October, 1914. Provided with a 120-foot flying-deck she was commissioned in April the following year and put under the command of Captain Oliver Schwann. Schwann, an enthusiastic advocate of naval flying, had been involved in early airship development and was among the most experienced of seaplane pilots. In 1911 he achieved the first water take-off in an Avro biplane mounted on air-bags.

Compared with some of the sleek cruisers and destroyers surrounding her, Stubby thought the *Campania*, with her disproportionately tall smoke stacks and flat flight deck, was the ugliest ship he had ever seen. After a later conversion she grew even uglier! Nevertheless, she and other ship conversions of her type were the forerunners of more advanced aircraft carriers that were to follow, leading eventually to the colossal vessels of the Second World War – the nucleus of the modern war fleets and a development that superseded the battleships which eventually became so vulnerable from the air.

Shown to their quarters, Stubby and the seventeen other recruits discovered that RNAS personnel had messing facilities separate from the rest of the ship's crew. Introduction to the regular supply of rum, traditional in the Navy when the 'mainbrace was spliced', was a pleasant surprise, as was the plentiful supply of duty free tobacco and cigarettes.

Stubby felt he had done the right thing in choosing a life in the Navy rather than waiting to be called up in the Army. Throughout his career with the RNAS he enjoyed good food, comfortable quarters and warm showers. Some of the things that his companions found irksome never troubled him and, because of his early familiarity with sailing, he was never seasick. The roughest sea held no terrors for him, which was just as well, because the *Campania* was a bad sea ship. As her triple expansion engines drove her through the water at 18 knots she pitched alarmingly and rolled up to 55 degrees, enough to take many other vessels completely over. Fortunately, because of her heavy engines and other equipment, she had a low centre of gravity, so always recovered. In stormy conditions it was an acquired art to climb the companionway or make progress across the deck. To survive aboard *Campania* required an above average constitution.

It may seem surprising, but up to that time no aircraft had ever taken off from *Campania* even in the calm waters of Scapa Flow. This was because she was a *seaplane* carrier. The system was to raise the machines through open hatchways from below decks by steam winches, open the folded wings and then lower them into the sea after the ship had heaved to, broadside to the wind. The seaplanes were always put on the water to leeward of the ship to give them maximum shelter. The pilots and observers were rowed out to their machines by dinghy.

The flying range of seaplanes in those days was generally greater than that of land planes because of their more powerful engines – essential to 'unstick' the machines from the water. The 'Babys' Sopwiths and Hambles, and the various types of Short aircraft all averaged a duration of 4 to 5 hours' flying, giving them a reasonable range for that period of the war. On return, the aircraft came down on the sea and taxied alongside the *Campania* to be winched aboard with their aircrew.

When a seaplane landed in rough weather it only needed one 'roller' to swipe off the floats. In these circumstances a Thornycroft motorboat, a superb seacraft, was immediately lowered and raced to the stricken plane, which might already be no more than a tangle of wooden struts and waterlogged canvas. The priority, of course, was to rescue the pilot and observer. This done, if there was time before the seaplane sank, efforts were made to unbolt the engine and even haul out the petrol tank.

The *Campania* rarely accompanied the Grand Fleet. The following year, during the Battle of Jutland, she even missed the confrontation with the German High Seas Fleet because of a muddle over signalled orders. However, during that year she was instructed by the Admiralty to carry out an unescorted aerial raid on the enemy port of Cuxhaven. This was considered by those on board to be nothing short of a suicide mission. A lightly armed ex-liner off the enemy coast, hove to as it lowered seaplanes into the North Sea, would be the epitome of a sitting duck. The crew were convinced that enemy destroyers would attack them from every quarter, while fast-moving light craft launched torpedoes into her unprotected hull. There were even mutters below deck that the Admiralty, having nothing but contempt for the air arm, had thought up the hairbrained scheme as a way of getting rid of this newfangled toy.

Leaving Scapa Flow early on the afternoon tide, the *Campania* sailed out into open waters. After a few hours they steamed close by a Dutch fishing fleet. The men on the smacks cheered vociferously as the strange British vessel glided past, but hardly had their wellwishers faded from sight when the radio officer picked up a message in morse: the fishermen were passing on information to the Germans about the *Campania*'s position, giving her estimated speed and course. Their one advantage, surprise, had been snatched from them. The enemy now knew they were coming. It would be lucky, as dawn broke the following morning, if they were able to launch just one or two of the seaplanes to bomb Cuxhaven before their ship was blown out of the water.

That night, as they continued to steam towards the enemy port, they contacted the Admiralty by radio, explaining what had happened. To everyone's relief a signal eventually came back from on high ordering them to turn about and head home to Scapa.

By now it was almost dawn, but it was hard to judge when the new day had actually broken as the sea was blanketed in dense fog. From the bridge of the *Campania* it was impossible to see for'ard to the end of the flying deck. In those pre-radar days no one knew who or what was surrounding them. Captain Schwann, putting himself in the place of his enemy, concluded that the Germans would expect him to scurry back to base by the shortest route possible and would surely be following that same westerly route across the North Sea, praying the fog would finally lift to reveal their defenceless quarry.

So, maintaining strict radio silence, he did the unexpected. He turned *Campania* northwards, steaming steadily up the coasts of Germany, Denmark and Norway, where he changed course again, this time out into the North Atlantic. His assumption had been right, the German navy *were* searching for him in force – but further south. With engine speed reduced to save coal, she battled through force 9 gales, pitching and tossing in her inimitable way. Meanwhile, the Admiralty, having heard nothing, assumed she was lost. But the old *Campania* surprised everyone by sailing over the boom defences at the entrance to Scapa Flow ten days later.

In July, 1915, Admiral Jellicoe, Commander in Chief of the Grand Fleet, wrote to the Admiralty to complain that 'no seaplane had yet succeeded in flying off the *Campania*'. He continued, 'We will not only be powerless to carry out aerial spotting, but I am afraid we shall also be unable to prevent the Germans doing so by means of their Zeppelins since our seaplanes are incapable of engaging the Zeppelins owing to their insufficient lifting power.' With commendable insight he concluded, 'I regret that I am unable to propose any means of meeting this menace, unless it is by the use of *aeroplanes*, rising from the deck of the *Campania*, capable of climbing above the Zeppelins and able to land on the water and be supported sufficiently long by airbags to allow of the rescue of the pilots.'

The impetus of authority had been applied. The following month, not an aeroplane but a *seaplane* with wheels fitted to its floats was held back by Stubby and his mates until the engine was revving at flying speed; with *Campania* travelling into wind at 17 knots it was released. It sped along the flight deck and rose into the air after 113 feet with only 7 feet of flight deck to spare. With so small a margin, and with larger, heavier landplanes in prospect it was decided to send *Campania* off to Cammell Laird's, on the Mersey, to have a longer flight deck fitted.

When she came back in April the following year the old girl looked odder than ever. Her 120-foot flight deck had been extended to 200 feet. In order to accommodate this, her forward funnel had been moved further aft, split in two and re-established as two separate smoke stacks on the port and starboard outer extremes of the ship. Meanwhile, her after funnel remained in a central position. Obviously, with such an obstacle sticking up amidships no one had contemplated the idea of aircraft actually *landing* on the flight deck!

In spite of Jellicoe's recommendation for the use of landplanes, the *Campania* returned with a complement of three Shorts, three Babies and four others, all floatplanes. She also sported a rather fine-looking observation balloon designed to be towed astern. Again the seaplanes, particularly the Short 184s, were to be launched with a wheeled carriage attached to their floats. After take-off these could be jettisoned by the pilot and picked up for further use by attendant destroyers.

During *Campania*'s refit Stubby was posted even further north, 30 miles beyond Scapa, to the small island of Westray in the North Orkneys. This was a remote shore station established in a sheltered bay on the east side of the island. The complement consisted of three flying officers, fifteen ratings and three seaplanes.

By this time Stubby had gained a reputation as the man to call on in any matter connected with aero engines. Mastering every detail relating to this new development in engineering he had become a largely self-taught expert. He completely understood these machines which still remained a mystery to most sailors and his growing knowledge had been reinforced by the far-sighted decision of his Commanding Officer to send him on training sessions to both the Sunbeam and Rolls Royce factories. In recognition of his value the Navy had promoted him to Petty Officer, one of the youngest in the service. In this position he was able to pass on his rare skills to others and introduce workshop practices that improved maintenance efficiency.

During his time on Westray he had the opportunity to enhance his well-earned reputation. The engines on seaplanes were started by compressed air. (Swinging the propeller, the landlubbers method of firing up motors, was not a practical proposition at sea!) On one occasion Henry was aware that the air bottles on his CO's machine needed replacing. On the precept that if you want a job done properly do it yourself he ordered a cutter and was rowed out to the seaplane. Climbing into the cockpit he replaced the old bottles with new ones and then noticed that a stiff breeze was moving out to sea at a steady rate. The sea anchor had come adrift and the seaplane, attached by a rope, was dragging the cutter with it. There was a strict rule that only pilots were entitled to start engines on the grounds that they alone knew how to control a plane once it was under power. Stubby was a strong believer in breaking the rules when necessary and at this moment he considered it very necessary. He stood up in the cockpit and, waving his arms, semaphored the situation to shore and asked permission to start up. Commander Tompkinson, his CO, was there and signalled an order to carry on, having no idea who the gesticulating figure far out at sea might be.

Ordering the cutter to cast off and stand clear, Stubby slipped down into the cockpit. Priming the engine, flicking the ignition, setting the throttle, turning on the compressed air took only a moment. The motor fired and purred sweetly. He was drifting broadside to the ever-freshening offshore wind in a sea that had become decidedly rough. He realized that the wind under his port wing might lift the plane at any moment and turn it over, so he used the elevators to counter this by getting maximum lift under the starboard wing. Accelerating out to sea he gradually brought her round until she was pointing diagonally across wind on course back to the island. At this point he was about three miles from shore and the sea was rising by the minute, but Stubby was in no doubt that he would make it. He knew all about the sea and the winds and understood instinctively how far he could edge across the wind without capsizing, realizing the importance of speed to skim the waves rather than allowing the floats to plunge into them and founder.

He glanced at the figures on the shore. The CO was jumping up and down, shouting unheard instructions. As he brought the seaplane towards the beach, the landing party seized the machine and ran it up onto terra firma. As Stubby climbed down from the cockpit the CO said, 'Well done, Stubbington,' and walked off. The Chief Petty Officer looked at Henry: 'Clever exhibition, Stubby. I wouldn't have missed it for worlds!'

It was not long before he and his mates, under Commander Tompkinson, left their temporary station and returned to the improved *Campania*. The seaplanes, with their more powerful V8 'Arab' and V12 'Maori' Sunbeam engines, were able to climb higher, while larger fuel tanks had increased the range. Stubby, having already completed the course on Sunbeams, considered them more than adequate, though not, of course, in the same league as the unmatchable Rolls Royce engines.

By the end of 1916 Allied merchant shipping was suffering terrible losses as vessel after vessel was sent to the bottom by U-boats or German surface raiders. The enemy's policy of bringing Britain to her knees by cutting off her vital supplies was edging perilously close to success. At one stage essential stores of food were within weeks of exhaustion. Every possible means of countering the menace was brought into force: convoys were escorted by destroyers and cruisers; searches were carried out by seaplanes and airships, (see Chapter 5); Q Ships with their volunteer crews manned strange, heavily armed vessels disguised as innocent merchantmen whose outline and identity changed day by day.

A new anti-submarine aid had arrived in England from the United States of America in the shape of fifty Curtiss H12 Flying Boats. Their design owed much to John C. Porte, a former British Naval pilot. Each of these was being re-engined for use by the RNAS with twin 250 hp Rolls Royce Eagle 1s at the seaplane and flying boat experimental station at Felixstowe. Flown by a crew of four, there was a forward machine-gun station in the bow with two Lewis guns and a rear defensive position with a single gun. The underwing bomb load consisted of either two 230 lb or four 100 lb bombs.

To distinguish these machines from their smaller predecessors, the H4s, the Curtis H12s were known as 'Large Americas'. They proved to be first-rate flying machines, although they still exhibited certain hull weaknesses inherited from the earlier types. (A British re-designed version, again inspired by John Porte, and known as the Felixstowe, eventually overcame these problems.) Climbing higher than any operational seaplane, not far short of 11,000 feet, and flying considerably faster, nearly 100 mph under favourable conditions, with an endurance of 6 hours, the H12s were all set to play an aggressive role in the war at sea. On 14 May the following year H12s shot down their first Zeppelin, flying at an altitude previously unreachable by seaplanes, and six days later sank a U-Boat. They became the first aircraft to operate the 'spider's web' system of maritime patrol (used extensively in the Second World War) in which the patrol area was divided into geometrical divisions and covered systematically sector by sector.

Two Curtiss H12s were flown up to the seaplane and kite balloon section at Houton Bay on the curiously named Orkney Mainland. A Commander Holmes, with four flying officers and fifty men, was dispatched by the Admiralty with orders to set up a unit to service and operate these new machines. Unfortunately, in true service tradition, the sailors had no clue how to handle this relatively sophisticated equipment. Worse than that, there was not a single aero engineer among them, let alone anyone with experience of caring for refined Rolls Royce engines. So Holmes sent an urgent signal to *Campania* requesting Petty Officer Stubbington's immediate presence. Realizing the urgency of the situation, Commander Tompkinson reluctantly allowed Stubby to go, on the understanding that it was only to be a temporary posting.

Arriving at Houton Bay Stubby was disappointed to find the pilots and crews who had delivered the boats from Felixstowe had taken one look at the surrounding wilderness and hastily departed south. So he had lost the chance of gleaning information on the 'Large Americas' from the only men qualified to answer his questions. Adequate operation and maintenance manuals were still a thing of the future. With painstaking care he carried out a minute examination of the H12s from stem to stern, and from wing tip to wing tip. The familiar Rolls Royce engines were the least of his concerns. Noting the five 70-gallon petrol tanks, he saw that fuel was gravity fed to the two engines via a small auxiliary tank mounted on the top wing and holding only 4 gallons. To this the fuel was fed from the main tanks by what looked to him like a totally inadequate little pump.

And so it proved to be. In flight these pumps had a habit of seizing up, leaving only the 4 gallons in the small tank. This was sufficient for no more than six minutes' flying before both engines coughed to a stop.

Within a week Stubby had both Curtisses tuned and fit for flying. He took off with each of the pilots in turn, explaining the intricacies of switching tanks in the correct order to maintain trim. There was a lot to learn in the air as none of the aircrew had had experience of multi-engined aircraft before, let alone the handling characteristics of flying boats.

Houton Bay was only a short distance from the *Campania*'s mooring, so when Captain Tompkinson saw the two Curtiss H12s flying overhead, their engines purring sweetly, he knew that his star engineer had done the job he had been released to do and signalled for his immediate return to the ship. Commander Holmes replied that before he could let Stubby go he must have a replacement from the *Campania*'s crew equally experienced in handling aero engines. Stubby knew that no such man existed and secretly he wanted to stay on dry land. After so many months incarcerated between steel walls with few pastimes other than reading, playing cards or clicking dominoes, and with only two weeks' leave per year, he had had enough of life aboard ship.

When Holmes learned the name of the replacement he sent for Stubby to ask about the man's qualifications. 'There's no doubt he's a very good fellow, sir,' said Henry truthfully, 'but he's only a workshop hand and he knows absolutely nothing about aero engines, let alone Rolls Royces.'

When the man arrived Holmes questioned him at once and the man confirmed what Stubby had said: he had no idea about aero engines. Without hesitation the Commander sent him back. It was an impasse – both Commanders were determined to retain the services of their skilled Petty Officer.

However, within days the matter was resolved, at least temporarily. A signal from the Admiralty ordered a crew to be sent to Felixstowe to pick up another Curtiss Flying Boat and fly it back to Houton Bay. This was Holmes's chance to get his PO out of the way, if only for a week or two. That day Stubby and Flight Lieutenant Cutler left on their journey south by boat and by train, both looking forward to the flight back up the long east coast of the British Isles. Stubby was feeling particularly pleased with himself as he recalled Commander Holmes's parting remarks: 'Bring our new boat back in one piece, Stubbington, and I'll make you up to Chief Petty Officer.'

At Felixstowe he gave the machine a thorough check before assuring Cutler that everything was in order. By then it was well into the afternoon and the two men flew north as far as the Humber before alighting at RNAS seaplane station, Killingholme. As dusk settled they moored the 'Large America' to a buoy with a 20-foot wire hawser.

That night it came on to blow in the region of force 7.

While her crew slept, the Curtiss, lightly loaded, had been planing on the surface. Pulled down by the restraining wire she had been bouncing against the buoy hour after hour throughout the night. By the time the flyers came to inspect her the following morning the wind had abated. Although the hull was undamaged, large holes had been punched in both her lower planes. Hauled up the slipway, patches were soon placed over the torn fabric and once again they were on their way. (It is hard to imagine the application of such a simple remedy in today's world of high tech' aviation!)

They now had an extra crew member. The Admiralty had decided to establish a new flying boat base in the north of Scotland. Before completing their flight back to Houton Bay they were to investigate the suitability of a saltwater lake inland of the Moray Firth. With this in mind, Squadron Commander McKenzie, who was reputed to be an expert in such matters, joined them at Killingholme. They found the lake covered in a green carpet of coarse couch-grass and surrounded by sand dunes. The only sign of civilization was the single track of the Highland Railway that skirted its shores. After a careful recce, flying low over the water from different directions looking for possible obstacles, McKenzie decided they would attempt a landing. The boat alighted on the water without a hitch and they taxied to the far end of the lake before switching off. The average depth of water was no more than eighteen inches but this was sufficient to operate flying boats.

As if from nowhere, they were met by a dinghy weighed down with naval officers and a huge stack of lead ingots which were hauled aboard the Curtiss until the load represented the all-up combat weight: guns, bombs, full tanks, and a complete crew of a 'Large America'.

'Now see if you can take-off with that lot,' the naval officers said.

Hauling the seaplane hard back against the shore, the throttles were opened wide as the machine roared across the surface. To the relief of the men on board, the hull came 'unstuck' with a fair stretch of water still to spare. Completing the circuit, they alighted again and, even fully loaded, had enough depth to stay clear of the lake bottom.

'That was fine,' said the ground party. 'Now we'd like you to try the same thing *across* the lake.' This was an interesting proposal as the width was only about half that of the length and was made even narrower by the abundance of couch-grass on either side. However, in the Navy 'orders is orders'.

With engines roaring they belted across the narrow stretch and just managed to get airborne, but in doing so they had ploughed through the couch-grass on the far side ripping a foot-square hole in the underside of the hull. Re-alighting on water was now out of the question and to add to their predicament it would soon be dark. Setting course for the nearest seaplane station, which happened to be Dundee, some 110 miles over the mountains, they prayed it would be an establishment with adequate rescue services.

By the time they reached the Firth of Tay night had fallen. Everywhere was blacked out and not a light was to be seen. They flew low up river hoping to make out a shallow enclave where they could beach their boat, but all they could see were unbroken rows of high stone wharves on either bank.

Flying up as far as the railway bridge before turning about they spotted the outline of a drifter making her way down stream. They flashed her with the Aldis lamp but it soon became clear that the crew were unable to read morse. A moment later, flying even lower, they had the good fortune to make out a RNAS Thornycroft powerboat crossing the river ahead. Tracing the powerboat's wake back to the northern bank, they saw a steeply angled wooden launching slip set into a gap just wide enough to alight between the landing stages. Circling once, they came down on the water about 40 yards out and aimed for the slip ahead of them in the gloom. It was high tide. By great good luck the 'Large America' careered up the wooden structure, tipped at an angle and came to rest in front of a row of seaplane hangars.

By this time they had made enough noise to arouse everyone on the station. The first man on the spot was the CO, a Commander Wilberforce, well known to Stubby from early days on the *Campania*. The three visitors were made welcome, fed and bedded down for the night.

After breakfast Stubby made his way down to the slip to set about repairs to the hull and to his horror he saw a group of sailors in charge of a Chief Petty Officer about to raise the flying boat by means of a 5-ton jack placed under her tail. He had arrived in the nick of time. If pressure *had* been applied the flying boat would have broken her back. Running towards the men he yelled at the top of his voice, 'What the hell do you think you're doing, you blithering idiots? Get away from that bloody jack!'

The sailors looked at him in bewilderment. The CPO white with rage, stomped off to his quarters. This was fine by Stubby as it left him to instruct the men how to raise a flying boat correctly. This was done by placing a trestle under each lower wing root, where the wing joins the fuselage, inserting a baulk of timber between the two and jacking up from the central position. When she had been raised 18 inches Stubby was able to set about repairing the hole.

McKenzie and Cutler came along to inspect the work and, to his surprise, they then wished Stubby goodbye. McKenzie was returning to the Admiralty to make his report on the lake, while Cutler made his way back to Houton Bay.

Stubby soon learned that the 'Large America' was not, after all, to be taken on to the strength of the air station at Houton Bay, probably because of lack of trained maintenance staff. Instead, two young flying officers, accompanied by a wireless telegraphist rating, turned up from Killingholme with instructions to fly the boat back to that station. Stubby was to accompany them as flight engineer.

The flight was postponed for several days because of fog, which still persisted on the day they finally left, but the meteorological experts assured them they would fly out of it once they had cleared the river and started to head south over the sea, but after flying east for half an hour they were still shrouded in impenetrable gloom. Assuming they were well away from land they turned south. Confidence was not improved by an unreliable magnetic compass that seemed at times to have a life of its own. After an hour and a half of nil visibility the pilot decided to fly west to see if he could make out the shoreline. Flying towards land at only a 100 feet Stubby considered nothing short of lunacy.

All at once they were confronted by a tall factory chimney a few feet off their starboard wing. This so shook the pilot that for the second time he headed resolutely out to sea. But after 20 minutes the shock must have worn off because once more he turned west, searching for the coast at low level. This time Stubby had an even lower opinion of his behaviour.

Looming out of the fog without warning high cliffs suddenly towered above them. Banking steeply to port they missed the rock face by inches. The big boat wobbled, began to stall, then flopped down as if exhausted into the sea. They had survived. It was nothing to do with flying skill – they had been exceptionally lucky.

The pilots had had enough; they were not going to fly any more that day. They worked out a course to taxi all the way back up the coast to Middlesborough on the River Tees. Stubby's suggestion that they should continue the short distance further to the Humber was ignored. Bouncing through the sea at 8 knots, it took them 14 hours to make the mouth of the Tees.

At one stage a coastguard signalled, asking if they needed assistance. With bitter feelings Stubby flashed back that help was unnecess-

17. A pilot and his mechanic of the *Corpo Aeronautic Militare* stand proudly before their Caproni C42 Triplane Bomber with its three 270hp Isotta-Fraschini engines.

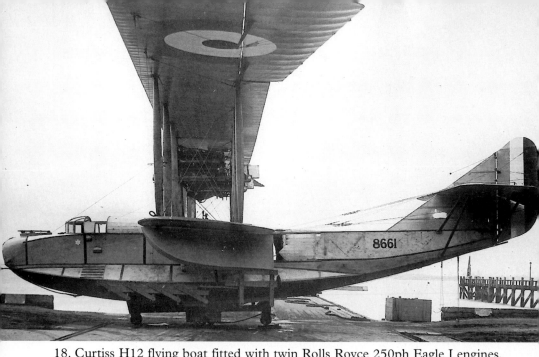

18. Curtiss H12 flying boat fitted with twin Rolls Royce 250ph Eagle I engines. Known as the 'Large America' and built in the USA it was based on designs by John C. Porte, a former British Naval pilot. Henry Stubbington won the Distinguished Flying Medal while flying in an H12. *(Imperial War Museum)*

19. Former RNAS gunlayer, later RAF sergeant observer 'Tiny' Wardrop is 7th from left, back row. Major Brackley, MC, his pilot, and also 214 Squadron's commanding officer, is standing immediately in front of him. Behind the group the Handley Page 0/100 displays its reliable twin Rolls Royce 250hp Eagle engines. Note the 230 pound bomb on left of picture. *(Norman Gilham)*

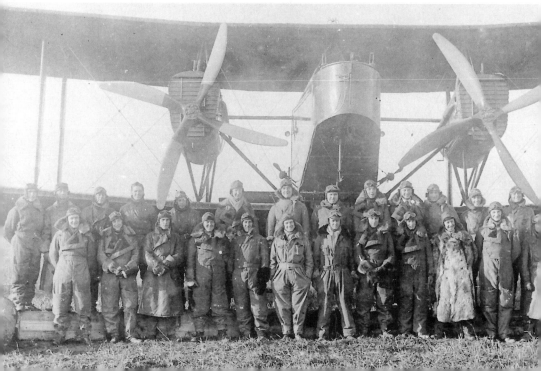

20. Handley Page 0/100s operating from the beach near Calais while their aerodrome at Coudekerque was being repaired after a German air raid. These massive RNAS, later RAF, heavy night bombers were of similar dimensions to the World War II Avro Lancaster but of somewhat different configuration! (Norman Gilham)

21. Bombers' moon. Aerial photo of Ostend docks taken by 'Tiny' Wardrop. A frequent target for 214 Squadron's bombers, the port is virtually devoid of shipping. German U-boats, however, continued to slip in and out of this convenient 'bolt-hole'. *(Norman Gilham)*

22. F.J. Powell sitting in the cockpit of his F.E.8, the only machine of this type in the world when the photo was taken. It had been hastily repaired after a crash following an attack by an enemy aircraft. Powell, one of the RFC's finest pilots, was entrusted with trying out prototype aircraft under combat conditions. Here he is checking his newly fitted upward-firing Lewis gun removed from a useless position that almost cost him his life. (*Imperial War Museum*)

23. The German reconnaissance and bombing aircraft, the Aviatik, powered by a 160hp Austro-Daimler engine. It was the Schwarzlose machine gun of the observer that all but destroyed Powell's F.E.8. This illustration is of an early type. *(Imperial War Museum)*

24. A rare wartime picture of Hugh Trenchard, (on extreme left), who was notoriously camera-shy. He is seen with Queen Mary and a squadron commander in France. The VIPs are watching a pilot looping his machine. *(Imperial War Museum)*

25. Robert Loraine, a Cornishman, was famous before the war both as a West End actor and also as a pioneer aviator, the first pilot to fly from England to Ireland. As a wartime squadron commander he achieved fame of another sort as one of the RFC's most eccentric officers. *(RAF Museum)*

26. A typical S.E.5a squadron of aircrew and groundcrew with a line-up of their machines on an airfield near St Omer in the summer of 1918. The S.E.5a was arguably the ultimate World War I fighter - equal to the Sopwith Camel, but with none of the latter's 'tricky' flying characteristics. *(Imperial War Museum)*

27. Wounded on the Somme, Archibald Yuille convalesced for more than a year before being passed 'fit for light duties'. Joining the RFC, he became a highly successful Sopwith Camel night fighter pilot, first in England, then in France. *(Imperial War Museum)*

28. The Avro 504k. After a short spell of service at the front in the early days of the war, the 504 soon became established as *the* RFC's basic trainer. In improved forms it continued in this capacity with the RAF until the end of the 1930s. As the picture shows, even in those days some women were only too happy to have a go. Note the Bessoneaux hangar. *(Imperial War Museum)*

ary; the engines were running perfectly and the hull was undamaged. Coming up river Stubby made fast to a buoy on the south bank near to an ancient 12-inch gun Monitor currently serving as a landing stage. He borrowed a hammock and prepared to kip down for the night feeling no concern for the others. They had forfeited his respect many hours earlier.

At first light he got through to the nearby RNAS station at Seaton Carew and begged 300 gallons of aviation spirit. The petrol arrived later in the day contained in 150 × 2 gallon cans. These had to be rowed out in batches to the 'Large America' and poured one at a time into the aircraft's tanks. Fortunately the Monitor's caretaker crew were glad to have something to do.

By the start of a fine, clear afternoon, the task was completed and, although the tide had reached its lowest ebb, a narrow channel flowed between the mud banks leaving just enough water for take-off. A naval motor launch chugged half a mile ahead to make sure the passage was clear. As the Curtiss gathered speed it came nearer and nearer to the launch. At 70 knots they were bearing down on the slow-moving vessel whose captain, a young lieutenant, and his crew, stared in apprehension at this fast-approaching predator. Banked in by acres of glutinous mud there was no escape, but, when all seemed lost, the 'Large America', hard astern, lifted into the air, murky water streamed from its hull deluging the boat's occupants. The sailors' furious gestures hardly expressed a loving admiration for flying boats.

Flying south of Flamborough Head, they followed the Humber up to Killingholme, which was to be Stubby's new station. His first act on arrival was to obtain permission to return to Scapa to collect his gear. Originally expecting to be away only a few days he had little more than his weekend kit to sustain him. All his possessions were aboard the *Campania*. He was still on the ship's strength and the purser owed him five months' pay! With a duty travel warrant from Killingholme to Houton Bay he was granted ten days to make the round trip. (He managed to retain this valuable document, later using it to good purpose to travel hundreds of miles by rail to many parts of the country. None of the officials had the faintest idea where either Killingholme or Houton Bay were and always assumed he was en route somewhere between one or the other.)

Reaching Houton Bay, he boarded a drifter out to *Campania*, still anchored in Scapa Flow. A chorus of 'Where did *you* get to? You've been adrift for months!' greeted him as he stepped aboard. After visiting the purser's office, collecting his back money and getting his clearance papers stamped, he gathered up his two hammocks, suitcase, a brand new uniform, tool box and ditty box, and was back on the drifter like lightning. His main anxiety had been the thought of bumping into Commander Tompkinson. Helpful voices kept chiding him, 'If old Tompky catches you he'll clamp you in irons to keep you on board!'

As the drifter pulled away from *Campania* he let out a heartfelt sigh of relief. To Stubby it was not far short of saying farewell to a prison ship.

Killingholme consisted of three flights. 'A' Flight was the operational unit known as War Flight. Maintenance was in the charge of a Chief Petty Officer who knew nothing about aircraft engines. 'B' Flight was the School Flight responsible for training, while 'C' Flight looked after General Overhauls and Major Repairs. Stubby, still a Petty Officer, was put in charge of all 'A' Flight maintenance, replacing the CPO who, in the traditional way, had transferred from the RN to the RNAS without knowing anything about the job.

Taking over this position as soon as he arrived created a groundswell of resentment, not because the CPO had been replaced, but because he, as a new arrival on the station, had done a skilled young engineer out of the job he had expected to inherit. The mechanics stood four square behind the leading hand who, in all but name, had been running the flight. Sullen anger simmered among the ranks and for some time Stubby faced a barrier of passive resistance whenever he ordered a job to be done. It was only the continual display of his skill when he cheerfully completed tasks off his own bat that brought about a gradual thaw in the atmosphere.

It was hard work keeping eight large flying boats up to operational standard as they carried out patrols from dawn to dusk, seven days a week. Another problem that confronted the 'A' Flight CO, Commander Moon, DSC, was the difficulty in providing a regular supply of volunteer flight engineers to fly with the crews. Although this was an essential aircrew category on Curtiss H12s, regulations at that time stipulated that no engineer could be ordered to fly against his

will. Two shillings a day extra flying pay was an attractive induce-
ment, but even so, once the novelty began to wear off men began to
complain about going on afternoon flights as these cut into their
evening 'shore leave.' So Commander Moon decided to offer the
engineers an extra day's leave for every two hours' flying time. After
this there were no further problems.

Stubby, who would happily have flown for nothing in any weather
conditions, considered this 'bribe' far from justified. On one
occasion, in the depth of winter, he was ready to take off with a
Lieutenant pilot who decided at the last minute that the weather was
too stormy. The officer voiced his opinion to Commander Moon.
The CO turned to Stubby, 'Is the boat fit to fly?'

'All in order, sir.'

'Right,' said Moon, 'we operate on timed take-offs and we should
be patrolling by now. Let's go!'

Commander Moon, Stubby and a W/T man climbed aboard and
were soon in the air carrying out the scheduled four-hour flight.
They returned without incident.

One of the 'Large Americas' was always standing by as the
'Emergency Boat', ready for any eventuality. It was early April when
a message came through from Flamborough Head at 11.20 am to say
that a Zeppelin had been detected flying in low cloud just off the
coast. Manning the 'Emergency Boat', a crew of four-Pilots Pattinson
and Mundy, W/T Rating Johnson and Stubby as engineer – was
airborne in twenty minutes with orders to seek out the German
raider and, if possible, destroy it.

As on so many occasions the flying conditions were foul. Almost
impenetrable cloud lay in layers above them. They were tuned into
the enemy's wavelength and could hear her morse signals distinctly,
but they tracked her for several hours without seeing a thing, while
all the time she was somewhere close above them. At 9,000 feet the
gloom lightened a little and the cigar-shaped dirigible suddenly
loomed alongside their port beam, close enough to see she was the
R26. Immediately Stubby and the wireless operator opened up with
their machine guns, pouring some 200 rounds into her flanks. Pulling
her nose sharply upwards the Zeppelin disappeared into the clouds
and, although they searched and searched, they never found her
again.

Now the flying boat was in trouble. By this time they were some three hundred miles from base and Stubby noticed that their starboard engine was losing oil fast, flowing aft and coating the tailplane. He was well aware that the cooling tanks to each engine carried no more than 4 gallons each. Any moment the supply to that engine would be exhausted and the machinery would seize solid.

He yelled to the first pilot to shut down both engines and make a gliding approach on to the sea. After this was accomplished the crew later told him they thought he had fallen overboard as he was nowhere to be seen. Actually he was already out of sight on the top wing sorting out the problem. Almost at once he had discerned what was wrong. The $\frac{1}{2}$-inch copper oil pipe which ran between the V of the cylinders had split at the front main joint. Without doubt it had been caused by bad workmanship where it had been brazed into the brass bearing during which the pipe had been filed too thin. Under pressure it had burst open. Lying on the top plane as the flying boat rolled and plunged in the rough sea he effected a secure emergency repair. Clambering back into the hull he reported to his astonished companions, who assumed he had gone for ever, that they were now ready to take off.

Unfortunately, as far as the pilots were concerned, they were not ready to take off at all. The captain was convinced his flying boat would break up in the heavy seas and they would all perish far from land. Stubby lost his cool. Regardless of rank he shouted 'Of course we'll be lost if we stay here. Whose going to rescue us in this lot? We'll be waterlogged long before anyone finds us.'

'And we'll be waterlogged if we try to take off into these waves,' replied the captain gloomily.

Determined to make them see sense, Stubby persisted. 'We took off in far worse than this in Scapa,' he lied, 'and that was in flimsy little seaplanes. Rev up your engines, keep her facing into the wind and go for it. Whatever you do don't attempt to pull her off or you'll break her back. Just plane over the waves until she rises of her own accord.' Such was the strength of his personality and his obvious knowledge of seafaring matters that they finally agreed.

As he claimed, the flying boat skimmed flat out over the crests of the rollers never once sinking into the troughs. Within moments the 'Large America' was back in its natural element and heading for base.

Next morning, when the story leaked out, Stubby was grabbed by his erstwhile disgruntled mechanics and carried shoulder high round the station. It was rumoured that Commander Moon had sent a report on the incident to the Admiralty but nothing more was heard until 10 September, 1918. On that date the *London Gazette* reported:

'His Majesty the King has been graciously pleased to award the Distinguished Flying Medal to Chief Mechanic Henry Robert Stubbington for conspicuous gallantry in the air against the enemy. The incident occurred during an attack on a Zeppelin. His emergency repair to one of the engines in a very rough sea saved the lives of the crew and enabled the flying boat to return to her own base.'

Not long afterwards Commander Moon buttonholed Stubby and started questioning him about every aspect concerned with engineering and flying operations on the station. For over an hour the two men strode back and forth over the concrete in front of the hangars. At last Moon came to the point: 'The Admiralty in their wisdom have realized they do not have a single engineering officer in the Flying Boat Service. I intend putting your name forward for a commission. What do you say, Stubbington?'

Stubby thought hard. He was happy in his present situation; he enjoyed his work, had plenty of authority and was reasonably well paid. As a junior lieutenant he could not imagine what his role might be; his authority would be considerably less and his pay very little more. On the other hand he had great respect for Commander Moon and was unashamedly flattered by the offer. Whatever his own feelings it would be wrong to turn it down.

'Thank you very much, Sir. I'll be glad to give it a go.'

A little oddly, he and another NCO were interviewed at the Admiralty by a Brigadier. Stubby alone was accepted as a Temporary Lieutenant and posted on a thirteen-week course to the Royal Air Force Technical Officers School of Instructors, Henley. There he stood out in his navy blue uniform amidst a sea of khaki.

To his disappointment he found the instruction was years out of date. On the day of the final examinations the documents arrived from the Air Ministry in sealed envelopes. The questions bore no relation to what had been taught during the course. He felt sorry for his fellow pupils who had taken copious notes and studied hard but had little idea how to answer what was being asked in the exam papers. Not surprisingly Stubby was top scorer in Engineering, while another RNAS Petty Officer came first in Aircraft Maintenance. His future career in the Royal Naval Air Service was assured.

# CHAPTER NINE

# W. E. D. 'TINY' WARDROP

By the middle of 1915 William Wardrop was reaching the end of his tether. He still had two years to go before completing his apprenticeship with the Edmonds Electricity Corporation. The pay was poor, the hours were long and meanwhile there was a war to be fought.

As a Londoner with Scottish antecedents he had gone along to the recruiting office in the hope of joining the London Scottish Regiment, but had been refused on the grounds that he was already being trained for essential war work as an electrician. Then he tried the Royal Engineers – again the same result. They were unable to accept him because he was irrevocably committed to the company that was teaching him his trade.

Continuing to badger his employers they eventually appeared to give in by saying they would release him from his indentures for the duration of the war provided he joined the Royal Naval Air Service in a flying capacity. He was convinced that this was the management's idea of a joke because 'Tiny' Wardrop, as he was known to everyone, although still in his teens, was already approaching heavyweight status and growing fast towards his adult height of 6 feet 4 inches. It was unheard of for a young man of such proportions to be accepted for flying duties.

Nevertheless, armed with his permit from the company, on 5 August, 1915, he went along to Spring Gardens in Whitehall to try his luck. To his astonishment and delight, after passing his medical with flying colours, he was accepted without further question and posted to Sheerness, still in civilian clothes.

At the end of a week he and his fellow recruits were judged fit to wear the King's uniform, during which period the would-be aviators had not been near anything that even vaguely resembled an aeroplane.

But a lecture by the medical officer on the dangers associated with strong drink and the evils of certain houses of ill repute in France encouraged the lads to think they would soon be on their way to the Continent to see a bit of action. In reality they were scattered along the English coastline to various air stations. Tiny was sent to Felixstowe.

Languishing at this seaplane and flying boat experimental station for over a year, he became more and more depressed. He penned request after request to his commanding officer pleading to be sent on aircrew training. All to no avail.

As the member of a launching and landing party under the charge of a petty officer his duties consisted of manoeuvring seaplanes down a concrete slipway into the water and then hauling them up again when they returned. In winter he and his companions wore heavy thigh-length sea boots and were muffled up to the eyebrows. In summer swimming costumes were sufficient working gear. Although his physical strength was well suited to this work it was not an occupation calculated to inspire a bright young man who nursed a burning desire to fly.

At one time he developed a 'couldn't care less' attitude to the service. If it chose to ignore him, then he would ignore them and their ridiculous rules. The Navy, of course, had well worn remedies for curing such behaviour. Not only was he subjected to stern physical punishment, such as endlessly scrubbing floors with a brick, but was also 'awarded' a regular series of 'North Easters'. The 'North Easter' was designed to hit the 20th century sailor where it hurt most – in the pocket. N.E. actually stood for 'Not Entitled' and was meted out for various lengths of time according to the seriousness of the 'crime'. The sailor to be punished joined the usual pay parade, cap in hand. But when it came to his turn the paymaster would shout 'Not Entitled', and the unfortunate man, unlike his better behaved ship-mates, was left without a penny in his headgear.

After kicking over the traces for some time Tiny realized he was getting nowhere and decided to toe the line. Playing the part of a good boy was not easy, but he relieved his pent-up feelings by submitting even more requests to fly.

To most of his mates one of the most welcome consolations of naval life was the regular rum ration. It was a prized tradition that meant nothing to him. He hated the stuff and always gave his tot away. At moments of ritual celebration such as 'splicing the main-brace' he sat in a cocoon of morose isolation surrounded by a noisy gang of depressingly cheerful spirits.

On one occasion, and one occasion only, he managed to scrounge a flight in a Curtiss flying boat from Felixstowe to Great Yarmouth and back – a trip of about 45 minutes. They flew in heavy rain the whole time and he saw very little, but when they alighted at base his enthusiasm for flying was greater than ever.

Then one day in October, 1916, after more than twelve months of purgatory, a minor miracle happened. Tiny was posted to Eastchurch on a gunlaying and bomb-dropping course. The training also included a six-week visit to Whale Island off Portsmouth to practise firing twelve-pounders at sea. It would be difficult to visualize the use of such weapons in aerial combat given the fragile structure of the existing flying machines!

At Eastchurch real flying training began at last. Sitting on a six-inch plank in the rear cockpit of a Maurice Farman, the novice bomb-droppers tried their skill by peering into a Negative Lens Sight set in the floor between their feet. It consisted of a square plano-concave glass plate through which four sighting wires were visible. The sight was pre-calibrated for different altitudes and speeds, and could be used during bombing either up or down wind. When the target appeared in the sight a toggle was pulled and the 25-pound dummy bomb was released.

The target itself was in the form of a ten-foot cross made up of discarded aeroplane wings. When not actually flying, one of the pupils stood by the target to mark with pegs the accuracy of his airborne colleague's aim. Apparently this was not as dangerous as it sounds because the 'bomb' was made of wood and could be followed, like a cricket ball, throughout its trajectory, allowing, in theory, plenty of time to get out of the way.

Tiny and his fellow pupils were given thorough exercises not only in firing the .303 mm Lewis machine gun, but in stripping it down, curing faults and unblocking stoppages. In flight they fired at targets on the ground and at sea and at small balloons in the air.

The final examination consisted of dropping four practice bombs from 1000 feet and another four from 2000 feet, all in broad daylight under good weather conditions. Hardly a thorough preparation for bombing enemy installations during a foggy night.

When Tiny's turn came, his score was assessed as being exceptionally high. The cloud layer had descended almost to ground level and the pilot flew back and forth searching for the target. At only 100 feet they suddenly spotted what they had been looking for. Tiny took aim and dropped all his bombs in quick succession. The hits were as near perfect as could ever be expected!

His reward was not what he had anticipated. Instead of being sent to a squadron, like the others who had passed, he was retained as an instructor at Eastchurch and, much to his chagrin remained there, in spite of many further applications to be posted for active service.

At long last, in August, 1917, he was transferred to No 14 RNAS Squadron (later to become 214 Squadron, RAF), at Coudekerque in France. He stared in wonder at the giant Handley Page 0/100s, twenty of them, (half operated by a sister squadron) standing in rows on the airfield. These massive twin-engined biplanes were the biggest bombers to be used by Britain during the First World War. (The even bigger 0/1500 arrived just too late for combat.) Tiny had not realized that aeroplanes could be so huge, (of similar dimensions to the Second World War Lancaster) or, being such a size, could manage to stagger into the air.

'The Bloody Paralyser' (see Chapter Three) had undergone development since the early days of the war and only began arriving on RNAS squadrons in September, 1916. It was powered by two Rolls Royce Eagle engines which had been purposely derated to 250 hp each, well below their total capacity, to ensure reliable running under all conditions. A later version, with 350 hp Rolls Royce engines, and a revised fuel system with tanks transferred from engine nacelles to the fuselage, but otherwise unchanged, was designated the 0/400.

Originally the crew of three were accommodated in an armour-plated cockpit fitted with a glazed bullet proof cover. Under operational conditions most of these refinements were removed because of their excessive weight. The fuselage was exceptionally strong, being constructed of cross-braced metal girders covered in fabric. The wings, with a total span of 100 feet, could be folded back to allow the bomber to be accommodated in the standard Bessoneau canvas hangar.

The release gears for the normal bombload of sixteen 112-pound bombs, or eight 230-pound bombs, were mounted internally on four crossbeams in the fuselage above the bomb-cell floor. This was a 'honey-comb' grid with sixteen spring-loaded flaps separately pushed open by each bomb as it fell. As is so often the case with good ideas, in practice these flaps caused trouble and were sometimes replaced by brown-paper rectangles that the bombs simply broke through when released – a rough and ready solution, but one which caused the crew acute discomfort from the freezing draft sucked up through the open apertures.

The HP 0/100 was formidably armed with a Scarff ring mounting in the nose with either one or two double-yoked Lewis machine guns; the upper rear cockpit housed either one Lewis gun on a rocking post mounting, or, more usually, two Lewis guns, each on an individual bracket on either side of the cockpit. A further Lewis gun was mounted to fire backwards and downwards through a trapdoor in the floor of the fuselage abaft the mainplanes.

At the time Tiny joined the squadron it was engaged on night bombing raids against enemy installations, such as U-boat bases, docks, railway centres, enemy aerodromes, canal locks and industrial targets. In relation to the massive strategic bombing of the Second World War such missions were mere pinpricks. The colossal industrial war-making capacity of the Ruhr lay within practical flying range of the allies during the latter years of the First World War, yet, although plans were envisaged by the far-sighted to cripple that prodigious output from the air, the prejudices still occupying most military minds, with the notable exception of Trenchard and a few others, still ensured that the aeroplane remained for the most part a mere adjunct to the fighting on the ground.

One of the largest raids ever mounted came within weeks of the armistice when all the night bomber force was engaged against targets in Cologne, Frankfurt, Coblenz and Trier. Losses were high; seven aircraft brought down over enemy territory and three forced landings behind Allied lines.

After a week's acclimatization, Tiny was selected by Major Brackley, DSO, later to become CO of the squadron, as his observer/ bomb aimer/gunner to fly in machine No 3130. Brackley was a taciturn character, a leader by example and, like Tiny, a keen sportsman. They hit it off from the start and from then on flew together until the end of the war.

With the inauguration of the Royal Air Force on 1 April, 1918, when the RFC and the RNAS became one service, Tiny became an RAF Sergeant, and was later awarded one of the first newly instituted Distinguished Flying Medals.

Preparation for a raid was very much a personal matter concerning each individual crew. The overriding factor was the weather. With no navigational aids other than a compass and maps, it was essential to see the ground in order to make out distinguishing features such as rivers, canals, lakes, railways, roads, buildings and, of course, the coast. Over the months Tiny became intimately familiar with the terrain over which they habitually flew.

Flying at a maximum ceiling of 8500 feet, bombing at 4000 feet or less, and operating always at night, it was comparatively straightforward to track a route to the target when the moon lit up the countryside. Tiny discovered that the bomber often cast an intriguing double shadow of itself – one racing across the underside of the cloud the other keeping pace along the ground. Reflected from the light of the moon, roads showed up white, railways lines shone as silvery ribbons, while water sparkled an attractive shimmering blue. On darker nights forests became black patches and roads and rivers were picked out in varying shades of grey. During nights when the weather was bad the bombers remained on the ground.

About an hour before a raid crews met in the Mapping Office to be briefed by the CO, who indicated the size and type of bombs to be carried, the targets for the night, perhaps the docks at Zeebrugge or Bruges, enemy aerodromes, or a roving commission bombing trains. After pre-flight study of maps and photographs Tiny discovered in practice that he had no difficulty finding most targets. He used the Dutch and Belgian coast as his datum line.

The route to the target was never stipulated at the general briefing. Individual crews would get into a huddle afterwards and decide which way they were going to approach, according to prevailing circumstances of wind and weather, and also based on their previous experience of where enemy guns and searchlights were situated.

They took care to empty their pockets of all personal possessions, removing anything that might give valuable clues to the enemy, should such items fall into his hands. They spoke to no one, not even the ground crew, giving not the slightest hint as to where they were going.

Retiring to the Crewroom the flyers pulled on their heavy leather gear and fleece-lined boots. Tiny always wore a silk stocking under his flying helmet and donned silk gloves before putting on his thickly lined gauntlets. Anything was welcome that helped to keep out the intense cold when racketing through the freezing night air.

On one occasion over the target Tiny had been forced to remove his gloves in order to release a couple of bombs that had become jammed in their recesses. These bombs stood in their usual positions, nose up, ready to somersault and point earthwards on leaving the aircraft. Struggling to get them away with bare hands he sustained severe frostbite. Afterwards he walked ceaselessly round and round the airfield in an agony of pain, the skin from his hands to his elbows swollen and blistered as though badly burned. After three days the Medical Officer lanced his bloated arms and the relief was exquisite. The aircrew were supposed to be issued with whale oil to protect their skin from the cold but it was never issued to their squadron. Instead, when they remembered, they rubbed their faces with vaseline.

Snuggled into the front cockpit, the pilot and observer, although in the open, were reasonably protected from the elements by the high screen. The gunner responsible for the three machine guns to the rear was kept reasonably warm by the hot gases from the engines as they flowed along the fuselage. But when Tiny lay prone in the nose over the target this *was* a bitterly cold position. He pressed buttons to operate a series of lights – two green to tell the pilot he wanted him to edge to starboard, two red to go to port, and a white light in the centre to indicate that they were on course. This was an adequate method of communication in the days before the electrical intercom system had been invented.

Because of the absence of night attacks from enemy fighters Tiny never needed to climb into the most exposed place of all, the nose gun position situated in front of the pilot. There was no oxygen supply for the crew, but this would have been unnecessary anyway as they never flew above 10,000 feet.

Before setting off on a raid the first crew in the air above Coudekerque made an assessment of the weather conditions, the strength of the wind and the prevailing cloud situation. If it seemed good weather for bombing they sent a signal to this effect to the rest of the squadron waiting to take-off. If conditions were considered unsatisfactory then the single Handley Page returned to base and the operation was scrubbed for the night.

Whenever possible, instead of flying over enemy territory, especially on the return trip after bombing, to avoid attention from the enemy Tiny would set course out to sea then come back to base crossing the coast on the safe side of the Allied lines in the vicinity of Dunkirk. True, this often necessitated crossing neutral Holland and the Dutch sometimes responded with token anti-aircraft fire, but it was usually of a desultory nature and not seriously intended to cause any damage.

Meticulous care was taken not to bomb civilian dwellings in enemy-occupied territory. Only military and industrial installations were classed as legitimate targets and if, for example, a hospital was identified near a chosen place of attack the operation would be abandoned rather than risk hitting it by mistake. Punishment for disregarding these regulations was severe, although mutterings in high places at a later date suggested that setting fire to one or two cities in Germany itself might not be a bad thing in helping to lower the morale of the enemy's munition workers.

On occasion they carried the largest bomb manufactured during the war, a gigantic cylinder with fins at one end and a point at the other. It weighed a staggering 1650 pounds and was slung externally beneath the fuselage, rather as the 22,000-pound 'Grand Slam' was secured beneath the Avro Lancaster in the later war. The bomb-sight, a Wimperis High Altitude Drift Sight Mk1 mounted in the nose, took account of the bomber's height above the target, its airspeed, the wind velocity and the amount of drift when flying across the wind. But, calibrated for the smaller pear-shaped bombs normally carried, it was found to be wildly inaccurate when dropping these big bombs. To Tiny's dismay, when he released the first one, he estimated it must have landed some five miles off target.

Later, with a freshly calibrated bomb-sight, they took one of these monsters to attack a railway marshalling yard. To make doubly sure of their aim they flew well below the stipulated height. The bomb, smack on target, erupted with a blinding flash as it struck an ammunition train, the blast concussing the three crew members. When Tiny and his pilot, Brackley, recovered, the Handley Page was flying *itself* over Holland. The gunner, in the rear of the machine, only regained consciousness after they landed back at base.

Whereas searchlights and anti-aircraft fire were a major hazard to the bombers, Tiny and his crew, as already said, were never attacked by night fighters. On two occasions only they had fleeting glimpses of single-engine aircraft as they flashed past and were swallowed up in the dark. In practice it was always difficult to pick out other machines, even their own big bombers, in the night sky. On the other hand it was surprising how small objects could be observed on the ground, even something as insignificant as a man lighting a cigarette. It was important for the crew on their part to keep all lights carefully masked, even shielding the glimmer from their tiny pea-lamps while map-reading.

On 20 September, 1917, Tiny logged a particular success by hitting and destroying a bridge, never an easy target, at Namur. To the Germans it had been a key element in the supply of arms and ammunition to the front. Its destruction enabled the Allies to carry out a planned advance which could not have taken place while the bridge was intact.

On 20 October they were not so lucky. Setting off in high hopes of bombing targets in Cologne, they were forced to turn back when they ran into fierce thunderstorms over Belgium.

When attacking enemy airfields it was the practice to fly around first trying to ascertain whether or not the German aircraft had left the base. If they were away from home then the ruse was to switch on the bomber's landing lights pretending to be one of their own machines returning. With luck the runway would then light up obligingly, helping them to aim the bombs more accurately. This, of course, worked both ways. One night the following year German machines came over in force and bombed the squadron's airfield at Coudekerque knocking out hangars, workshops, offices and the mess. The ground itself was so badly pitted that the Handley Pages had to be diverted to a stretch of firm sandy beach near Calais from which they continued to operate until repairs had been carried out.

In retaliation, on 6/7 June, 1918, Squadron Leader Brackley, Tiny and a gunner called Thomas took off from the sands to attack an enemy airbase in northern Belgium. Arriving over their chosen target they switched on their navigation lights in the prescribed manner. Unexpectedly, the Germans replied by shooting off blinding white flares which lit up the sky like day. Searchlights and flak followed within moments. Dropping their bombs on the runway, the crew hastily set course for home. Unknown to them they must have sustained some damage to their control lines because, as they were coming in to land and were some 200 feet above the beach, they suddenly dropped like a stone. Tiny, squatting in the nose, was completely buried in sand. Scrabbling free, he reached back to assist his pilot. Seeing a leg protruding from the cockpit, he pulled and thought it had come away in his hands. Fortunately it was only a flying boot and Brackley was completely unhurt. Not so poor Thomas. When the two men extricated him from the broken fuselage they saw he was badly injured. The MO took immediate steps to have him flown back to England for intensive care, but he died the following night.

Under such circumstances uninjured aircrew were normally sent back to flying duties without delay. The Royal Air Force, as it had recently become, found this procedure the most practical way of helping flyers to get over the effects of a crash. But Brackley, by then commanding the squadron, decided that he and his observer, who had both flown without respite for nearly a year, were entitled to a few days' break.

Back in England Tiny marvelled at the apparent tranquillity of people's lives. he worried whether his mother was getting sufficient to eat, blatantly taking advantage of the prestige his uniform lent him to buy more food than would normally have been allowed. He was glad to return to the squadron, the comparative inactivity at home making him restless and uncomfortable. On 15/16 June, only nine days after the crash, they set off to bomb the docks at Bruges. Searchlight activity and anti-aircraft fire over the target was intense. The Germans had developed their defences to a frightening degree and now, in the final year of the war they had 10.5 cm guns that could fire shells up to a height of 20,000 feet.

On this occasion the Handley Page was straddled by the brilliant flashes of bursting shells as jagged metal splinters rained down on wings and fuselage, accompanied by sharp tearing noises. The crew breathed in the pungent smell of cordite, a sure sign that shells were exploding close by. The port engine was hit and ground to a stop as steam poured from its fractured radiator. Thrown off balance and veering sharply to port, Brackley had to throttle back the remaining engine in order to keep a straight course. From then on the machine was descending in a long shallow glide, the crew desperately hoping that by the end they would have reached Allied territory.

The miracle to them was that, although the bomber was riddled with shell holes, they had escaped injury, especially as searchlights and ack-ack fire continued to harass them. Eventually they crash-landed near Nieuport on muddy ground just short of their own lines. Within moments they were surrounded by soldiers they assumed to be Germans. Drawing their revolvers, they tried to look as menacing as possible. It was fortunate they made no attempt to shoot as the infantrymen turned out to be Belgians. They were quickly bundled away to a dugout, the reason for the urgency becoming apparent when German artillery sent over shell after shell completely destroying the Handley Page.

Although the British were happy to accept their rescuers' nationality, the Belgians were not nearly so sure about them and gave every sign of believing that they were German spies, that this was an elaborate bluff and that the Handley Page was in reality a giant Gotha. With the aircrew not knowing a word of Flemish and the Belgians professing to speak no English, communication was difficult. After a couple of hours of menacing grunts, florid gesticulations and fractured French phrases, sandwiches and beer were handed round. One of the 'non-bilingual' Belgians turned to Tiny and said in good English, 'Are you a Londoner?'

Surprised, Tiny replied, 'Yes, I am.'

'Do you know the Strand?'

'Yes, I do.'

'Do you know "The Black Hole"?'

'Of course. I've eaten there many times.'

The Belgian grinned. 'I used to be a waiter there before the war!'

Their rescuers apologized for being suspicious and for making out they understand no English, but said they had to be doubly sure that these unexpected visitors were who they said they were.

A signal was sent to the squadron and next morning a car arrived to bring the crew back to Coudekerque where an enraged armaments officer tore them off a strip for not bringing back the machine guns from the Handley Page. They wasted no time enlightening him on the facts of war and assuring him that if they had lingered to dismantle any equipment they would not have returned at all.

With a replacement aircraft they continued the war for another four and a half months. A rather unusual mission was to fly to Zeebrugge to take part in a combined raid with the Royal Navy. In a sense the aircraft acted as bait, drawing off the guns and searchlights while the Navy steamed inshore in the darkness ready to attack the coastal installations. As soon as the big guns of the seaborne offensive opened up all enemy attention was diverted from the bombers on to the ships. It was pleasant to fly around unmolested watching the firework display taking place thousands of feet below.

Tiny's last raid was on a railway station a few miles behind enemy lines. They encountered no opposition to speak of – an anti-climax after so much danger and excitement. This was on the night of 9/10 November, one day before the Armistice was signed and the war came to an end.

In the new year, on 20 January, Tiny left the Royal Air Force and returned to the Edmonds Electricity Corporation to complete his final two years as an apprentice electrician. He rose to become an important member of the company and was later awarded the MBE for his services to the community.

# CHAPTER TEN

# F. J. POWELL

Joining the Duke of Lancaster's Yeomanry on 3 August, 1913, as a trainee officer, at the age of 17, F. J. Powell was mobilized with his regiment almost exactly one year later on the outbreak of the First World War. As everybody said at the time, 'It will all be over by Christmas,' so there was an overwhelming desire among servicemen to get out to France to have a go at the Boche before peace returned.

After some months endlessly touring the mill towns of Lancashire, Powell, as he was always known, reckoned that he stood very little chance of crossing the channel, so in frustration, he transferred to the Manchester Regiment; but this was no better. By November he was certain he was not going to be in France by Christmas.

Then, by chance, he saw a notice asking for one officer from each battalion to volunteer as an observer with the newly formed Royal Flying Corps and put his name forward at once. Never having seen an aeroplane, he had no idea what he was letting himself in for, but it seemed a more likely way of getting to France. He certainly had no burning desire to fly.

The only qualification was that applicants must not weigh more than 10 stone and by the time he was posted to Farnborough some strenuous exercise had brought him down to the required weight.

On arrival, the adjutant, a major, put him on duty as orderly officer, showing him into a small room, complete with camp bed, adjacent to the office. While there, Powell eavesdropped on a conversation between the major and the colonel that probably changed the course of his wartime career. He heard the colonel say, 'This chap I'm seeing tomorrow. Is he an observer or a pilot?'

'He's an observer, sir,' replied the major.

We've got more than enough damn observers. Cancel his transfer at once.'

Powell worried all night about this and next morning he reported to the adjutant and asked, 'Is there any chance of being remustered for training as a pilot, sir?'

The major beamed at him. 'Really? You'd rather be a pilot? Well done, my boy! We'll arrange it immediately.'

Within hours he found himself sitting in the forward cockpit of a Maurice Farman Longhorn receiving instruction from a pilot called 'Willie' Strugnell, a rare character at Farnborough, being the only sergeant instructor among a group of officer pilots. (By the time this sergeant ended his career in the RAF he had risen to the rank of Group Captain and had won a Military Cross.)

Strugnell must have taught well because, after only four hours' dual flying, Powell went solo. He was absolutely terrified. Waiting to take off, his mind went blank and he was unable to remember what any of the controls were for. Staggering into the air, he managed a circuit and came back towards the airfield over the adjacent golf course. Two players were staring up at him. He thought, 'If only they knew what a crass amateur is flying over them at this moment they wouldn't be standing there gawping, they'd be running for their lives!'

Coming in to land he did remember not to bang open the throttle, which could result in the engine cutting, but allowed the machine to glide in gently – too gently as it happened. At the last moment he realized that he was too low and was going to drift smack into the line of hangars. Immediately forgetting what he had been taught he pushed the throttle lever fully forward, just managing to hop over the buildings and make a passable landing on the airfield. Luck had been with him on this occasion; the engine did not cut out.

No blame was attached to him for this performance. Strugnell, who had been watching, assumed that the manoeuvre had been made necessary because of a dangerous air pocket and further flying was promptly cancelled for the morning.

On non-flying days the pupils' only alternative activity was to retire to a cramped hut, really no more than a packing case, to learn morse. Morse keys fixed to table tops were tapped in listless boredom; lacking supervision, progress was painfully slow. The subject was soon neglected and the place became a rendezvous for playing cards and swapping blue jokes. One day an enterprising character suggested that, in the interest of improving their skill, all stories should be 'told' in morse. Anyone infringing this rule would have to contribute half-a-crown towards the beer fund. Within days proficiency improved beyond measure as they moved from thinking in single dots and dashes and progressed to the almost subliminal recognition of an intelligible rhythm. Consequently, when someone turned up to test them they nearly all passed well above average.

Two personalities at Farnborough made a particular impression on Powell. One was Gordon Bell, credited with dreaming up so many of the phrases that have become part of the everyday language of the flying fraternity. In Gordon's terminology a sharp manoeuvre to port or starboard was described as 'a split arse turn', while the high-necked double-breasted RFC tunic he dubbed 'the maternity jacket'.

The other man whom Powell came to admire was an Irishman, Mervyn O'Gorman, who, as a Lieutenant-Colonel, had taken over from Colonel J. E. Capper as Superintendent of the Royal Aircraft Factory in 1909. This brilliant engineer was largely responsible for steering the onetime Army Balloon Factory towards armed military aircraft.

One day Powell had reason to report to his office. The Colonel was sitting behind a large desk in the centre of the room. Suspended from the ceiling on a length of string, and held by no more than a drawing pin, was a beautifully engineered connecting rod. He asked O'Gorman why it was there.

'That,' said O'Gorman, 'is a masterly example of engineering. I hope one day that we will equal it here at Farnborough.'

In a short time Powell qualified for his Royal Aero Club certificate. This 'ticket', written in French and English, was recognized as a kind of passport among flying men, ensuring a ready welcome and any help that might be needed by the holder the world over.

Early in 1915 he was posted to Netheravon for further training prior to being awarded his pilot's wings. Here he flew machines designed by Maurice's brother, Henry Farman. On one of his first solo flights he came in to land on what was sloping ground leading down to a track that ran across the aerodrome. Because of this extraordinary arrangement his aeroplane, not fitted with brakes, continued to roll down the hill until it collided with the track's rough surface, at which point the spindly undercarriage collapsed.

This was his first accident and he was sternly reprimanded by his CO, Major George Dawes, for bending one of his precious machines. Under the circumstances Powell thought the blame was a little unjustified.

But the incident was not serious enough to affect his career and in due course he passed his engine exam to add to his flying qualifications already affirmed by his ticket. The rigging test was taken by an RFC captain who led him into a hangar housing a Maurice Farman Longhorn and a Henry Farman. Powell knew he would be asked about the length of various control wires. It was difficult to learn the dimensions of every component of several aircraft, so he had concentrated on familiarizing himself with the details of one machine only. He virtually shouldered the captain towards the Longhorn, but his examiner, a knowing gleam in his eye, beckoned him towards the Henry Farman. The ruse had worked. It was the Henry Farman that Freddie had studied and he came through with flying colours.

But, in the end, he failed because of low marks in one subject – 'The Formation of Troops' – hardly an essential piece of knowledge for a pilot, but all part of the curriculum. At the weekend he brushed up on parade ground procedure, took the exam again and passed. The following day he was awarded his wings.

Introduced to the Vickers Fighter with its strange 100 hp Monosoupape Gnome engine, Powell quickly realized that this was a machine that was flown, not by the seat of the pants, but by ear. In order to survive, pilots had to concentrate on the sound of the engine. After flying these aeroplanes for some time it was possible to tell from the engine note whether the mixture was too rich or too weak, or a plug had cut out, or, most serious, a rocker arm had broken, possibly resulting in a rogue con rod flying through the air and cutting off your tail.

The Monosoupape (French for 'one valve') had no throttle. The engine ran flat out at full revs from the moment it was started. The only method of control was to 'blip' it on and off with a small switch. The fuel mixture also needed constant adjustment from the moment of take-off, reducing the richness in the carburettor as the aeroplane climbed higher into more rarified air – reversing the procedure, of course, when returning to land. The hand control for this procedure was less than conveniently situated on the floor near the pilot's left foot!

This early 'pusher' Vickers was slow, had a low ceiling and only a limited flying duration. It was armed with a single Lewis machine gun fired by the observer seated in the forward cockpit. Freddie loved it. It was deceptively strong, the longerons (in this case rods that attached the main planes to the tail) being made of high tensile steel. Being a 'pusher' the all-round visibility, so vital in a war plane, was far superior to the faster, more manoeuvrable 'tractor' type aircraft that superseded it.

What he particularly appreciated about this aeroplane, unlike machines he flew later, was that it lacked a 'mind of its own'. In other words, when he pushed it into a certain position it stayed there like an obedient dog without trying to correct the situation by returning to straight and level flight.

In the Spring of 1915 he was posted to France. As he was driven in the RFC tender towards his new home, 5 Squadron at Abeele, he became aware of the rumble of heavy gunfire growing ever louder as they approached.

5 Squadron consisted of three flights: 'A' and 'C' flew Avros, responsible for artillery observation, while 'B' was made up of Vickers fighters assigned to the more dramatic-sounding offensive patrols.

Soon after he joined the squadron the Avros were replaced by B.E.2cs, but the four old Vickers remained; they were known in official circles, a trifle euphemistically, as the Vickers Fighting Armoured Biplanes. The armour was a square steel plate under the pilot's backside. No such luxury was considered necessary for the observer. In practice, because it added unwelcome weight, the plate was discarded anyway.

Each aeroplane had its own portable canvas hangar, while the officers' mess was installed on the ground floor of an old farmhouse. The sleeping quarters, well stuffed with warm dry hay, were in the loft.

Powell's eccentric flight commander was the famous Robert Loraine, later to become the squadron's CO, and previously well known as a star of the West End Theatre and also as a pioneer aviator, perhaps more noted for his spectacular mishaps rather than any outstanding exploits in the air. Flying with his 5 squadron team, Loraine became frustrated at having to leave all the shooting to his observer so he installed a second machine gun on the rim of the pilot's cockpit. He considered this a more justifiable use of extra weight than the piece of armour plating.

An offensive patrol could only last for a maximum of two hours, and this was cutting matters fine enough; the tank held fuel for no more than 2 hours' flying under favourable conditions.

Flying up and down the trenches Powell and his companions often felt they were serving the enemy's cause by providing German anti-aircraft gunners with useful practice. Flying perhaps at 4000 feet, the pilot of a Vickers fighter might hear a sudden 'pop, pop, pop' overhead. Looking up, he would see three shell-bursts some 500 feet above him. This would immediately be followed by three bursts a similar distance below. The next explosions would be perilously close, bracketing the aeroplane approximately 100 feet above and no more than 100 feet underneath. It was time to leave that unhealthy patch of sky. Without any additional engine power, the only resort was to dive as fast as possible. Looking back, and up, the pilot would see the six most recent shells bursting in the space his aeroplane had occupied only moments before.

Powell admitted to a degree of disappointment if, during his two-hour patrol, he was unable to spot any opposition in the form of a German aircraft. When he did have the opportunity to show a bit of aggression and actually knock an enemy plane out of the sky he always gave the credit to his gunner/observer, a flyer particularly skilled at his job.

Their best day came while flying a little to the east of Ypres when they spotted a German flying *below* them, which was unusual. It was an Aviatik biplane of the early reconnaissance type which, given time, could have climbed high above the Vickers. That is, after an hour or so of steady ascent, it was capable of reaching 10,000 feet!

But the two men gave him no time for that. Diving on his tail, Powell's gunner raked him with his forward-mounted Lewis gun. The Aviatik went into a spin and appeared to be heading earthwards with no chance of recovery. Wanting to confirm their victim's fate,

142

they began to follow him down. But for once the Vickers decided differently and started pulling hard to the right. It was as if, for once, the machine had determined to exert its own will and, as it happened, save the lives of its occupants, because, in the end, Powell gave way to its demands and allowed it to turn in a steep bank. In doing so he and his companion were saved from a fate similar to the one they had just inflicted on the Aviatik. Coming down hard behind them to attack was what seemed an enormous aeroplane, twin boom, twin tractor engines, twin tail, and a central gondola in which sat a pilot with a gunner in front and another to the rear.

Swinging the Vickers hard round and coming up under the belly of this unfamiliar enemy machine, Powell yelled to his gunner to point his gun upwards and keep firing. A stream of machine-gun bullets hit the big aircraft in the fuselage and put at least one of the engines out of action. The German spiralled over and began a long uncontrolled tumble through the skies. At the end of its last journey they saw the powerful-looking aircraft crash on open ground near a pre-war racecourse just behind the enemy lines.

Seeing his opponent crash was always enough for Powell; he never felt any desire to gloat by flying over the area of the disaster. In fact he often experienced a mood of sadness that the combat had been necessary in the first place. He could not understand the aggressive attitude of a pilot like 2nd Lieutenant Gilbert Insall, VC, of 11 Squadron who, on one occasion (also flying a Vickers) followed his victim down, saw it crash behind the German lines, then entered into a gun fight with the surviving enemy pilot and observer and various other troops who happened to be in the vicinity.

In addition to the four Vickers, 'B' Flight soon received the very first D.H.2, also powered by a Monosoupape. In fact this was the only RFC flight operating in France at that time whose machines were fitted with these engines. The D.H.2, like the Vickers, was another 'pusher' type, but designed as a high speed, single-seat fighter. With an outstanding rate of climb for those days, it outmanoeuvred its contempories. It was extremely successful during 1915 and the early part of 1916, (when it was then supplied in quantity to 24 Squadron), until being replaced by 'tractor' fighters with synchronized guns firing through the propeller arc.

The D.H.2, designed by Geoffrey de Havilland, had been sent for the specific purpose of acting as squadron scout – seeking out enemy aircraft and destroying them. By this time Powell had shown a particular flare for knocking down German machines and, out of a group of enthusiastic teenage pilots, he was chosen to become the 5 Squadron scout pilot in sole charge of this exciting new machine. When Loraine told him of his decision, Powell marked it down as the happiest day of his life. His joy was shared by his fitter and rigger. By RFC tradition the team of pilot, ground crew and machine always stayed together and could not be separated by anything other than disaster.

Within a short time yet another prototype single-seat fighter arrived on the squadron to be war-tested. Again this machine was a 'pusher', again powered by a Monosoupape, so again it was allocated to 'B' Flight. This was the first F.E.8 to be manufactured.

Powell was told he could hang on to his D.H.2 or swap it for the new arrival. In flight he found it hard to discern any marked superiority in performance between one or the other. But on the ground, after careful inspection of both aeroplanes, he came to the conclusion that the F.E.8 was much better put together. In small details, too, it won hands down. The pulleys that worked the ailerons on the D.H.2, for example, were covered by some beaten-out aluminium nailed to the spar whereas on the F.E.8 the pulleys were encased in beautifully streamlined metal tunnelling. The Royal Aircraft Factory, he concluded, had done a good job. He chose the new F.E.8, while Loraine took over the D.H.2. These were the only two single-seat fighters on 5 Squadron.

Unfortunately for Powell, he had not paid overmuch attention to the armament arrangement on his latest acquisition. The machine gun was secured to the floor of the nacelle, the muzzle pointing through an aperture in the nose, and it was fired by a remote-control pistol grip. A curious contrivance consisted of two bars that came up from the fulcrum of the gun supporting a foresight and a backsight. As the gun was swivelled by the pistol grip the gunsight moved with it. In spite of assurance from the manufacturers that this sight was accurate, their confidence was ill founded, as was the positioning of their gun. So he found to his cost.

Powell was on dawn patrol. Climbing up fast under a cumbersome two-seater reconnaissance Aviatik flying above the Ypres Salient, he positioned himself close underneath the German's fuselage, in exactly the right spot to pour lead into his enemy where it would do most damage. Then he realized that, because of his gun's placement, he was unable to fire effectively. If he pulled back on the stick to point the gun upwards he would either crash into the Aviatik's underside or stall. He was in no position to dive away either, because the German observer, now well aware of his presence, was desperately trying to depress his own gun on its rotary mounting to draw a bead on him. Once out of the shadow of his opponent, the F.E.8 would present an unmissable target. Intelligently, the Germans decided to turn east and head back to base, no doubt puzzled by the lack of aggression from the British scout so ominously close beneath them. Powell reckoned he would shortly be eating sauerkraut in a prisoner-of-war camp.

In the end, having crossed the enemy lines, he realized he had no alternative but to break away. At a moment when he judged the gunner's concentration was waning he put his machine into a vertical bank. In the same instant the gunner, who was obviously as alert as ever, opened fire and hit everything in sight except, miraculously, Powell himself. His fuselage was in ribbons, his engine out of action and the German bullets had burst his petrol tank and pinged apart most of the beautifully streamlined wires that Powell had admired so much.

As the Aviatik dwindled in the distance, the F.E.8, still well in the wrong sector of the map, was on the edge of total disintegration. At 5000 feet, Powell knew he had to handle his aeroplane with a delicate touch if he was to complete the long, infinitely gentle glide back to the safety of his own lines. To avoid the slightest strain on the broken structure there could be no turns to left or right – just an unhurried forward motion slowly losing height as he studied the distant horizon. Spotted by a Hun fighter, his chances of survival would have been those of a tattered tom tit attacked by a golden eagle. But by good fortune all his enemies seemed to have gone home for breakfast.

In the end he managed a forced landing just inside friendly territory. At least he thought it was friendly until an irate Royal Artillery officer came storming up to him and greeted him with, 'You bastard! Do you realize my battery's been digging a concealed site here for the past two days? Now, we'll have to up sticks and move somewhere else. The Boche will have seen you come down here and is sure to shell this area to bloody smithereens!'

Even as he spoke all hell was let loose. After hastily expressing his sympathies, Powell wasted no time in making a rapid withdrawal on the start of his long trek back to 5 Squadron.

The dogged Recovery Team from No 5 later retraced his steps, found the F.E.8 and lovingly transported their unique prototype back to base. After only a few days in the skilled hands of the repair boys the wreck was transformed and emerged once more, if not as good as new, at least capable of flying again.

On Powell's instructions the gun was installed on a quadrant mounting with enabled him to point the weapon upwards. He also persuaded the fitters to dispense with a silly sort of cowling fitted round the four-bladed airscrew. It rotated with the engine and if it got out of trim by as little as 1/16th of an inch, which it often did, the whole machine vibrated as though suffering from a fit of the palsy. It had no apparent use, being added, presumably, as a cosmetic afterthought to enhance the appearance of the aeroplane.

Hearing about these unauthorized modifications, the mighty 'Boom' Trenchard himself arrived at the station unannounced. He brought with him the aeronautical engineering genius, Mervyn O'Gorman. Called to their awesome presence as the two men stood in the middle of the aerodrome, Powell wondered what lay in store for him. Trenchard looked down from his impressive height and thundered, 'O'Gorman, this is Powell. Go with him and he'll tell you what's wrong with your rotten machine!'

As they walked towards the hangars Powell felt a strong impulse to turn and run. As a young lieutenant, barely out of his teens, he had just been instructed by his supreme commander to point out shortcomings in an aeroplane designed by one of the foremost experts in aviation. But the Lieutenant-Colonel soon put him at his ease. He explained that theory was all very well, but he needed someone who had flown his machine in war to learn about its weaknesses and how it could be improved. Encouraged by O'Gorman's attitude, Powell told him everything he had in mind regarding the F.E.8. Apart from the inappropriate positioning of the gun and the useless cowling, he stressed that the dihedral of the wings was too great. They pointed upwards towards the tips at an acute angle, thus creating an excessive amount of lateral control. With ailerons on upper and lower wings, it required real physical strength, applying not only both hands to the joystick but knees as well, in order to force the machine over into even the shallowest of banking turns. Powell suggested that the ailerons could be dispensed with in favour of a tiny flap, about two feet wide, mounted on the edge of the upper wing.

O'Gorman was thoughtful. 'Do you know why I designed it that way? I had so many unfortunate experiences with my earlier B.E.s – pilots being killed because of the machines' lack of stability, not enough lateral control – that I made sure it wouldn't happen with this one. Now I see I've gone too far towards the other extreme.'

The two men remained in conversation for a long time, Powell expressing his ideas with moderation, knowing, as the only pilot to have flown the F.E.8 in combat, how much importance would be placed on what he said. When they reported back, Trenchard boomed, 'Well, O'Gorman, has Powell told you how to sort out your rotten machine?'

'He has made a number of invaluable suggestions. As a result there are several modifications I would like to introduce.'

To Powell's surprise Trenchard replied, 'That will be all right, O'Gorman, ... in the next war!'

Privileged to be the only man to fly what was then considered the fastest fighter on the Western Front, Powell was once detailed to lead a group of RNAS pilots on an introductory offensive patrol. The Naval airmen, stationed at Dunkirk, were flying the excellent French designed Nieuport biplane scouts, powered by tractor 160 hp Monosoupape Gnome engines. (More advanced versions of this aeroplane were used extensively by American pilots later in the war.)

By pre-arrangement, on a cold, clear day, he rendezvoused at 8000 feet with four Nieuports bearing naval markings. They were flying in line-ahead formation to the west of Ypres. Opening his throttles, Powell roared ahead of them to take up the lead position. Wishing to fly them over the lines, he signalled his intention to turn by dipping his left wing three times and then changed direction. But to his irritation the Nieuports flew straight on. Banking round, he climbed up behind the trailing machine and waited to see what they would do next. After a few moments they came about and he again assumed the lead, this time indicating they should follow him to the right. Again they carried on in a straight line.

Losing patience, Powell left them to their own devices and flew back to base where he filed his report on the strange incident. Such occurrences only reinforced the view in the RFC that the chaps flying for the 'Royal Naval Advertising Society' were an odd lot who avoided the smoke and sound of battle by always flying out to sea – *away* from the action over the trenches.

Back in Britain, too, the men of the RFC felt that it was the RNAS who got the glory because it was largely they who were responsible for home defence. Powell remembers an incident when he was on a rare seven days' leave immediately after a Zeppelin raid on London. He was entering the Savoy hotel dressed in his RFC uniform when he was booed and hissed by angry civilians.

It was irritations far removed from aerial combat that sometimes prompted Powell to get hot under the collar. Robert Loraine, his flamboyant flight commander, adopted an autocratic posture that annoyed every one of his pilots. Despite the unwritten rule that a man's machine was regarded as his own, Loraine would order fitters to carry out modifications without consulting the pilots first. In the end Powell was delegated to speak to his flight commander on behalf of himself and all his fellow pilots. After hearing him out, Loraine conceded that it was only right to inform the officers of his intentions and leave them to pass on the orders to their ground crew, but on the understanding that his wishes were implemented anyway.

Promoted to Major on taking over the squadron, Loraine, always the actor, decided to adopt a monocle. Powell, while on leave popped into Harrods and bought a boxful. On his return every officer turned up for dinner wearing an elegant eyeglass with broad black ribbon attached. It was noted in his favour that Loraine took it all in good part.

Powell actually refused a precious leave because Loraine said he would fly his even more precious F.E.8 while he was away. He felt certain that his CO, a notoriously ham-fisted pilot, would bend it out of all recognition during his absence.

When he was due for leave again he said to his rigger, 'The old girl's fabric is soggy with castor oil. Strip her frame down completely and then carefully rebuild her. Take your time – do it well. Make sure she's not ready to fly until the day I get back!' His rigger got the message.

In the Spring of 1916, after about a year in Abeele with 5 Squadron, Powell was posted back to England and finished up in Cambridge where a new squadron was being formed. The outfit consisted of three or four pupils but no aircraft apart from a couple of tiny single-seater Bristol Bullet tractor biplanes, with a wing span of just over 24 feet and powered by 80 hp Gnome engines. The CO flew one and Powell flew the other.

Powell protested that he was wasting his time and requested an immediate posting back to France so he could get on with the war. This was refused with the words: 'No you can't go back to France. It's time you did a job of work.'

Bored out of his mind, he determined to do something unusual, something so spectacular that it would be recognized as a 'first' in world aviation. After long reflection he came up with the idea of doing a loop off the ground! Anything more foolhardy could hardly be imagined.

Strapping himself tightly into the cockpit of the Bristol Bullet he set about putting his plan into action. His idea was to hold the machine down just above the grass until it reached maximum speed, about 70 mph, then climb up through the first half of the biggest loop he could manage; on reaching the top he would pull the stick hard back into his stomach, whip the tail over and, with the help of engine and gravity, complete the loop with room to spare above the ground.

The initial part of the plan went well. He climbed to the top and flipped over. Then he realized that the lower extremity of the loop would be below ground. There was absolutely nothing he could do about it. The end was preordained.

Powell claimed that it was a flock of sheep at the edge of the aerodrome which saved his life. As he dived towards them they scattered in all directions and he was so fascinated by this unexpected woollen starburst that he failed to tense up when, moments later, his machine plunged into the ground in an adjacent bean field. His belt broke and his upper body smashed through the instrument board, finishing up in the nose of the aeroplane. The engine ended up nestling neatly in his crotch. If the motor had rotated one quarter turn more both legs would have been severed.

The CO rushed across the airfield to investigate, first warning a group of students to stay put, imagining he was about to view a scene of carnage guaranteed to put young aspirants off flying for ever. As he drew near he could make out nothing more than the small tail plane sticking up above the bean stalks. Reaching the spot he was astounded to hear Powell's voice faintly singing a popular tune:

> Sprinkle me with kisses,
> A lot of loving kisses,
> If you want my love to grow.

He was swiftly extricated from the mess and rushed to hospital. During his convalescence he received a wire from Loraine: 'Currently in Gosport – about to return overseas – have a flight for you to command – can you come?' His immediate reply was: 'Yes.'

Still suffering from a broken ankle, he made his way to the War Office, praying that a medical examination would pass him fit for active service. Leaving his crutches outside the MO's surgery he walked as normally as possible into the room.

MO: 'Well old man, how's the ankle?'

Powell, sitting down and extending left leg: 'Completely mended, thank God.'

MO, examining ankle: 'Excellent. But according to the records it was your *right* ankle that was broken.'

Powell: 'You know the forces. Always cocking things up.'

MO: 'Always. Happens all the time. Happy to pass you fit for service.'

Ignoring the pain in his right ankle he marched out of the room. Within days he had joined Major Loraine on his new squadron. He was still on crutches.

In the summer of 1916, stationed at Leonvilles, where, unlike his previous billet, the officers were housed in a magnificent chateau, 40 Squadron was engaged in offensive patrols and the escort of bombers. On these escort duties the bombers flew at around 6000 feet, while their four guardian fighters flew in diamond formation

29. The F.1. Night Fighter Camel differed from the standard type in having twin
    Lewis guns mounted on the upper wing and with the cockpit set further back
    to aid visibility. On this war-battered example even the fabric from the centre
    section has been removed to enhance the pilot's upward field of vision.
    *(Imperial War Museum)*

30. Checking the nose gun of an R Type Gotha with its twin 260hp Mercedes
    D.1Va water-cooled in-line engines producing a maximum speed of 80 mph
    on a good night. Like the Zeppelins it was the scourge of London and the east
    coast of England for a time. The Albatros DV in the foreground was among
    the best of the German fighters, though it suffered from fatal structural
    weaknesses that limited its manoeuvrability. *(Imperial War Museum)*

31. This 'Giant' R.29 was powered by four 245hp Maybach engines, two tractors and two pushers in twin nacelles. The R.43 shot down by Archibald Yuille was *even bigger*. It spanned 138 feet and had *five* engines, the fifth being in the nose.

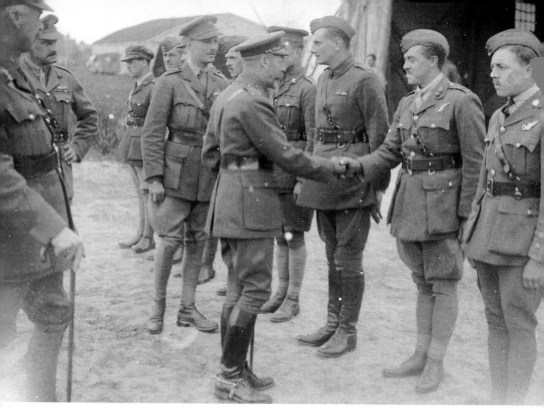

32. King George V meeting pilots and observers of a front-line RAF squadron. The King, among many other witnesses, saw the R.43 'Giant' crash in flames after Yuille destroyed it in his Sopwith Camel. (*Imperial War Museum*)

33. F. Donald Bremner joined the RNAS as a pilot after serving for a year at sea as an ordinary seaman on his friend's yacht, sailing in the service of the Admiralty. (*RAF Museum*)

34. The Bristol Scout on the Aegean Island of Thasos. Although really too tall to fit comfortably into this diminutive fighter, Bremner loved it dearly. Archibald James (see Chapter 14) loathed it.

35. The French Voison 3 (Type LA). Worthy old warhorse with a formidable 37mm Avion canon. In service throughout the war. Bremner and his observer were shot down over Gallipoli. They were lucky to survive. *(Imperial War Museum)*

36. Looking particularly innocuous in this shot, the 'Eindecker' nevertheless instituted the 'Fokker Scourge' of Allied flyers for nearly a year with its gun trained to fire through the propeller arc. It was this type of fighter that destroyed Bremner's Voison. *(Imperial War Museum)*

37. Like a number of French-built machines, the fast and manoeuvrable Nieuport stayed in front-line service throughout the war; it was constantly uprated in power and armament as the war progressed and was much favoured by American pilots. Here Charles Nungesser, one of France's high-scoring aces, alights from his cockpit. (*Norman Gilham*)

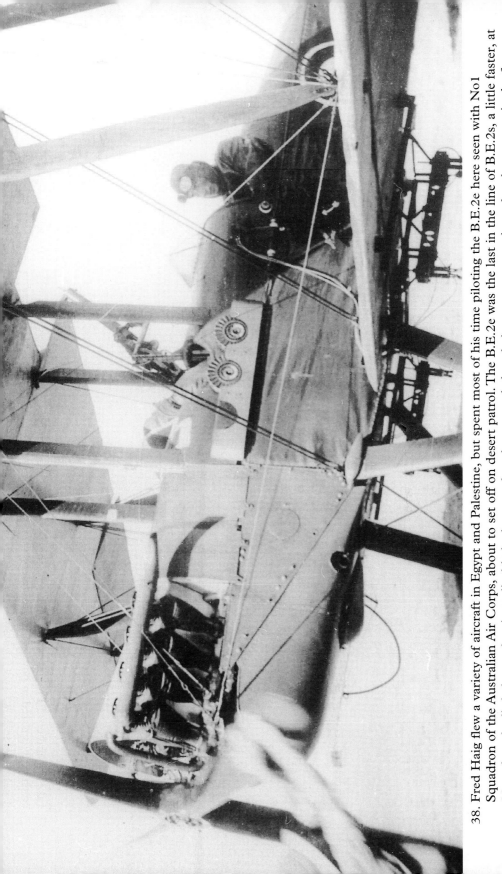

38. Fred Haig flew a variety of aircraft in Egypt and Palestine, but spent most of his time piloting the B.E.2e here seen with No1 Squadron of the Australian Air Corps, about to set off on desert patrol. The B.E.2e was the last in the line of B.E.2s, a little faster, at 82 mph and a little larger, but inexplicably had reverted to the outmoded cockpit arrangement, where the observer sat in the front seat, thus severely restricting his defensive field of fire. (*RAF Museum*)

39. Archibald James fought as a cavalry officer in the trenches, but soon volunteered to fly with the RFC. After serving as an observer he trained as a pilot. He maintained that a man who could handle a horse properly would have no trouble in flying a plane. *(Imperial War Museum)*

40. The Vickers F.B.5 first put in an appearance on the Western Front early in 1915. It was an efficient 'pusher' aeroplane where the observer sat in the nose with a .303 Lewis machine gun. Colloquially known as the 'Gunbus'. *(Imperial War Museum)*

4000 feet above them keeping an eye open for attacking German fighters.

Up to the time Powell had left for England he had never encountered a Fokker Eindecker, often considered the world's first true fighter, with its ingenious interrupter mechanism enabling the gun to fire forward through the propeller arc. Now the so called 'Fokker Scourge' was at its zenith and many allied flyers had fallen as a result of its aggressive activities.

This monoplane's main advantage, apart from the forward-firing machine gun, was its extraordinary ability to climb to over 17,000 feet, an altitude much greater than that officially achieved by any current RFC fighter. The Fokker hovered like a hawk in the upper skies, then plunged on its prey firing into the virtually defenceless bombers. Legend was beginning to cloak the Fokker in an aura of invincibility. Yet such was the speed of development in the air war that within a few months it too would become obsolete.

It was a cloudless July day and Powell was leading his flight at 10,000 feet high above their formation of F.E.2b two-seat bombers, pushed along by their ponderous 160 hp Beardmore engines. Atmospheric conditions must have been ideally suited to his F.E.8 because when he started to climb the plane responded readily. He eventually reached an unprecedented height of 16,000 feet. Almost immediately he spotted a Fokker only a few hundred feet higher than himself. As it dived towards him all he could see was the single set of wings, so held his fire; perhaps it was a French Morane monoplane, but a burst of fire from the fast-approaching machine convinced him it was not and he pulled away and banked round, now positioned a few feet above his enemy. As he in his turn opened fire he saw the pilot swivel his head and look up as if in disbelief. Raked from stem to stern the Fokker fell away in an uncontrollable spiral. It went down and down until, after falling 10,000 feet, it came level with the bombers whose gunners, not to be left out of the action, all opened up on the hapless fighter.

Under such circumstances Powell felt unrestrained by the disciplines of formation flying. Such close flying, he reckoned was wrong for fighters, with only the leader able to keep an eye on the surrounding sky while his followers had their time cut out concentrating on avoiding collision with their nearest neighbour. Such flying had become something of a fetish on some squadrons with aircraft even taking off in formation – very spectacular but of no practical use.

On one occasion he was returning to Abeele after a patrol when he saw a number of upended machines sitting on their noses dotted around the airfield. At first he thought they were the victims of an enemy air attack, but on landing discovered they were the remnants of a reinforcing squadron led by a Major Sholto Douglas (later to become marshal of the Royal Air Force Lord Douglas of Kirtleside). On the insistence of their leader they had attempted to land in formation on the aerodrome's rough grass with catastrophic results. Only Douglas himself, landing in the central, well-used and consequently flattened area of the aerodrome, came down unscathed. In the mess that evening he tried to discuss the vexed question of fighters flying in formation with Sholto Douglas, but the major seemed disinclined to pursue the subject with a mere 20-year-old captain.

Later in the war Powell was all in favour of larger formations of D.H.4 bombers flying close for the self-protection afforded by concentrated fire-power. But that was a different matter – they flew on daylight raids, sometimes unescorted, in exactly the same way as did the American B17s in their early European missions during the Second World War.

In contrast to the previous year, enemy activity in the air had increased dramatically. Before, it had been almost the exception rather than the rule to encounter a German aeroplane over the trenches. But now, in the summer of 1916, all that had changed. The Hun had increased in numbers and aggression to the point where at least a sighting and very often a combat was virtually guaranteed during every patrol.

Nature afforded the Germans a distinct advantage in this aerial warfare. The prevailing wind blew in over the war zone from the west. Consequently, although allied aircraft were wafted quickly over enemy territory, they were invariably faced with a long slow struggle back to their own lines. More than once, in the early Vickers scout, Powell had the disconcerting experience of being pushed backwards by a stiff breeze while attempting to get home before his petrol ran out. Conversely, the enemy was aided in his flight back to base by a friendly tail wind, often when he needed it most.

As the air fighting intensified so casualties mounted and many young officers sought solace for the loss of friends by consuming ever greater quantities of alcohol. This, of course, led to a deterioration in the sharpness of their reactions and increased their chances of being killed.

Powell was never without his hip flask. Encased in a freezing open cockpit on a bitter dawn patrol a swift swig of rum worked wonders. At high altitude morale was instantly raised. Returning to lower levels produced an immediate sobering effect. It is hard to imagine the cumulative stress of twice daily patrols, four hours in all, with so many attendant dangers.

Although the Allied and German aircrew did their best to destroy each other during aerial battles, a genuine comradeship existed between all those who flew during the war, notwithstanding their nationality. On one occasion, after a friend of Powell's, Maxwell Pike, had been shot down in flames, a German plane flew low over their aerodrome a few days later and dropped a message. It read, 'The gallant Captain Pike, shot down in mortal combat, has been buried behind our lines with full military honours.'

There was humour too. An elephantine F.E.2b flew at height over a German airfield and released a deadly looking missile. The Boche airmen scattered in all directions. On hitting the ground, instead of exploding, the object bounced several times. After cautious examination it was discovered to be a rugby ball with the inscription 'April the 1st!'

When weather was bad and flying impossible the airmen made their way to nearby towns such as St Omer and even as far south as Amiens. Here the young men learned more about life than they would ever have done back home if peace had prevailed.

Major Loraine, casting round for alternative diversions, purloined a large Red Cross hut that appeared to be abandoned. Re-erected on the edge of the aerodrome, he converted it into a very presentable theatre capable of holding an audience of 250. The first productions, acted by the airmen themselves, under the professional direction of their theatrical CO, were two unpublished plays by Bernard Shaw.

Powell had developed a marked antipathy towards the playwright after reading an article in the magazine *John Bull* in which Shaw had urged young men not to enlist. He was so incensed by this that he said to Loraine, 'The government ought to train assassins to take care of people like him!' To his amazement the great man himself turned up on the squadron to spend a week as a VIP guest. Loraine introduced him to Powell with the words, 'Shaw, this is Powell. He would very much like to shoot you!'

Shaw replied in his strong Irish brogue. 'How do you do? I'm very pleased to meet you. You know, you might have chosen somebody worse.'

At dinner Loraine excused himself to attend a dress rehearsal of *The Inca of Jerusalem*. He delegated Powell to bring his guest to the theatre when he had finished his meal.

During the performance he sat watching Shaw convulsed with laughter, tears streaming down his cheeks, his great auburn beard wobbling with merriment. Powell thought it was rather bad form for an author to express such obvious amusement at his own words. Afterwards he said to Shaw, 'I'm so glad you appreciated our poor efforts in putting. on your play.' Shaw replied, 'Do you know, if I had known it was going to turn out like this I wouldn't have written it!'

In February, 1917, Powell was posted as Chief Fighting Instructor to 7 Group Training Establishment, commanded by General Dowding. He was stationed at Upavon in Wiltshire where he chose a comfortable little single-seater D.H.2 for his personal transport, while his fitter and rigger were provided with a motorbike and sidecar to follow him round on his tours of inspection to aerodromes all over Southern England. At each station his duty was to quiz the school's fighting instructor to see that the officer was doing his job satisfactorily. It was not long before he put in a hard-hitting report saying that the training was useless. It was based on classroom lectures and solo aerobatic demonstrations by the instructor; about as much use as a member of the public paying half-a-crown to watch a flying display and then departing with the idea that he had become a fully qualified pilot. He suggested setting up a special Fighting Instruction squadron with three flights, the first to teach aerobatics, the second to practise air fighting against another aircraft, and the third, consisting of single-seat fighters, for final advanced training in aerial combat.

Instead of getting the chop as he had feared, Powell was promoted to Major and given command of 43 Flying Training Squadron, flying Avro 504s, at Ternhill, north-east of Shrewsbury. His suggestion was taken up in a rather different way when a squadron was formed at Gosport to give advanced instruction to pilots already qualified in the teaching role. They were taught how to break all the rules of flying and get away with it – how to land in a cross wind or how to take off down-wind and never lose control of the aeroplane.

In spite of his reservations about formation flying, he occasionally led a flight of his best pupils on a trip to a resort such as Blackpool, landing on the sands and spending a day in the funfair. He should, of course, as Commanding Officer, have spent more time at his desk shuffling the many papers that arrived from head office. After four months he had had enough and put in a request to return to a front line unit, even if it meant demotion. After a great deal of demurring by the powers that be he was posted to command 41 Squadron flying the ill-reputed Airco D.H.5s, now a much respected veteran of twenty-one.

Within months his new team of pilots crowded round telling him what a frightful machine the D.H.5 was. It was far too dangerous to indulge in aerobatics and trying to loop the loop meant certain death. Powered by a 110 hp Le Rhone rotary engine, this single-seat tractor biplane had a backward-staggered upper wing to give the pilot an increased field of vision.

Always one to find out things for himself, Powell took off the next morning and flew the D.H.5 up to 3000 feet where he proceeded to try a loop. Diving, he built the speed up to 100 mph before pulling the stick back. Upside down at the top of the loop it seemed to him as if a giant hand had reached from the heavens, caught hold of the machine and was shaking it as a child might rattle a toy. It was a terrifying experience, especially in those days of no parachutes. As he fell out of the loop he wondered if it was his fault for not getting up enough speed initially. Diving again, this time he achieved 120 mph before zooming upwards – only to encounter an even worse buffeting as he flipped over, actually to the point of being bodily bruised. He found the experience quite terrifying and wasted no time coming in to land. Members of the squadron watching below were more than impressed to see their new CO stunting D.H.5, something previously unheard of among reasonable men.

By the end of November that year the D.H.5 was relegated to less demanding duties after sustaining particularly heavy losses on the Western Front. Mercifully, 41 Squadron was re-equipped with far superior S.E.5s much sooner than that, only a few weeks after Powell's arrival.

The S.E.5a, by contrast, was a delightful machine to fly, no more difficult to handle than the docile Avro 504. A 200 hp Hispano-Suiza engine was later replaced by the more efficient high-compression Wolseley Viper of the same power. The performance was light years ahead of any machine Powell had flown in battle before. At sea level the S.E.5a was capable of a then phenomenal 138 mph and had a service ceiling in the region of 19,000 feet. It proved a steady gun platform for the .303" Lewis gun attached to the upper plane, and its fuselage mounted .303" Vickers with Giurgiu Constantinescu's reliable interrupter gear enabling it to fire straight through the propeller arc. The S.E.5a is to be ranked among the very best fighters produced by any country during the First World War, yet in size it was less than 21 feet long with a wingspan of only 26 feet 7 inches.

Orders for patrols came down from Wing HQ and the nature of their implementation was then left to the commanding officers of the individual squadrons who detailed the flights under their command for specific flying duties. Apart from this main task, Powell believed that a vital function of the CO was to keep up the morale of his pilots. With this in mind he took over a spare hangar, procured some bags of cement, a rare commodity on the Western Front, and ordered his airmen to lay a smooth floor. He then instructed his officers that they should each come back from leave with at least two pairs of roller skates. The rink proved a great success and roller-skating, Badminton and even 'roller rugby' became popular features among members of 41 Squadron, undoubtedly the only unit in France to possess its own rink.

As CO, Powell's least pleasant task was writing letters to the next of kin of men who had been killed. In losing friends with whom he had shared so much danger, he fully understood the grief experienced by their families. A visiting officer showed him a cutting from *The*

*Times* in which a bereaved father quoted an excerpt from one of Powell's letters which, he said, had brought his wife and himself great comfort. Powell had written: 'Knowing your boy as I did, I can only say I am sure that he died happily when he laid down his life for his King, his Country, and for You.'

Casualties meant replacements, and at that stage of the war most of the replacements were half-trained pilots with no experience of war. With unpractised eyes, they seemed incapable of seeing the enemy in the sky and returned from offensive patrols to report no activity on the part of the Germans. When, as happened all too frequently, they did not come back it was odds on that they had been shot down without even knowing what had hit them. It was, after all, a period of maximum effort on the part of the Germans. The Albatros D V was everywhere; Richthofen's notorious Flying Circus ranged across the skies shooting down outgunned bombers and reconnaissance machines in their dozens.

Powell knew that, almost as soon as he crossed the lines, he was sure to be surrounded by swarms of opposing aircraft. Realizing that some of his new pilots were barely getting over the lines when out on patrol he arranged to lead a flight of novices himself. With absolute confidence he told them, 'You are going to follow me and I can assure you that before the patrol is over each and every one of you will have been involved in a fight.'

Planning to cross the lines at 14,000 feet followed by his pupils, he instructed one of his flight commanders to lead another flight 3000 feet above them ready to pounce on the Boche as soon as he attacked. In other words Powell's flight was to act as bait. To make his own S.E.5a doubly visible he attached a 6-foot yellow streamer on his rudder and two red, yellow and blue streamers to either wingtip.

Crossing the lines at Amiens he banked right, heading for Douai, then on, ever deeper into enemy territory. He had told his pilots that if, in the unlikely event that they failed to engage any German aircraft, then they would descend to ground level in order to strafe some enemy aerodromes. This would have been a suicidal venture which he only threw in feeling sure it would never have to be implemented. But as they flew on he began to wonder if every German flyer had taken the day off. He need not have worried.

Making a wide turn prior to descending, the skies were filled with black crosses. Albatros were everywhere, particularly above. He saw his high-flying flight commander fire a red Very light, a rather tardy warning that enemy aircraft had been spotted.

Coming up behind an Albatros, Powell lined up his tail in his Aldis Telescopic Sight. As an old hand, he decided not to blast away, but conserve ammunition by getting an accurate bead on the pilot's head before despatching him with two or three rounds. To achieve this it was necessary to manoeuvre his machine with precision so that the man's flying helmet was dead in the centre of the sight. The German slipped to one side, momentarily out of his line of fire. Powell counter-ruddered and brought him back into the middle of the graticule. His finger tightened on the trigger and he was within a milli-second of firing, when another Albatros, who had been stalking *him*, blasted his S.E.5a with his twin Spandau 7.92 mm machine guns. The double stream of armour-piercing bullets hit the instrument board, pierced Powell in the arm and leg, and went on through the V of the engine cutting out one entire cylinder block. Shells screamed into the radiator sending up clouds of scalding steam.

Powell, who felt no pain from his wounds after the initial hammer blows, was most afraid of fire. Having seen so many stricken aircraft spiralling helplessly down in flames, his one thought was to get down from 14,000 feet to ground level without a moment's delay. Diving as steeply as he dared he glanced back to see three Albatros on his tail. Executing an Immelmann turn without engine, he was able to evade the less manoeuvrable German machines, and so proceeded with a series of such turns until he was only a few hundred feet above the ground. To his immense relief he saw a broad open field ahead of him and wasted no time in landing. Then he realized that it was a German aerodrome. The pilot who had shot him down came in and taxied alongside him while his two companions continued to circle the airfield keeping an eye on their captive.

He stepped out of his cockpit, strolled to the rear of the aeroplane and fished in a small locker for his cap which he donned in place of his flying helmet. Then, going over to the German, still sitting in his Albatros with the engine ticking over, he held out his hand to give his victor a formal handshake. It was then, for the first time, he noticed the blood running out of his sleeve.

Later, when bandaged up and interviewed, he had great difficulty in convincing his interrogator that he was indeed a major. To the German an officer holding that rank was invariably a middle-aged gentleman with a white moustache – certainly not a fresh faced youth of twenty-one whose war had suddenly come to an end!

# CHAPTER ELEVEN

# ARCHIBALD B. YUILLE

On 1 July, 1916, after a sustained artillery barrage that had lasted for seven days, the men of the British infantry launched themselves against a well-entrenched German Second Army. Struggling forward through a non-stop hail of machine-gun bullets, hard-won gains were measured in no more than yards. By the end of the first day of what became known as the Battle of the Somme the British Army had suffered losses of around 60,000 men, 19,000 of them dead – the greatest one-day loss in the history of the British Army. The author's own father became a casualty on that terrible day. As a nineteen-year-old subaltern he sustained many wounds and lost his left arm.

But the British continued to press slowly forward. On 15 July, south-west of Bapaume, they launched an attack spearheaded by a few of the earliest tanks. Used prematurely before they had been properly developed, these machines were underpowered and too few in number to bring about a decisive victory. Once again it was the 'poor bloody infantry' who had to bear the brunt.

Another nineteen-year-old subaltern, Archibald Yuille of the 8th East Lancashire Regiment, also fell wounded. He crawled into the relative safety of a shell hole and waited until he was at last guided by medical orderlies back to his own lines.

Overwhelmed by the never-ending legion of broken and dying infantrymen crowding the casualty clearing station in the small town of Albert, south of Bapaume, the weary medical staff were doing their best to cope. Their only consolation was the almost sublime patience of the waiting men, many dying before their time came for treatment.

After twelve hours Archie received an anti-tetanus injection. Although his arm was in a mangled condition and he felt nauseous to the point of collapse he was, somehow, able to remain on his feet. Because stretchers were at a premium he was classified as 'walking wounded'. Crowded inside a rickety canvas-topped Commercial lorry, converted into an emergency ambulance but more suitable for carting sacks of coal than human bodies, he and his companions, more dead than alive, were bumped and shaken over rough roads on solid tyres some twenty miles to the railway station at Amiens. Here they were loaded into railway carriages with red crosses painted on their roofs and sides.

They sat in compartments crushed five on each side, while stretcher cases were hoisted onto luggage racks above their heads. In these conditions the sixty-five-mile journey from Amiens to Rouen took another twelve hours. Archie never forgot that journey – the agonized groans of the injured, the stench of gangrenous wounds, the unbearable heat.

In Rouen he was sent to one of the two overflowing hospitals for another long wait. When his wounds were eventually examined the doctor shook his head: 'That arm of yours is very bad. There's nothing we can do for it here. We'll have to get you back to England for further treatment.'

After a restless night he was put into another crowded ambulance and driven a further forty-five miles to Le Havre. Here on the quay wounded men lay unattended on row after row of stretchers, or sat in crumpled heaps on the cobbles swathed in bloodstained bandages, their heads drooped in dejection. They waited with stoic resignation for the ship that would take them home. Anyone seeking proof of the futility of war had to look no further than the docks at Le Havre.

The hospital ship was filled to more than ten times her peacetime capacity. A nursing sister advised Archie to keep moving as best he could. 'Keep the circulation going,' she said, 'You'll feel better that way.'

After a voyage of little more than a hundred miles over a mercifully calm sea they sailed into Portsmouth waters. Finally, a train journey in rather greater comfort brought them to Waterloo Station where lines of ambulances were waiting to receive them. They were home.

Archie was taken to a small private hospital run by Canadian women in Roland Gardens, South Kensington. Most of the patients were Canadian officers. After he had been cleaned up and his wounds dressed he was put in a bed with crisp white sheets the like of which he had almost forgotten existed.

As he lay in a semi-coma he became aware of a figure bending over him. 'Well, Archie, my boy, we must get you sorted out and take good care of that arm of yours.' To his amazement he was staring into the kindly face of Dr Mengies, his own family doctor. By a strange coincidence the doctor had taken up work in that very hospital for the duration of the war. It was a fortunate meeting. Mengies managed to save his arm, although it was a good year before it had healed and Archie was declared fit for duty by the medical board.

During his long convalescence he did a great deal of thinking. He had volunteered before his eighteenth birthday on the outbreak of war and had no difficulty in deciding that there was no future in returning to the mud and horror of the trenches, and having escaped death more than once, tempting fate yet again would be madness. Yet he still had the urge to do his bit, but if possible in a more constructive way.

He had plenty of time to read about the exploits of the 'aces' of the Royal Flying Corps and soon realized the contribution they were making towards winning the war. During his time in the army he had paid little heed to what was taking place in the skies above him. If he thought about aeroplanes at all it was only to view them as aerial spotters directing the artillery. Now he realized that their duties were more widespread than this and he decided to volunteer for training as a pilot as soon as he was well enough.

An essential criterion when applying to fly with the RFC was that the volunteer should be of a high physical standard, so it came as a shock to Archie, when he was released from hospital, that he was classified as only fit for light duties. However, losses among aircrew on the Western Front had recently been so great that replacements were desperately needed and he was promptly accepted for pilot training.

He was posted to the Ruffy-Baumann private flying school, a grass area adjacent to the Great West Road in Acton, West London, (a site later occupied by the Renault works). The training establishment was run almost entirely by French civilians, under the command of an English lieutenant, who did their best to impart the theory of flight to their current intake of some fifteen pupils. Flying instruction, such as it was, was given in dual-control Caudrons. These French-designed aircraft (a few were built in the United Kingdom by the British Caudron Company) had been largely withdrawn from active service by 1917 but were being used extensively as trainers. Most nacelle-and-tail boom biplanes of that time were 'pushers', but the Caudron G111 differed in having its engine, an 80 hp Gnome, Le Rhone or Clerget, at the front. This machine, with its stubby canoe-like fuselage, lacked the more conventional control by ailerons and was manoeuvred in the air by the simple expedient of 'warping' the outer wing areas with a joystick control. The noise from the motor excluded any chance of communication between instructor and pupil.

Training consisted of revving up the engine, charging across the field, pulling back the stick, lifting into the air and, after flying a few hundred yards, descending once more on to the grass. The aircraft was then turned round and the exercise repeated in the opposite direction. On one special occasion, when the weather was exceptionally good, he was permitted to make a few shallow circuits of the field. The course lasted for two weeks and Archie, in the light of his later training, considered it a complete waste of time.

The fledgling pilots were then transferred to Shoreham, one of the older established flying schools. The atmosphere of service efficiency was in marked contrast to the casual approach of the Ruffy-Baumann school. Now, for the first time, pupils were introduced to the realities of flying by veteran RFC pilots in a machine that had already become a legend in aviation circles. The Avro 504, an outstanding trainer, was instrumental in producing thousands of RFC and RAF pilots during its long career lasting well into the 1930s.

Archie learned to fly in the rugged 504J dual-control version of the Avro. His instructor demonstrated each action and then gave an explanation as to how and why these actions were carried out; each machine was fitted with a 'Gosport' speaking tube so he was in vocal contact with his pupil at all times. The Avro 504J was fully aerobatic and its light and powerful controls quickly showed up any faults in the pupil's flying.

It was not long before Archie was considered competent to fly solo and, after a series of exercises involving 'circuits and bumps', he was ordered to set off on his first cross-country exercise. It was a straight-forward route from his base at Shoreham to Crowborough, south-west of Tunbridge Wells, and back again to base, an overall distance of little more than fifty miles over the ground. Navigation had to be accomplished by squinting at the sun, if it was visible, and looking over the side in the hope of spotting some useful landmarks. There were no helpful instruments whatsoever, not even a compass.

Archie became hopelessly lost. Assuming he had reached Crowborough he headed south, as he thought, and, on seeing a large stretch of water, concluded that he was over Southampton. Turning left, he expected to head comfortably back to base. In reality he had continued to head north on reaching Crowborough. What he had thought to be Southampton Water was actually the mouth of the Thames. He then continued up the east coast for some while until time and dwindling fuel convinced him that he must have made a mistake. Coming to a decision he circled a convenient field and landed.

Approached by a farmer, he asked where he was. 'You be near Great Yarmouth,' came the reply. He was in Norfolk, some hundred and seventy miles north of base! After giving the farmer a few instructions on how to swing the propeller he managed to start the engine and make the short hop to the Royal Naval Air Station at Great Yarmouth. A message was relayed to the RFC in Shoreham and, in due course, one of his instructors arrived to fly back with him as an observer. Such was the length of the flight that his cautious passenger ordered him to complete it in three hops, landing first at Martlesham Heath, near Ipswich, and then at Hendon before returning safely to base. A round trip of close on four hundred miles was something of a record for a pupil flying on his first cross-country. It made an impressive entry in his log book.

Archie looked back on his days at Shoreham with considerable pleasure. It was thrilling to zoom at zero feet along the shore at Brighton, hopping first over the Palace Pier and then over the West Pier, or flying straight at the windows of hotels before climbing hair-raisingly a few feet above the roofs. There were many complaints from civilians, and officially the RFC condemned such antics, but in reality low-level flying was encouraged as an essential element of pilot training.

Completing twenty-five hours on Avros, Archie had the excitement of piloting a Sopwith Pup biplane at Shoreham for about twenty minutes. Known at the time as the 'pilots' dream aircraft', it was small and highly manoeuvrable, with a ceiling around 17,000 feet, fast and a joy to handle. With an 80 hp Le Rhone engine it was no more powerful than the Avro 504, but, being smaller and lighter, it was a lot nippier.

Under normal circumstances he would have spent much more time on these machines, being sent for three months to an advanced flying training school, graduating eventually on to Sopwith Camels, before completing a course at gunnery school. But it was now March, 1918; on the Western Front the Germans had launched the first of their attempts to split the British and French forces and push their way through to the Channel ports. The brunt of the attack had fallen on the British Army and during the fighting the RFC had taken heavy losses. There was a desperate need for aircrew to replace those lost in the recent conflict and all flyers then in England and experienced in combat were quickly shipped over to France. Freshly or partially trained pilots like Archie were immediately recruited to fill the gaps left in the Home Defence squadrons.

Posted to 112 Squadron then operating the potent twin-gun Sopwith Camels at Throwley, on the downs west of Canterbury, Archie was introduced to his new CO, Major Quintin Brand MC, who had previously achieved fame as an outstanding aviator in combat against the Germans. (By the outbreak of the Second World War Brand had received a knighthood and risen to the rank of Air Marshal.)

Brand, a South African, had lost an arm during the war, a disability that never seemed to detract from his considerable flying skill. A natural leader, he inspired confidence in his young untried pilots offering them every chance to achieve mastery over their machines and themselves. And, as Archie was later to discover, the Camel was more difficult to master than the aeroplanes he had previously flown. In fact it was 'a vicious little devil' that probably killed more novice pilots than any other aircraft.

In the meantime there were a few Sopwith Pups on the airfield and their understanding CO gave his new arrivals *carte blanche* to fly them all day and every day, encouraging them to really learn their trade by clocking up as many hours as possible. Sometimes he flew alongside them instilling the skills of formation flying which he considered an essential aspect of air discipline. Giving Archie the confidence to get in close to other aircraft was a valuable lesson that stood him in good stead later on.

Archie flew over large tracts of Southern England, occasionally mixing business with pleasure. On one occasion he landed at Eastbourne, called at his sister's school and took her out to lunch. Generally, he preferred flying from place to place rather than stunting, although he did practise stalling and occasionally looping the loop as he had been taught on the Avro.

Judged competent in daylight flying and still piloting the Pup, he was sent up to gain experience in night flying. No longer able to distinguish objects on the ground, although large areas of water such as the Thames were normally easy to pick out, he learned to depend on what was nearly always a clearly defined horizon. (Flying at night only took place under favourable weather conditions.) Although towns and villages in south-east England were blacked out, coloured beacons were installed at identifiable locations as an aid to navigation.

One of these lighthouses flashed a signal in morse at his base in Throwley, while three red lights in the form of an arrow indicated the perimeter of the airfield and the direction to land. Coming in at night was a tricky operation; with no instruments it was often impossible accurately to assess one's height above the ground. It was all too easy to land with a tremendous bump and damage an undercarriage.

Transferring on to Sopwith Camels, Archie was introduced to what was arguably the most successful fighting machine of the First World War. A strongly constructed biplane, the night fighter version differed in several respects from the standard model. Normally twin synchronized Vickers machine guns fired through the airscrew, but it was discovered that at night the guns were too close to the pilot, the flash blinding him when he fired them. In their place two Lewis guns, with Neame illuminated sights, were attached to the top wing, firing over the propeller. A special mounting enabled the guns to be swivelled upwards from the horizontal, if needed, at an angle of 45 degrees. Many of the night-fighting Camels had their cockpits moved further aft so that the pilot was behind the fuel tank. This reduced the risk of his being soaked with petrol and burned in the event of a crash-landing in the dark. This new position also improved his field of vision. Camels were powered by many different engines during their time, but most night-fighting Camels were fitted with 110 hp Le Rhones. Later a 180 hp Le Rhone was introduced.

Compared with the sweet-tempered Pup, the Camel was not an easy aircraft to fly. Because of the powerful torque reaction exercised by the large rotary engine the aeroplane had a strong tendency to swing viciously to the left. Unless the pilot was on his guard this could quickly develop into a sideslip culminating in a spin from which few novices managed to extricate themselves. Those who lived to master the Camel's eccentricities learned to use them to advantage. The aircraft's lightning flick to the left in combat insured that the most skilled opponent would be quite unable to stay on his tail. Conversely it required physical strength to turn the Camel to the right. Veterans often found it quicker to allow their machines to following their natural inclination and complete a tight circle round to the left.

Care had to be exercised on take-off owing to these characteristics. To counteract the torque of the engine a pilot needed to apply full right rudder until he was moving through the air fast enough for the tail fin to play a part. Failure to do this often resulted in the aircraft whipping off to the left and ending in a fearsome crash. Thanks to timely warnings of these dangers by their CO, Archie and his fellow pupils survived to join the elite band of accomplished Camel pilots.

During the previous year, Major-General Trenchard, as he was then, was desperate to receive every new Sopwith Camel as soon as it left the factory. However, at that time the Germans were mounting bombing raids on London using the large twin-engined Gothas, so a number of Camels were retained in England for home defence. Now, in the early Spring of 1918, the raids against the capital and south coast towns had virtually ceased. The Gothas were concentrating on bombing military installations to the rear of the British lines in France. It was decided, therefore, to form a night-flying Camel squadron to counter these latest enemy operations. 151 Squadron was based on units drawn from the three Home Defence squadrons and placed under the command of Major Brand. This was one of the first new squadrons to come into being after the formation of the Royal Air Force on 1 April, 1918.

It was June when they took over a freshly prepared airfield, complete with hangars, near the forest of Cressy not far from Abbeville on the Somme. Initially the squadron's brief was to defend the town of Abbeville and surrounding areas from the German night raiders. After a time the Camels flew further afield, covering places such as Amiens and as far north as Etaples.

Navigation over unfamiliar terrain at night was not easy, but the Camel did have a compass, a clock, an airspeed indicator and an altimeter. The dials were treated with luminous paint but in practice were difficult to read. Essentially the three main aids were the compass, and, when seen at night, the sea and the River Somme. In addition six beacons had been erected at various points on the ground. Each flashed its individual letter in morse. It was essential for the pilots to memorize these signals and the exact location of these land-based lighthouses.

One of these beacons indicated the route to 151 Squadron's aerodrome in a rather cunning way. Circling the beacon at 1000 feet, pilots knew they had to fly north-north-west for twenty miles. On seeing the standard three red lights in the form of a T indicating an airfield they would again circle, this time flashing their own aircraft code letter. The 'airfield' was in fact a dummy designed to put the enemy off the scent. A man on lookout duty in a dugout then rang 151 Squadron's genuine aerodrome ten miles to the south-west. On getting the all clear he flashed a hand torch, signalling to the Camel overhead that it was all clear to fly to base and land. It was a simple and effective routine in theory, but more complicated to carry out in practice. For example it was often difficult to spot the light from the torch.

Landing was not an easy procedure either. Coming down between the two red lights which marked the aerodrome boundary, while keeping an eye on the other red light at the far end of the field was hard enough without trying to gauge height above the ground in pitch darkness. After a time a sophisticated landing aid was introduced. Just before the aeroplane touched down the headlights of a Ford motor car were switched on to illuminate the grass for the benefit of the incoming pilot!

The Germans had their problems in navigation too. To signpost their homeward route a series of fixed searchlights shone skywards, either in the form of a V or an X or in parallel. They also shot 'flaming onions' 1000 feet into the night sky – bright green orbs in the shape of onions in sequences of three, one, and two in quick repetition – to guide their Gothas home. Learning the locations of these various enemy devices was of great assistance to the British pilots in tracking down their quarry.

Making use of all this came only with experience. On Archie's first night flight in France he became hopelessly lost. He could not remember the positions of the various lighthouses and became completely muddled as to which signal applied to which beacon. Circling one of these flashing lights, and perilously low on fuel, he decided to come down by the small tower on the assumption that there was probably an emergency landing field located alongside. As he approached, the ground looming up in front of him appeared to be favourably clear of obstructions. Unfortunately he was mistaken. The authorities had not prepared for such an emergency and he ended up in a field of fully grown corn. The long stalks wrapped themselves round the undercarriage bringing the Camel to an abrupt halt and, as Archie put it, pitching the machine and its pilot 'arse over tit'.

A recent invention, known as the Sutton safety-harness, had been fitted to Camels. It consisted of support straps for the shoulders and thighs and incorporated a quick-release system. This device had saved many lives, both in the air and on accidental impact with the ground. Archie, instead of being flung from the cockpit with possibly fatal results, was held in place, unhurt. Releasing himself, he soon made contact with some patrolling British infantry and the following day was returned to base. After that he needed no encouragement from his CO to do his homework on lighthouses. From then on his knowledge of codes and flashing beacons became second to none.

The only factor that completely foxed all who flew at night, friend and foe alike, was fog. A dense mist would sometimes creep up at night from the Somme and drift across the marshy, low-lying areas of northern France to a depth of several feet. It obliterated all recognition points, hiding buildings, roads and railways.

The pilots were scheduled to fly on two-hour night patrols, just as they had done previously in home skies. A flight of three aircraft individually carried out each patrol and was then replaced by another three after their time was up. Again they only flew in decent weather, knowing that the Germans would also adhere to this sensible rule.

151 Squadron soon realized that there was something else to which the Gothas conformed. When raiding England they had always been able to climb to 10,000 feet by the time they reached their target, but on the shorter continental flight they only managed to lumber up to an altitude of 8,000 feet, and this was the height at which they invariably bombed – a useful piece of intelligence for the Camel pilots.

In further defence a number of anti-aircraft guns, previously used in the protection of London, were sent out and installed in the area. These were accompanied by searchlights whose operators had great difficulty in latching on to German bombers in the opening stages. This was hardly surprising as the human ear was the only aid available in trying to locate the aircraft high overhead. In an attempt to improve their performance Archie and his companions flew above them in the early part of the night, before the Hun was expected, in order to give them some practice in picking out high-flying aircraft. Over a period of time this led to greater proficiency. There were occasions when a 'mess in the sky', a combination of searchlight and anti-aircraft fire, helped Camel pilots to locate the Gothas.

It was almost the end of July and so far not a single Gotha had been shot down by 151 Squadron. Even if one was located, it was all too easy for its pilot to dive off and disappear into the darkness. On the 28th of that month Archie was patrolling at the regulation 8,000 feet over Amiens. Peering through the night he spotted a 'mess in the sky' to the north-west, over in the direction of Etaples, and decided to investigate. To his excitement he found himself coming up fast behind a large black shape which he identified as a twin-engined R-Type Gotha. These bombers had a wingspan of nearly 78 feet (more than 12 feet greater than the Luftwaffe's principal bomber, the Junkers JU88, of the Second World War). With a crew of five, these aircraft were powered by two 260 hp Mercedes D.1Va water-cooled in-line engines. With a bomb load of 1100 lbs they cruised at around 80 mph, well below a Camel's maximum speed.

Archie, remembering his formation training, flew in close behind the bomber. In the end he imagined he could almost reach out and touch its towering tail. Tightening his grip on the triggers of his twin Lewis guns he fired a steady burst into the Gotha's fuselage. His quarry immediately dived away beneath him while his Camel caught in the slipstream, went into a sickening spin. At that moment Archie thought he saw flames shooting out of the bomber but was not certain; they could have been from the exhausts of its Mercedes engines. After falling some 3000 feet Archie managed to pull out of his spin and fly straight and level. As if by a miracle in all that black night he again saw the Gotha dead ahead of him. Coming in even closer, he opened fire a second time and continued to pour bullets into the bomber until it finally broke away and was lost in the darkness. With petrol running low he flew back along the coast, turned inland on reaching the mouth of the Somme and landed back at his squadron airfield.

It was later confirmed that the Gotha had come down only a hundred yards within the British lines at Ypres. At least three of the crew taken prisoner were high-ranking German officers who had obviously been on a 'see for ourselves' outing. Unfortunately for them they had picked the wrong aircraft on the wrong night.

Archie was credited with shooting down 151 Squadron's first Gotha in France, but a short time later this achievement was to be eclipsed by an even more satisfying coup. On the night of 10/11 August Lieutenant, now Acting Captain, Archibald Yuille was again flying in the vicinity of Amiens when he spotted another 'mess in the sky', this time to the north in the direction of Doullens. Opening his throttles he charged off to investigate. By the greatest good luck, as he modestly insisted, he again came up behind a giant bomber. Although he did not realize it at the time this really was a Giant, the R.43, a five-engined RXV1 prototype built by Zeppelin. The R.43 had a defensive armament of six machine guns, one on each of the upper wings and two each in dorsal and ventral positions. Its wing span was a colossal 138 feet, 36 feet greater than the Avro Lancaster bomber of the Second World War. With a complement of eight crewmen, it was on a mission to bomb Doullens forty miles behind the British lines.

Archie closed to within 25 yards, coming up steadily from below and behind so that the bomber was silhouetted against the night sky. His first three bursts put one of the R.43's engines out of action.

Two more bursts of tracer and armour-piercing bullets at six hundred rounds per minute from each Lewis gun set the rear of the enemy's fuselage ablaze. The aircraft slipped sideways and then fell away in flames towards the earth.

Knowing that other Camels were flying in the vicinity, Archie fired his Very pistol, one green flare, one red, to identify himself as he followed the burning bomber to its fate. On this occasion there was no shortage of witnesses. Half the population of Northern France had been straining their eyes upwards trying to locate the source of the thunderous noise coming from the five powerful engines of the R.43. Many saw it crash in flames, including King George V, who happened to be visiting his troops at the time.

In five months' operational service up to the end of hostilities on 11 November, 1918, 151 Squadron shot down sixteen German bombers that fell in the British lines and ten that fell behind enemy lines. For his contribution Archibald Yuille was awarded the newly inaugurated Distinguished Flying Cross.

# CHAPTER TWELVE

# F. DONALD BREMNER

Contemplating the grandeur of the Norwegian fjords as he sailed the still, deep waters in his yacht, 21-year-old Donald Bremner was not surprised to receive news that Britain and France had declared war on Germany. It had been on the cards for some time. Hurrying home on a cruise ship he gave careful thought to how best he could serve England in the forthcoming war. Before the ship docked he had narrowed his choices to two: either to approach Tommy Sopwith, whom he knew slightly, with a request to teach him to fly or join the amateur crew of a borrowed steam yacht, the *Zarifa*, captained by Stewart Garnett, a friend from his Cambridge days when they had rowed together at Henley.

In the end, feeling that the Sopwith organization was not sufficiently advanced to give him proper instruction, he decided in favour of signing on with the *Zarifa*. Garnett had already offered his crew and the yacht for war service, an offer that had been accepted without hesitation. A grateful Admiralty even provided two three-pounder guns that were immediately installed either side of the bridge.

It was an era of amateur endeavour by no means confined to ships. Other ex-undergraduate friends had enterprisingly bought or borrowed vans and converted them into ambulances driven by themselves to care for the wounded in France. Like others with privately owned aeroplanes, Patrick Hamilton, for example, joined the RFC with his Deperdussin monoplane and was given the rank of captain.

The *Zarifa*, with its private enterprise crew, augmented by professionals such as the 1st and 2nd Engineers, an RNR Signalman and a number of enthusiastic sea scouts, took up station at Lowestoft with orders to contact the North Sea trawlers, passing on messages about the areas that were to be swept for mines, a necessary undertaking at a time when sending wireless signals was still at an experimental stage.

An early assignment was to take Admiral Charlton, in charge of minesweeping operations, out to review some of the trawlers. As a small boat enthusiast himself, he was impressed by the *Zarifa* and took her and her crew away from the Naval Commander at Lowestoft, commandeering her as his own flagship. Overcoming the problem of already possessing a flagship with the serial No 1, the Admiral designated the *Zarifa* No 01.

After this they ranged over the whole of the sea area bordering the east coast from Dover up to Scapa, delivering secret charts of minefields to various units of the Navy. On occasion the sailors of the 'real' Navy looked askance at this unusual little vessel. Destroyers, particularly, had a habit of 'bullying' the *Zarifa* by cutting close across her bow, leaving her plunging in their wake. Much to the annoyance of the Admiral this occurred one day when he was aboard. Ordering his flag to be hoisted, but not broken, he waited for the next destroyer to ignore the rules of the sea as well as exhibit bad manners. Sure enough, another swiftly moving warship came in, impudently cutting even more finely across *Zarifa*'s course. 'Break my flag', roared the Admiral. As his flag fluttered free at the masthead for all to see it was almost as if the destroyer was trying to apply non-existent brakes. As soon as it was able, the destroyer manoeuvred alongside and her captain signalled his abject apologies.

After being at sea for about a year the Admiral decided it was wrong for the volunteers to continue as highly educated ratings and he suggested that they should apply for commissions in whichever branch they chose. Donald, who had always been interested in flying and indeed in all things mechanical, had absorbed each copy of *Flight* as it came out, had watched Pégoud loop the loop in France, had entered his motorcycle in a road race in India and visited Tommy Sopwith at Brooklands. So for him it *had* to be the Royal Naval Air Service. The Admiral oiled the wheels, Donald was interviewed by Captain Scarlett at the Admiralty and subsequently posted for navigation training at Portsmouth, a course that was firmly rooted in the skills needed for finding one's way at sea rather than in the air.

From there on to actual flying training at Chingford (whose First World War aerodrome now lies at the bottom of a reservoir). Each cadet was taught on the unbelievably basic 50 hp Gnome-engined Bristol Boxkite, exposed to the open air while hanging like a monkey onto the instructor's back, and occasionally reaching forward over his shoulder to get a 'feel' of the joystick!

The oddest manoeuvre performed in the air came when the time was ripe for the pupil to take over. While climbing over his instructor's body, the latter had to relinquish control of the rudder bar while retaining his grip on the joystick until his pupil was in place. After a while the instructor had to decide whether it was less perilous to reverse the clambering procedure or permit the novice to stay where he was and try to land the thing!

Flying solo consisted of ground hops, followed by circuits, followed by a few brief cross-country flights – Chingford–Northolt–Chingford, for example – an accumulation of 27 hours in the air before being awarded his pilot's ticket. During the course he gained flying experience in other aeroplanes apart from the Boxkite:

The Maurice Farman Longhorn – clumsy but comfortable;

Avro 504K – beyond reproach;

B.E.2c – exceptionally stable but with one dangerous feature; if it stalled it was impossible to pull it out of a dive in less than 500 feet, a disconcerting situation if you happened to be flying at, say, 400 feet;

Curtiss J.N.4 – an American tractor biplane twin-seat trainer used extensively by the US Army. The particular model flown by Donald had been acquired by the RNAS at Chingford for trial purposes. It was powered by a bulky water-cooled V8 O.X. model engine of 90 hp. It had gained an unfortunate reputation at the station and was feared to be capable of going into an irrecoverable spin.

Sidney Pickles, the civilian test pilot, came to Chingford with the express purpose of killing those fears. He threw the J.N.4 all over the sky, stalling and spinning the machine with a nonchalant disregard for its supposed shortcoming. By the time he landed he had made a nonsense of the unfounded rumours. Donald, who had wondered what the fuss was about in the first place, always enjoyed flying the machine.

Apart from piloting aeroplanes, Donald was also introduced to some of the traditional customs of the Senior Service. Each cadet in turn had to act as mess president and, taking his place at the head of table, was obliged to maintain certain inviolable rules such as not mentioning a lady's name before the Loyal Toast had been drunk, or, most important, refraining from drinking soup with two hands – that is without tipping the plate. This latter regulation, like the tradition of drinking the Loyal Toast sitting down, stemmed from perfectly practical considerations established during the days when such functions were performed aboard a rolling and pitching sailing vessel with only limited headroom.

It was a disappointing day for Donald when he was taken by his CO to view a diminutive Bristol Scout. With a wingspan of only 24 feet, 7 inches, and fitted with a Monosoupape 100 hp Gnome engine, it was known affectionately as 'Barnwell's Baby' after Bristol's chief designer, Captain F. S. Barnwell, RFC.

'Right, Bremner. You are about to be drafted to Dover and this will be your service type from now on,' said his CO.

Unfortunately the CO's prediction appeared to be unachievable. It was rather like a fully grown man trying to squeeze himself into a child's pedal-car. Struggle as he may, Bremner's 6 foot 3 inches were unable to fit underneath the cross-bar inside the cockpit. At his height he would never have been accepted for the RFC in those early days, but the RNAS did have some larger machines to choose from and so his posting was amended. To his bitter disappointment steps were taken for him to be sent instead to Westgate to pilot seaplanes.

He need not have worried. Upholding another long-established Naval tradition the Admiralty totally ignored these sensible rearrangements and drafted him to Dover anyway, to fly – *Bristol Scouts*!

On arrival Donald set about solving the problem of how he could shoehorn his way into the machine and it was not long before he hit on a solution. By removing the padded cushion from the pilot's seat he was able to lower himself those extra few inches which allowed sufficient room to slip his legs under the cross-bar. It was an extremely tight fit but he made it. The discomfort of sitting on a metal seat with projecting bolt-heads was a small price to pay for the pleasure of piloting what he later came to regard as the best machine he ever flew.

Dover aerodrome in the bad weather of late November, 1915, was a testing ground for any pilot. It was built on a steep slope ending at the edge of a cliff. Landings were particularly tricky.

Always interested in the handling characteristics of unfamiliar machines, he enthusiastically climbed into an old Bleriot, a type little different from the one in which the great man had successfully flown across the English Channel six years previously. He reckoned that the French aviator had done exceptionally well when he twice tried to get this contraption of wire and canvas into the air. On both occasions the engine spluttered and konked out even before the machine had taken off. He also tried out a small 'stunt fighter' known as the 'Sparrow', but considered its performance nothing short of hopeless.

During that wet and windy month he barely had time to familiarize himself with the Bristol Scout before he was drafted with five or six other pilots to lend a hand in the ill-fated Gallipoli campaign.

The battles on the Western and Eastern Fronts had bogged down into a stalemate of trench warfare during the previous winter and the British War Council had looked round desperately for somewhere where mobility might be revived. To them a direct attack on Turkey seemed a viable possibility. After all, the significance of such an assault was well understood by the Germans. 'If the Dardanelles fall, then the whole of the Balkans will be let loose on us,' Grand Admiral von Tirpitz had predicted. He even believed that defeat in those waters could lead to Germany losing the war.

An Allied naval fleet attempted to force a way through the Dardanelles on 18 March as a preliminary to gaining control of Constantinople (Istanbul) and the 38-mile-long straits, thus opening a direct link with Russia and her fleet via the Black Sea. The plan very nearly succeeded, but in the end, after seven warships had been struck by mines, it was decided that the objective could only be achieved if the campaign was reinforced by land forces.

The landings on the Gallipoli Peninsula were marked by muddle and incompetence and the 78,000 men, mostly Australians and New Zealanders (Anzacs), but also including the British 29th Division and one French division, suffered the consequences of delays which enabled the Turkish defenders, under the brilliant tactician Mustafa Kemal, enough time to mount a savage opposition which inflicted crippling casualties on Allied troops. Within weeks this expedition, planned to break the deadlock of trench warfare, had itself sunk into a bloody battle of attrition.

In July Britain disembarked a further three divisions. This did nothing to break the stalemate but resulted in some of the fiercest hand-to-hand fighting of the entire war. Allied losses at Anzac and Suvla alone approached 30,000, while Turkish casualties were fewer than half that number. In addition, the men of the Commonwealth, Britain and France had to endure the blazing heat of Turkey's summer and the debilitating effects of dysentery and other endemic diseases.

In October the officer in command, General Sir Ian Hamilton, was recalled and his successor, General Sir Charles Munro, after studying the military situation, immediately recommended evacuation of the entire peninsula. This skilfully handled operation began during the middle of December just as Donald and his companions were on their way to join the campaign.

Crossing France, they travelled south in a packed civilian train, sleeping on the floor. Reaching Marseilles the pilots embarked on a ship for Malta. When they arrived the senior naval officer said he had no idea why they were there and advised them to book into a hotel for the night.

The following morning, there being no apparent urgency, Donald decided to visit a hospital where he knew a doctor of his acquaintance was in residence. There had been such a rush on leaving England that he had only had time to complete the first stage of his series of typhoid injections. After his medical friend in Malta had finished with him he strolled back to the hotel where, to his astonishment, he was told that a ship, with the other pilots aboard, was already leaving for their destination, an aerodrome on the island of Imbros. Rushing to the quay, he managed to leap aboard as the vessel was pulling away.

The mountainous island of Imbros, also known as Imroz Adasi or Gokceada, was strategically situated in the Aegean Sea some ten miles west of the entrance to the Dardanelles. It had become an important base for Allied operations and its airfield was also the HQ of No 2 Wing, RNAS.

The landing ground was sandwiched between the bay and the harbour on one side, a saltwater lake on the other, and sand dunes in the gaps between. Winds, which were fairly persistent, gusted clouds of sand across the aerodrome making landing and take-off difficult. With practice, back in England, it had become comparatively simple to gauge one's height above the ground from the size of the blades of grass. Here there was no grass, only baked mud which looked the same from whatever altitude you viewed it.

It was a bleak, forbidding place, lacking many of the amenities available on a home station. Although the flying officers ate in a stone-built mess, they lived and slept in aeroplane packing cases, 10 feet x 7 feet x 7 feet; each 'hut' afforded an area large enough for two camp beds. The interior walls were lined with tarred paper. A familiar feature was a scratching sound from behind the paper. Pinpointing the exact location, a slit would be made with a penknife revealing a six-inch centipede which was then extracted wriggling on the tip of the blade. A strip of sticky paper effected an immediate repair to the hole.

Occasionally the tranquillity of the camp was disturbed by enemy air raids. The quantity of bombs dropped was small and during Donald's time on the island no significant damage was done. Nor were the German machines ever intercepted. By the time the British pilots were airborne the raiding machines had disappeared from sight. A local graveyard set into the rock on the side of the hill had been provided with a concrete roof. It represented a secure air raid shelter for anyone who felt inclined to use it.

Donald's first take-off into a strong wind from Imbros was spectacular if not successful. Climbing above the aerodrome in a Bristol Scout, he was approaching 1000 feet when his engine cut dead. Flight Lieutenant Savery, his CO, was following him in a Nieuport, a faster machine. Fearing that his senior officer might crash into him, Donald threw both arms above his head, a recognized signal for an engine failure, and pushed the stick forward. In order to avoid the sand dunes he made a technically unwise move. Turning into wind, he executed a vertical bank over the salt lake where his wing almost skimmed the water, then brought her up to clear a small ridge. At that moment a gust of wind from the hills lifted him 50 feet, turned him over and landed him neatly on his top wing.

The main duty of the RNAS pilots and observers was spotting for the 15-inch gun monitors stationed at sea off Imbros. Most of this work was carried out in rugged but slow French Voisin 3s (Type L.A.), two-seater bombers powered by 120 hp Salmson (Canton-Unne) 9M radial engines. They were fitted with a Hotchkiss machine gun in the front of the nacelle fired by the observer. These unimpressive-looking pushers were actually extremely battleworthy, their strength being derived from a tough steel frame. They continued in operation on all fronts throughout the war and were fitted with successively more powerful engines as time went on.

Executing figure of eights between the naval monitors and their targets on the peninsula, the aircrew corrected the ship's line and angle of fire by wireless messages. Flying at no more than 50 knots they remained above the range of rifle fire from the ground.

If, on return, a pilot made a bad landing, the old Voisin exhibited its displeasure by hopping forward on its four pram wheels. To the discomfort of its two occupants it would literally gallop across the airfield to the point where it was often advisable to take off and try again. Even when back in the air it would continue to buck up and down until brought under control.

On one such exercise Donald had completed his spotting duties when his observer suggested they continue patrolling further up the Straits. They had been briefed to keep a weather eye open in case the modern German battle cruiser *Goeben*, the fastest naval ship in the whole Mediterranean region, accompanied by the equally up-to-date cruiser *Breslau*, decided to steam out of port and into the channel. The presence of these powerful naval units in the Straits could have caused havoc. Ostensibly both ships had been sold to the Turkish navy at the outbreak of war, but they were still manned by German crews who had merely swapped their naval caps for fezzes! Currently they lay in the Bosporus opposite the German Embassy.

It all happened in a matter of moments. As they flew at several thousand feet above the waters entering the Sea of Marmara they were attacked from astern by a Fokker Eindecker monoplane with a Spandau machine gun firing through the propeller arc. The poor old Voisin, with its single forward-pointing gun, had no chance to fight back. Bullets slammed into the cylinders of the pusher engine, which, after a series of vicious bursts from the Fokker, coughed painfully and stuttered to a stop. In its death throes the rear-mounted radial engine acted as a shield protecting the two aviators from injury. As the Voisin dived steeply away the German pilot, probably assuming he had dealt the *coup de grace*, flew away to the north.

Spiralling down towards the Straits, they had no hope of reaching base at Imbros. Pulling out of the dive, Donald managed to touch down on the sandy terrain of an emergency landing ground near Cape Helles at the extreme southern tip of the Gallipoli peninsula, a pocket still held by the Allies.

It was the late afternoon of 8 January, 1916, just a few hours before the final evacuation of Allied troops. If Donald and his observer had forced landed the following day they would have flown straight into the unsympathetic hands of the Turks. As it was they tried to set fire to the Voisin before it was seized by the enemy, but some British engineers rushed out and pushed the machine into a dugout. They explained that preparations for the evacuation had to be kept secret. Any fires would give the Turks the impression that stores were being burnt prior to pulling out.

For eight hours they sat on 'W' beach, as it was coded. As soon as darkness fell troops marched in a continuous column eight abreast on to a low pier and were marshalled into large barges moored on either side. These were then ferried out to waiting ships which took the men away to safety.

Throughout the operation a huge gun, 'Asiatic Annie', fired shell after shell from the Asian, that is the eastern, side of the Straits at the retreating army. At times there were earth-shattering explosions no more than thirty yards from the lines of soldiers who stood patiently waiting to be moved forward on to the pier. Mercifully the Turks sent over HE shells, which, although terrifying enough, did not spread the jagged white-hot splinters of shrapnel which would have decimated the troops.

The final phases of the evacuation of the Gallipoli peninsula, the only successful feature of that campaign, was carried out with quiet efficiency. Long before daybreak all the men had gone, leaving the beaches strewn with the tangled debris of war. Donald and his companion were taken off at 1.00 am and embarked on SS *Partridge* one of the last two ships to leave the area, and sailed back to Imbros.

The squadron was re-equipped with two types of the excellent French Nieuport, but Donald was allowed to hang on to his Bristol Scout, although he also flew the Nieuports on many occasions. These machines had arrived in packing cases from England without any form of armament, so the squadron armourers fitted the single-seat version with a Lewis gun above the pilot's head; it was fixed on a quadrant mounting which allowed the gun to be elevated above the horizontal. In order to accommodate the breech when the gun was in the elevated position a small section of the upper main plane had to be cut away. The twin seat version was already provided with a standard mounting to which it was only necessary to attach the observer's machine gun.

Donald had fitted his Bristol Scout with two Lewis guns, one each side of the fuselage, both firing through the propeller arc. As there was no interrupter gear he had bound his propeller blades with doped fabric in an effort to reduce the number of splinters whenever bullets hit the whirling prop. Naturally he fired his guns as little as possible!

One day he encountered another Fokker and flew towards his enemy intent on putting up a better show, now that he was in a fighter rather than a lumbering reconnaissance machine. The two aircraft approached each other head on. Donald counted on the German eventually breaking away to his left as he knew that to go right had a gyroscopic effect which would send the Fokker into a dive – and this is exactly what happened. At the last moment the Fokker executed a 180 degree turn to port while Donald followed him in a 360 degree vertical bank finishing up on his tail. The German weaved in all directions but the Bristol put several bursts of tracer into his fuselage. The Fokker dived away at a speed which the Bristol was unable to match and, although a fellow pilot in a faster Nieuport went after him, the German got away to live another day.

Frustrated by this incident, Donald fitted his 'Baby' with a more powerful Nieuport 90 hp Le Rhone engine complete with the larger propeller. This worked well enough, although, now nose heavy, it altered the landing characteristics of the Bristol.

Spotting duties continued for the big gun monitors although the intensity with which they fired at the peninsula had slackened. In fact, the great unwieldy lumps of metal, the worst of sea boats, now contented themselves with lobbing shells from their moorings in the harbour a couple of times a week. The guns only fired a flat trajectory so in order to achieve more elevation the naval crews flooded the hull's stern compartments to tilt the barrels upwards. Even so, they once managed to slice the roof from the sergeants' mess situated on a low promontory between the harbour and the peninsula.

The Turks, sheltering behind hills on the peninsula, had little to fear from this shelling. When Donald and the others reported these negative results the Admiral complained, 'Why do our RNAS chaps always put in more pessimistic reports than the French pilots?'

The Squadron CO replied, 'The French are politer than our fellows, sir.'

In the late spring of 1916 the squadron was transferred to Thasos, an island some 70 miles north-west of Imbros. Approaching from the sea, the only way in, the aerodrome presented tricky landing problems, being nothing more than a small flat area overshadowed by towering mountains. The two Nieuports ahead of Donald both crashed on trying to land, so he took the precaution of making a low slow pass over the landing ground before coming in and saw that what appeared to be a difference in ground level right in the middle was actually only a change in soil colour. Encouraged by this he approached and touched down safely.

The tented accommodation was already occupied by a French squadron flying Nieuports. The pilots were highly skilled and a close rapport was soon established between them and the British. The RNAS pilots had difficulty preventing their Nieuports from bouncing on landing and the French showed them how to overcome this by countering the bounce through rough use of the joystick to calm the machine down.

Among many outstanding characters in this French squadron was a pilot called Constantini, a former racing driver and first class mechanic. He made it his business to overhaul Donald's engine and presented him with an exquisitely made German Bosch magneto. This remained with him throughout his career and was transferred to whatever machine he was flying at the time. In return, Donald, who had taken on the role of armaments officer as well as his flying duties, provided his French friends with bombs and bread, two commodities of which they were short.

The tinsmiths from the monitors had provided the squadron with a supply of bomb-shaped containers. On arrival at Thasos these had been filled with petrol and armed with inertia plungers and Very cartridges. Lobbed through a hole in the floor, until bomb racks were fitted at a later date, they proved effective in setting fire to the crops grown by the Bulgarians, whose government, motivated by the fiasco at Gallipoli, had entered the war against the Allies. Many acres only a short flying distance from Thasos were devastated by these raids.

A Serbian pilot serving with the French had a fanatical loathing for all Bulgarians and begged Donald to give him all the bombs he could spare. Piloting a rickety Henry Farman Shorthorn, he clipped eight bombs into the standard racks under the wings and then loaded up the front cockpit with bombs as well. Having dropped the bombs from the racks in the normal way, he would then hook each bomb from the front cockpit with a walking stick, spin off the safety fans and throw them over the side.

Living conditions on Thasos were even more primitive than on Imbros. The swarms of flies were more than an irritation as they carried the ever-constant threat of disease. The primitive latrines were an ideal breeding ground and it was well understood that the best time to pay a visit was when meals were being served in the tented mess; then, and only then, did the insects depart to infest the food.

Like many others, Donald succumbed to malaria and dysentery. The MO had run out of quinine and sent his patient to an army hospital in Stavros. Here he writhed in fever, not helped by lying in the heat of a tented ward.

Good connections have their rewards and when he was on the road to recovery a friend of his father, Brigadier General White-Thompson, came to see him, lent him a horse and a groom and advised him to 'ride about and get his strength back'.

Posted back to England, Donald spent some time in and out of hospitals, acting, he felt at times, as a convenient guinea pig for medical practitioners who administered various drugs and injections with little regard for their potency. Surviving their ministrations, towards the end of 1916 he was posted to Redcar, soon to become executive officer for the station, responsible, under the CO, for administration and discipline. To his pleasure he found that the Commanding Officer had been his old CO on Thasos.

Early in 1917 he was given an extra duty which entailed travelling to London once a fortnight to sit on a selection board to choose prospective RNAS pilots. His colleague on these occasions was another of his old commanding officers, Colonel Samson, a well known character in flying circles who at one time had been in charge of 3 Wing on Imbros.

Their method of candidate selection would seem bizarre to exponents of present-day methods of separating the wheat from the chaff. During the interview he and Samson would fiddle with their pencils. If, at a certain stage, each man held the pencil point upwards this indicated that the applicant was to be accepted for pilot training without more ado. Pencil pointing downwards – not at any price! Pencil laid flat on the desk was a signal to ask the candidate to leave the room while they discussed him. Pencil held horizontally in the air – a borderline case who should be advised to try joining the RFC, which, as every RNAS officer knew, was an inferior service!

And the criteria on which these decisions were based: someone they both liked; preferably around 19 years old; a good horseman usually made a good pilot; a good oarsman also usually made a good pilot; he had to come from the 'right' school – so he knew how to behave in the mess.

Donald could not remember a single candidate coming from a working class background. He assumed that any who had applied must have been filtered out before that stage.

Throughout the year he had to return to hospital for further treatment and witnessed many cases of men suffering acute shell shock as a result of experiences in the trenches. These men were also used in the role of involuntary guinea pigs by medical staff who had no understanding of the problem. Often, though, the tenderness displayed by individual nurses did more than anything to allay their suffering.

In April, 1918, at the time when the RNAS and the RFC were amalgamated into the Royal Air Force, he was drafted to Orford Ness, close to the Aircraft experimental Station at Martlesham Heath. Whereas Martlesham, like Farnborough, concentrated on aircraft development, Orford tested and improved equipment in various sections devoted to bombs and bomb-sights, guns and gun-sights, navigational instruments and, in Donald's case, a 'general' section which included all the odds and ends that failed to fit into any of the other categories.

Among these items were parachutes. Pressure had increased in several quarters, particularly a group known as the Guardian Angels, to establish parachutes as a regular RAF issue to aircrew. One question that Donald's team tackled was how many times a parachute could be repacked and reused. A bomb case weighing between 11 and 12 stone was attached to a parachute and dropped from an aircraft over and over again from varying heights. It was discovered that after about one hundred descents the chute was liable to burst with a loud report.

They experimented with folding the parachutes in a variety of ways. One of the most efficient in speed of opening, a system of folding from the centre outwards and rolling it up onto a strip of canvas, was discarded. It was felt that because it opened so quickly it might impose a dangerous strain on the parachutist. In another test Donald fired a single bullet into a parachute pack lying on the ground. Opened out, the folds were found to contain no fewer than 150 holes from that single shot.

The men and officers from several branches of the services were aided by a number of gifted scientists, men such as Professor Frederick Alexander Lindemann who had been appointed Director of the Experimental Physics Station at Farnborough. At the age of 28 he had evolved the theory of aircraft spin and bravely proved it in a flying experiment. In the Second World War, as a close friend of Winston Churchill, he became the Prime Minister's chief scientific adviser and ended his days as Viscount Cherwell.

Another young man of equal brilliance was Dr R. V. Jones, whose brother was killed while attempting to execute a loop too near the ground. Dr Jones contributed much to the progress of aeronautical science during both world wars and in the years between. He became the head of the Air Ministry's Scientific Branch.

The flying men, too, were chosen for their enthusiasm for experimenting with new ideas and, where necessary, for taking risks. Such a man was a pilot named Hill whose ancestor, Sir Rowland Hill, had introduced the penny postage. Hill quizzed Donald and his team about the possibility of fitting his pusher machine with metal reinforcement strips along the leading edges of the wings. He wanted to see if he could sever enemy balloon cables by deliberately flying into them. After consideration, they decided such an idea was too hazardous and suggested an alternative – a pair of steel bowsprits or booms some 10 to 15 feet long extending outwards beyond each wingtip. These were soon put in place and the intrepid Hill flew off to attack a nearby balloon cable. Unfortunately no allowance had been made for the effects of static electricity. As one of the booms slammed into the cable there was a blinding flash and the aeroplane was thrown into a violent spin. Hill, outstanding pilot that he was, managed to right his machine before it hit the ground and landed safely. It was decided that the idea was not practical.

A very small, but exceptionally brave pilot, Major Charley, was somewhat miffed to learn that over at Martlesham Heath one of his colleagues was claiming to have achieved a world altitude record of around 25,000 feet, though it was, of course, unofficial. The last such record ratified by the recognized authority, the FAI, had been before the war, established by the Frenchman G. Legagneux in an early Nieuport when he achieved a remarkable 20,079 feet.

Charley, who regularly flew to heights of 20,000 feet to carry out weather observations, decided to better the Martlesham Heath effort and, what is more, to achieve it without the use of oxygen. With a minimum of preparation he heaved his 8-stone frame into the cockpit of his experimental 150 hp Monosoupape engined Sopwith Camel and took off. After what seemed an eternity, this non-smoking, non-drinking engineer/pilot achieved a height of around 25,000 feet breathing nothing but the rarified air at that altitude. Not surprisingly, he blacked out. The machine flipped over on her back – an attitude in which Camels attained maximum stability. Slowly, and fortunately for Charley, the machine decided to go into a spin. At around 15,000 feet he recovered consciousness. Most pilots in such circumstances would have shaken their heads, pulled out of the spin, thanked their lucky stars, and come in to land as soon as possible. But not Major Charley. He took a deep breath, heaved back on the stick and climbed once more to his previous height. This time he did not faint. He had almost certainly achieved a world record, even if it was never officially recognized – 25,000 feet *without* the use of oxygen. Possibly this has never been bettered, especially in an open cockpit.

Donald continued his experiments, investigating, for example, the best forms of underwater explosive to use against submarines. His team made good use of cocoa tins packed with graded amounts of TNT and set them off in a local river. They carried out tests to improve aerial photography at night by testing magnesium flare bombs dangling from black parachutes that had been lined inside with reflecting foil. An attempt was also made to turn night into day with searchlights but this was unsuccessful.

Interesting trials were made to improve navigation at night, based on timing along a given course, altering course at a pre-arranged moment and firing a Very light according to previous instructions so ground observers could assess the accuracy of the navigation. At no time was the pilot allowed to know his route in relation to the map – in other words he was flying blind. Pilots following these instructions, combined with the use of instruments and weather reports, became progressively more accurate. If only these promising beginnings had been sustained and built on by the RAF during the '20s and '30s, the lamentable inadequacy of navigation at night in the early years of the Second World War might have been avoided. For Captain Donald Bremner, participating in these fascinating developments was a long way from his life as an able seaman aboard the armed yacht *Zarifa*.

# CHAPTER THIRTEEN

# FRED HAIG

In mid-January, 1915, a force of some 20,000 Turks, in collaboration with the Germans, crossed the Sinai Desert with the express purpose of invading Egypt. Wisely they followed an inland route keeping well clear of the coast road which was within range of the Allies' naval guns.

One of the earliest examples of how useful the aeroplane could be as an aid to ground forces was demonstrated when British air patrols spotted all three advancing Turkish columns. Thus forewarned, the multi-national force along the Suez Canal put up a spirited defence and soon broke up the Turkish attack, inflicting nearly 2000 casualties against thirty-two Allied dead and wounded.

The Allies themselves then swept east across the desert to Mesopotamia (Iraq) to secure the British-controlled oil wells at Ahwaz. A two-pronged advance continued north up the Euphrates and Tigris and at first all went well, again considerably helped by accurate air reconnaissance carried out by the few aeroplanes available. But, as lines of communication lengthened difficulties increased. From their furthest point up the Tigris, overcome by Turkish reinforcements, the British were forced to retreat to the city of Kut, a hundred miles down river, where they were heavily invested by the Turks.

After three unsuccessful attempts to relieve their comrades, the British relief forces withdrew. They had suffered twice as many casualties as the numbers they were trying to save. What little food could be dropped from the air was not nearly sufficient, and on 29 April Major-General Charles Townshend surrendered to the Turks. His men were in a state of exhaustion from the heat and emaciated by starvation and disease. Many subsequently died in the hands of their captors. A promising campaign, partly designed to regain prestige in the area after the Gallipoli fiasco, had ended in disaster and lowered the Allies' reputation throughout the Middle East.

It was not until the spring and summer of the following year that Allied forces began the slow advance back through the desert and, eventually, once more into Mesopotamia. The part played by the air forces during this drawn-out campaign is seen through the eyes of Fred Haig, an Australian pilot.

After leaving state school in Melbourne, Victoria, Fred attended an 18-month course in mechanical engineering at the technical college in the city. It was a subject close to his heart and he passed with flying colours. In 1913, while still in his teens, he sailed for Fiji to take up his first job with the Fiji Shipping Company. Not required to sail on the banana boats, his duties were confined to maintaining the marine engines while the ships were in dock. More than content with this task, although the hours were long and hard, things went fair dinkum until Fred went down with malaria.

Hauling his once husky 6 foot 4 inches out of hospital and back to the port the foreman told him, 'You're too weak for this job, cobber. Here's a week's money. You're no use to us anymore.'

Fortunately one of the hospital visitors was a lady whose husband owned the local picture palace in Suva, the capital of Fiji. Could he play the pianola? Yes, as it happened, he could. After a successful audition he began work providing mood music for the silent films of the time.

Society in Suva consisted of the Government House elite, the staff of the Pacific Cable Company, the business community, and the 'me too's' of which, of course, Fred was one. War clouds were gathering by now and a meeting of the former Fiji Volunteer Corps was called one Sunday morning. The get together was poorly attended but there were sufficient present to elect a commanding officer, an adjutant and a sergeant major. Turning to Fred, who at the end was the only one left without an appointment, they asked him about his qualifications and he told them he was an engineer. They were delighted because they had just received an assignment of two Vickers machine guns from England and no one had a clue how to operate them, so they immediately put Fred in charge of the machine-gun section. He lugged one of the guns up into the hills and dismantled it completely, laying out every component in neat rows. Then, carefully cleaning and oiling each part, he re-assembled the gun and fired a number of experimental rounds. By the end of a week he felt he understood quite a bit about the Vickers, how to operate it and how to clear stoppages quickly and efficiently.

Then a fever broke out on the Union Steamship Company's banana boat *Manapourri* which decimated the crew. Fred, who now wanted to get back to Australia, signed on as a junior engineer and sailed back to Melbourne.

By this time the war was well under way and he wasted no time in joining 'F' Company made up of former public schoolboys of the 5th Battalion then being formed from local volunteers. For some reason, possibly because he had 'kicked around the islands and knew a thing or two', he was appointed company cook.

One day he was passing his CO's tent when he spotted a Vickers machine gun outside, still in its case. Unable to resist, he lifted it out of the box, assembled it and mounted it on its tripod. Captain Carter, sticking his head through the tent flap, said, 'Do you know about these things, Haig?'

'I certainly do, sir. I'm an expert on the Vickers machine gun.'

'Well, that's fine. I've got a Lieutenant Stevens joining us next week to form a machine-gun section. You can be his corporal.' With that quick promotion Fred ceased to be company cook.

Within a very short time he and his mates were crouching in a boat in the Eastern Mediterranean heading for the beaches of Gallipoli. It was 25 April, 1915. Stored in the boat was his precious supply of machine guns, destined never to be fired in anger. They went to the bottom when the vessel was sunk by a shell from a Turkish gun. Fred, his friend Nonny Cole and a few others who had survived swam for the shore and were at once absorbed into the milling crowd of infantrymen on the beach that was to become known as Anzac Cove.

At first the landing was largely unopposed, but after a brief period during which the Turks reorganized their forces and counter-attacked, it became a nightmare of explosions and confusion, with dead and wounded lying everywhere. The Aussies had struggled inland as far as they could go before being recalled to dig a line of trenches behind an almost imperceptible rise in the ground.

Thirsty after his exertions, Fred slithered down to a small creek and began drinking from a stream. The water tasted strange and then, rising to his knees, he saw to his horror the waterlogged bodies of two dead Australian soldiers only a few feet upstream.

The line bowed backwards in the centre and the men were told to straighten it in order to provide sustained fire-power along its full length. The Australians did their best to comply in the face of withering fire from the Turks. Nonny was killed outright and moments later Fred received a bullet in the right lung. Taken to the rear he was given rough and ready treatment before being sent to Alexandria aboard a hospital ship. Here he was declared unfit for further military service and shipped back to Australia. This would seem to be the end of his war and he had to sign a form to agree that, although he had been wounded, he relinquished all claims to any compensation from the Commonwealth Government. Although this was rescinded shortly afterwards, Fred never received a war pension.

He took a job with the Kenny & Lewis Company in Melbourne, making 18-pounder shells. On a day off he paid a visit to Nonny Cole's folks to pay his condolences and to let them know what a fine soldier their son had been. While he was there he had a chat with Nonny's younger brother, Adrian, who later became an air vice-marshal. Adrian Cole told Fred he had joined the recently formed Australian Flying Corps and that they were desperately short of engineers. How did he feel about giving it a go? Fred said he'd love to but he doubted if he could get through the medical. Calling at the town hall for a fitness test he was happily surprised when the MO passed him fit for ground duties.

Kitted out in uniform once again, Fred sported the prestigious brass 'A' for Anzac above his AFC colours, showing he was a veteran of the Gallipoli campaign. As soon as Major Reynolds, his CO of No 1 Squadron at Point Cook Air Station, saw this insignia he questioned him about his previous war service and his qualifications. 'Just the man we want!' said Reynolds. 'From now on you are our Armaments Sergeant.'

Before long he was back aboard ship on the six-week voyage back to Egypt. Still only of tender years himself, Sergeant Haig was able to call on his skills to keep his even younger charges occupied during the drawn out voyage. Apart from imparting the intricacies of machine guns and rifles, he taught them how to signal by semaphore and send messages in morse code. Above all he explained the mystery of aero engines, something he had mastered during his stay at Point Cook.

As the Allies pushed the Turks back from the Suez Canal, 1 Squadron moved across the Sinai desert to a point west of Jerusalem. Fred considered the aeroplanes on their strength were of inferior quality – a few B.E.2es and one or two D.H.5s apart from an assortment of other machines, all suffering from warping due to the excessive heat, and with engines affected by a constant intake of sand.

Better aircraft were promised, some fitted with the Constantinescu machine-gun interrupter gear. To prepare for their arrival Fred was ordered to return to Cairo to attend a course on this ingenious equipment.

Complete with rifle, pack and pass he reached the nearby railway station at midnight. The train to Cairo drew alongside and, although it was difficult to see in the dark, Fred realized he was standing opposite a first class carriage. This was much to be preferred to the cattle trucks in which NCOs and men were normally expected to travel. Without hesitation he tried the handle which was unlocked, climbed inside the empty compartment and settled down for the night, stretched out comfortably on one of the seats.

About six in the morning he was woken by a voice with an English accent exclaiming, 'I say George, there's a fellow asleep in here, an enormous Australian sergeant. How the hell did he get in here?'

The major wasted no time in interrogating Fred who explained that he had simply got into the nearest carriage when the train stopped and had been enjoying a good night's kip. What seemed to worry the major most was the fact that the carriage had not been locked. 'Can't understand it,' he said. 'Terrible breach of security. Do you know who this compartment belongs to?'

'No idea, sir.'

'It is part of the private quarters of General Salmond, who, as I'm sure you know, is the Officer Commanding all the air forces in the Middle East. At the next stop you'd better be out that door and off to the cattle trucks pretty damned sharp. Understood?'

'Sir!'

When the train did eventually grind to a halt, Fred was ready with pack and rifle to make a bolt through the door, while the major stood behind him to help him on his way. As he stepped down onto the platform a high ranking officer barred his way. It was General Geoffrey Salmond himself who, of course, wanted to know the whole story about the uninvited guest occupying his private compartment.

Major Dickson-Spain, who was the General's ADC, explained the circumstances and apologized for the lapse in security. This resulted in a long chat between Fred and the General. Salmond noticed during the conversation that the young sergeant, who wore an open neck shirt, had a badge of the Australian Automobile Club attached to the identity tags slung round his neck.

'Do you own a car, sergeant?' asked Salmond.

'Yes, I do, sir. A single cylinder de Dion Bouton.'

'What an amazing coincidence. I have the same sort of car,' said the General. 'I expect you're hungry, aren't you?'

'I certainly am, sir.'

Salmond turned to Dickson-Spain. 'Take Haig for a wash and shave, then bring him along to join me for breakfast in the dining car.'

Over the meal they chatted about cars and the development of motoring in Australia. Just as the General was leaving he said to Fred, 'I think you've got what it takes to become a good pilot. Would you like to fly?'

Fred, who had never had any inclination to take his outsize feet off the ground, nevertheless had enough nous to know which side his bread was buttered and replied, 'Yes, sir. I'd love to.'

Salmond asked him where he was staying in Cairo which happened to be the Heliopolis Palace Hotel and told him not to leave there before 10 o'clock the following morning. Before that time a dispatch rider arrived on a motorcycle and sidecar combination and took him to RFC HQ to be booked in for immediate training. It was a Thursday, and the six-week course, mostly classroom instruction in various aspects of the theory of flight, had already started the previous Monday, but by dint of hard work Fred soon caught up with the other forty trainees.

Then he was posted to an aerodrome near Alexandria for a six-week flying course on Avro 504Ks powered by le Rhone engines. After passing his tests he was awarded his wings and taken before the flying school's CO who told him he had a problem. The CO had learned that all Australian Imperial Forces personnel who flew held commissioned rank. 'There's only one solution I can think of,' said the officer, 'and that's to kit you out as a sergeant in the RFC; we do have a few pilots in that rank.'

And so, armed with a rail warrant and some money from RFC funds, he returned to Cairo to rejoin his unit. As he was walking past Shepheard's Hotel on his way to the railway station he met a couple of lieutenants from his own squadron. They were staggered to see him wearing wings and dressed in British RFC uniform. They told him that when he failed to turn up for the armaments course in Cairo he had been posted as missing with every possibility of being shot as a deserter. Even now he had the distinct impression that his outlandish explanation was not really being swallowed. But he persuaded the two officers to accompany him in a taxi to Royal Flying Corps headquarters. Fortunately Major Dickson-Spain was in his office. 'By Jove, we must have forgotten to inform your squadron CO about what was happening to you.' At that moment Salmond walked into the room which gave Fred an opportunity to thank his benefactor for giving him the chance to become a pilot.

'I told you you'd do all right,' said Salmond. 'I've read the training reports and you've made the most of it. Well done.'

His ADC explained the difficulty that had arisen because of his absence from the squadron, and the General ordered him to sort it out straight away. A signal explaining the situation was sent to Major Williams, who had taken over from Reynolds as CO of 1 Squadron, and Fred caught the next train back to camp. Unfortunately Williams never forgave him for the way in which he had become a pilot and, in spite of Fred's protestations, he continued to consider the whole thing some labyrinthine wangle on the part of his sergeant.

Fred was ordered to take his place in the sergeants' mess and revert to Australian army uniform, although still wearing RFC wings, thus becoming the only NCO pilot in the AFC. After a few weeks the squadron was lined up on parade to receive an inspection from a visiting general – none other than General Geoffrey Salmond himself. Fred was standing stiffly to attention behind his ground staff flight when the General reached him. The VIP winked at him as he marched past.

After a short address in which Salmond praised the good work being done by the Squadron, he turned to Williams and said a few words. Fred was then called to the saluting base and Salmond said, 'Sergeant Haig, your CO has something to say to you.'

'Yes, I have,' said Major Williams. 'We have decided that as there are no NCO pilots in the AFC you are to be promoted to Second Lieutenant forthwith.'

Fred had already taken part in a couple of bombing raids and a few reconnaissance flights before his promotion. Now, in the spring of 1918, the promised Bristol Fighters had arrived to escort the two-seater B.E.2es, and, with the Nieuport Scouts and S.E.5as of the RFC, permanent air superiority was achieved over the German Air Force in Palestine.

Sir Edmund Allenby, Commander of the Egyptian Expeditionary Force, had been making steady progress since the previous year in spite of recent setbacks, not so much from enemy activity as through the loss of many of his seasoned troops, removed to the Western Front to reinforce the Allies who were desperately trying to repel the currently successful German offensive.

A combination of bad weather and the demands for more and more men to pour into the insatiable war machine in France brought further advances to a halt, but by early summer the German offensive in Europe had petered out and, on 14 July, on the Palestine front an enemy attack, mainly by German troops, was repelled in the Jordan valley. After that Allenby's plan to break the Turkish hold went steadily forward.

Fred, on reconnaissance with his observer in a B.E.2e, was normally protected by a Bristol Fighter, but on this occasion was escorted by a B.E.2c flown by a Captain D. W. Rutherford, the same Rutherford who, early in the previous year, had been attacking a railway in the area of Gaza when he was forced down by engine trouble. He was spotted by a Lieutenant McNamara flying a Martinsyde Scout from the same squadron. McNamara descended under heavy rifle fire in an attempt to rescue him and, in spite of being severely wounded in the thigh, landed about 200 yards from Rutherford's machine but, owing to his injury, was unable to get out of his cockpit to help Rutherford restart his engine. As Hostile Turkish cavalry were approaching, Rutherford climbed onto the Martinsyde's fuselage behind McNamara but in taking off the latter, because of his injured leg, was unable to keep the aeroplane straight and it turned over. Both officers extricated themselves and set the machine on fire. While the pilot of two other aircraft attacked and held off the cavalry with machine-gun fire, Rutherford assisted McNamara to his B.E.2c and lifted him into the pilot's seat. Still under heavy fire he swung the propeller and climbed into the observer's seat. The wounded McNamara took off successfully and, although weak from loss of blood, managed to fly the 70 miles back to base.

Lieutenant F. H. McNamara, an Australian officer of 67 Squadron of the AFC, later to be redesignated as 1 Squadron, AFC, (Fred's squadron), became the first pilot operating in the Middle East to be awarded the Victoria Cross.

And now, over a year later, a surprisingly similar incident occurred. The two AFC machines were pounced upon by three German Halberstadt fighters. Fred had always impressed on Rutherford that he wanted him to fly behind and above him during reconnaissance missions, but to come alongside to double the fire-power, both behind and in front, if the enemy attacked.

For some reason Rutherford's machine had disappeared, but by dexterous manoeuvring and accurate firing on the part of his observer, Dick Challenor, they managed to shoot down one of the Halberstadts. This was enough to frighten off the other two German machines who soon disappeared over the horizon. The two then looked round for their companions in the B.E.2c and within moments had spotted the missing machine burning on the ground below. They picked out Rutherford and McGilligan, his observer, standing a little way off, apparently unhurt. 'What do you think, Dick?' yelled Fred. 'Shall we go in and try to pick 'em up?'

'I'm game,' shouted his observer. 'After all, we're bloody short of aircrew!'

So Fred came down in the desert well behind the Turkish lines, making a perfect landing, and taxied over the rock-strewn ground to within a hundred feet of Rutherford and his observer. Meanwhile, Dick Challenor leapt out of the aircraft and removed some largish stones from the area in front of the machine. When he was back on board Fred shouted to Rutherford and McGilligan to climb onto either side of the fuselage and put their feet on the rear spar of the lower wing, then lean as far as possible in towards the centre section and grip hard on to the centre section spar.

'It'll never get off the ground with the weight of all of us,' yelled Rutherford.

'Of course it will,' Fred shouted back. 'Just hang on!' Opening the throttle wide the overloaded machine began to bounce across the sandy waste. Unfortunately Rutherford, obviously in a bad state of nerves, began to lean outward as if to jump free of the aircraft as it gathered speed. Fred grabbed him with one hand while trying to control the machine with the other, but it was useless. Rutherford fell off, the B.E.2e swerved to the right and tipped over on its nose. The rescue mission had ended in disaster. Four aviators were stranded in the Jordan Valley with no means of transport.

The only consolation was that, although the aeroplane was a write-off, no one was seriously damaged. Fred had injured his nose and was missing two teeth, but to an outsize Aussie who had survived the holocaust of Gallipoli these were small matters. They collected the maps from the cockpit, then fired a Very pistol into the tank setting the aircraft ablaze.

As they were trying to estimate the distance they would have to trek to reach the British lines a bunch of Arabs galloped towards them firing as they came. Mercifully the bullets stopped when their attackers realized the airmen were unarmed.

Although neither Fred nor any of his companions could speak Arabic it was uncomfortably clear what the Arabs were jabbering about. They were trying to make up their minds whether to shoot their captives or take them back to the Allies and claim a reward, but before they had come to a decision a patrol of Turkish troops arrived and took the matter in hand. As the brigands slunk away the new captors wasted no time in impressing on the airmen that they were now prisoners of war. This unwelcome status was reinforced by the arrival of four German officers who immediately took charge.

Taken to an aerodrome near Amman, the Australians were treated with utmost courtesy by fellow flyers in the German Air Force. Fred scribbled a note to let his own people know that he and his three companions were in good health and being well treated. A German pilot took the message and, at the risk of his life, dropped it over the Australians' airfield. A day or so later a Bristol Scout appeared, flying low over the enemy airfield, taking a similar risk. It dropped a large package containing spare boots and socks for the Australians, and a note of thanks to the Germans.

After three or four days, during which they were even entertained in the officers' mess, they were put in the charge of a scruffy posse of Turks under the leadership of a villainous looking 'bimbashi' and led away on moth-eaten mules towards the distant hills. After several stifling hot days trekking through rock-strewn mountain passes, they eventually arrived at Nazareth, then the Turco-German General Headquarters of the Palestine front. The crumbling dwellings and the cowed, half-starved inhabitants squatting in putrid doorways did nothing to evoke Fred's memories of bible stories told to him in childhood.

Here, in filthy quarters, they joined company with two British prisoners. One, Withers, was a balding middle-aged officer in the Yeomanry with years of experience in South Africa who wore a row of campaign medals for service during the Boer War. For many months since his capture he had lain in hospital recovering from serious injuries. On one occasion General Liman von Sanders, Commander-in-chief of the Turko-German army, had paid a visit to the ward and, after a brief speech in which he praised all present for their courage and fortitude, had then spent a moment with each bedridden officer individually, assuming all were either Turks or Germans, and presented each with an Iron Cross – including Withers!

The other prisoner was an unusual man. Wearing the battered uniform of an RFC captain, Alan Bott spoke several languages with remarkable fluency. He had become known as an author and journalist, and at the age of twenty-three had written a book, *An Airman's Outings*, about his experiences as a pilot on the Western Front earlier in the war. It had become a best seller.

As time went on, Fred and the others grew convinced that Bott was in some way associated with the British Secret Service. When they eventually ended up in Constantinople Fred was frequently staggered by the number of contacts Alan seemed to have in the city and the ease with which he obtained money, food and clothing when needed.

He told them how, when chasing a two-seater Rumpler over

199

mountainous country near Nablus, a stray shot from the German observer fired at the extreme range of 300 yards had holed the petrol tank of his Nieuport Scout. Almost at once he was soaked in petrol just as some sparks licked into ominous flames across the centre of the fuselage. Not wishing to go up in a blaze of glory, he switched off the engine and descended as rapidly as possible side-slipping onto a tiny patch of grass on the edge of a boulder-strewn slope. Crashing into an enormous rock, the Nieuport disintegrated and Bott was knocked out cold, for how long he would never know. He had come round to find himself surrounded by Arabs. (It appears to have been a regular experience among downed aviators in that part of the world!) Fortunately, as in the case of the Australians, some officers and men in Turkish uniform had turned up and taken charge. One of the officers, claiming to be a doctor, bandaged Alan's injured thigh on which the weight of the engine had been bearing. After this he examined his head which had been badly knocked about, one eye swollen and completely closed.

He was treated with every consideration, which slightly puzzled him until he learned that the soldiers were not Turks but Armenian conscripts forced into service by cruel masters who they loathed. To a man they longed for an Allied victory.

Since his capture, in spite of having to walk with a stick and suffering from blinding headaches, Alan had made more than one unsuccessful attempt to escape. This was his over-riding preoccupation. Without hesitation the rest of the group accepted him as their leader.

Very soon each of them was brought in turn before a German intelligence officer for interrogation. By the end of the session he must have been a frustrated lieutenant as, without exception, they played the role of idiots, unable to remember the numbers of their squadrons and quite incapable of pronouncing the names of the places they had come from.

After this the Germans tried a more subtle approach. Placed on parole, the four Australians and two British were taken on a day's outing to Haifa, providing a welcome opportunity to splash around in the Mediterranean. It was not until later, while taking tea in the Mount Carmel Hotel, that the Germans tried some gentle questioning with the aid of RFC squadron photographs.

'Do you perhaps recognize some of your friends?' they asked. Their guests, eyes glazed, merely gazed longingly at some fishing boats lying on the beach as they wondered whether these vessels might provide a possible means of escape.

Changing the subject, one of their captors then enquired about the latest exploits of the famous Colonel Lawrence. Fred denied all knowledge of such a person and proceeded to bore the company stiff with a drawn out rambling discourse about a man called Lawrence he had once known in Australia who, interestingly enough, owned a couple of pigs. To shut him up the whole party, friends and enemies, went off for another swim. It had been a good day for the prisoners but a waste of time for the Germans.

Any chance of escape via the Mediterranean was thwarted when the six POWs were told to prepare for a move to Damascus. But someone had whispered to Alan Bott that the Armenians ran secret caravans from Damascus to Akaba at the north-eastern extremity of the Red Sea which, of course, was the base for Lawrence's Arabs.

They were transported in grubby railway trucks and, no arrangements for food having been made by the military authorities, they were sustained on the two-day journey by bread and eggs given to them by the Syrian Arab officer in charge who bought them with his own money. He listened intently while his prisoners told him how much better the Arabs were faring in those areas of Mesopotamia and Palestine then occupied by the British.

Chugging through the wild hills of Samaria, the train halted many times. After crossing the River Jordan they eventually arrived at Deraa and stopped for an hour. While there they had a visit from an over-polite Turkish doctor who assured them that the British Army was rife with cholera – news that was greeted with cynical laughter. But the laughter faded when he drew out a rusty, unsterilized hypodermic needle and proceeded to inoculate each of them in turn – 'to protect the people of Damascus against this filthy disease'. They later discovered that, whereas the British Army in Palestine was completely free of cholera, Damascus was riddled with it.

When at long last the train came within sight of its destination, distance lent enchantment to this city crowded with mosques and minaret spires glowing in the rose-coloured hue of a magnificent sinking sun, all set against the silhouette of a far off mountain range.

Reality came all too soon when they were hustled from the train to Baranki Barracks, a large forbidding building used as a prison for military offenders. Alan Bott whispered a word of comfort to Fred: 'There are a lot of people in this city friendly towards the British, and believe me, they hate the Turks' and Germans' guts.'

Worn out and hungry, the six men fell asleep on the bare bedsteads, but within hours were awake again, scratching, writhing and cursing. The beds, the floor, the walls, the ceiling were swarming with bugs. This was only the prelude to a prolonged and squalid sojourn in the far from fair city of Damascus.

Plans were hatched for an escape. Fred still favoured the idea of trekking to the coast, possibly Acre or some other port, then stealing a boat and sailing it to Cyprus or Jaffa. Alan thought there was a better chance if they tried journeying south to Akaba by joining up with one of the caravans. This would require money of course, and he hatched a plan to enlist the help of the Spanish consul who had charge of British interests in Damascus. This latter plan was adopted after a great deal of discussion and it might well have succeeded, especially as the Spanish consul came up with a useful fistful of 'baksheesh' for each of them. Sadly, at the very last moment a trusted intermediary was caught by the Turkish authorities and had the truth bashed out of him. Surrounded by no less than twelve guards they were marched to the railway station and put into another squalid truck for a further journey across Syria, this time to Aleppo.

Smarting at their failure, Fred and Alan sat in the wagon hatching plot after plot. They toyed with the idea of jumping train if and when it slowed down, making their way to a German aerodrome, stealing an aeroplane and flying it to freedom. Discarding this idea, they still made attempts to walk off the train and out of the station whenever it came to a halt. On at least one occasion it was only bad luck that prevented them from getting away.

At Aleppo they were amazed not to receive some form of punishment after making such a nuisance of themselves in Damascus. On the contrary they were taken to an hotel regularly used by Turkish officers when breaking their journeys between Constantinople and the war zones.

On their way from the station their morale was raised even more when some khaki-clad Indian soldiers wearing turbans saluted them smartly from a hospital balcony. The officers returned their salutes, as did a passing German major who thought the salutes were for him.

During meals Fred kept his eye on a supposed fellow prisoner in the same hotel, a Mohammedan official of the Indian Postal Service. At first they accepted him as someone in the same situation as themselves, but when Fred said, 'Don't like the look of that joker. Let's watch him,' they all clammed up and took care not to say anything of importance in his presence. It was just as well.

Apart from having a comfortable room to himself, he was seen walking about Aleppo without a guard. Although these facts were not proof of treachery in themselves, the snippets of information that filtered through during various stages of the journey almost certainly confirmed the man's perfidy. He went out of his way to have conversations with prisoners who had just arrived by train. There were reports of him turning up lying in hospital beds suffering from unspecified illnesses, but always well enough to try getting information out of the genuine patients. Later, in Constantinople, he was seen engrossed in conversation with men in cafés and bars, undoubtedly gathering whatever crumbs were available to tip onto the plate of his paymasters.

Leaving Aleppo for an unknown destination they were herded towards an overcrowded, windowless, third class carriage. Airless and full of peasants, it was hardly the ideal transport for a journey of untold length. Alan, who spoke fluent German, had noticed a clean, covered truck occupied by no more than half a dozen German soldiers. He struck up an instant friendship with a Feldwebel who, within moments, was explaining in graphic detail the intimate details of his love life in Paris before the war. Needless to say, as fellow Europeans, the POWs were invited to share the ample travelling accommodation with their German hosts.

During the journey across Asia Minor the German soldiers provided them with tea and loaned them a small spirit stove to boil water. The endless games of poker were enlivened on several evenings when groups of Turkish soldiers rushed from the train in an effort to desert. Some got away, others did not. Those that escaped were running off to join the numerous groups of brigands then roaming the countryside of Anatolia. It would have been a perilous undertaking for any POW to have attempted escape along such a route where a man could be slaughtered for a lot less than his boots.

After four days the passengers were transferred to a curious little narrow-gauge train that ran westwards via a seemingly endless series of tunnels cut right through the Taurus Mountains. In between the long periods of darkness they would suddenly shoot out into startling sunlight and gaze down on to a valley floor thousands of feet below.

The journey took eight hours. It paused at Belamedik where a strange sight met the travellers' eyes. Much of the work on the railway had been done by British and Indian soldiers, the few survivors from the siege of Kut. They had been overseen by a handful of German technicians and some Turkish guards. As time went by more and more Turkish labourers were employed to reinforce the project, while the Tommies, trustworthy and intelligent in the eyes of the officials, had gradually taken over the supervision of the project. Now dressed in civilian clothes, each was respectfully addressed by the labourers as 'Effendi'. In their time the British soldiers had worked far harder and with more efficiency than any of the others, and now they were in charge – well paid and with plenty of freedom.

One Tommy was responsible for all the Greek clerks on the office staff. The paymaster for this section of the construction project was an Australian sergeant. Thousands of pounds passed through his hands each month and the officials representing the German engineering company trusted him without question.

The little train rattled on to Bosanti where the narrow gauge ended. Here they were greeted by more Tommies anxious for news of what was happening in the outside world. What the flyers had to tell them was not encouraging – Allied setbacks on the Western Front, even worse concerning the Italians, and thousands of tons of shipping still being sunk by U-boats. They tried to cheer them by telling them about the huge numbers of American troops arriving in France to bolster the war-weary British and French armies.

The Tommies told them how a party of two Australians, two Englishmen and a French petty officer had carefully constructed a beautifully engineered collapsible boat. It had taken many months to build and when they escaped they were successful in tramping through the heart of bandit country, eventually reaching the coast.

204

Here, by sheer bad luck, they were apprehended and returned to captivity.

Next morning Fred and the others were puzzled as they watched the British soldiers loading crates containing German aeroplanes onto railway trucks with what seemed like unjustifiable enthusiasm. In the end Fred could stand it no longer and asked them, 'Why the hell are you doing the enemy's work so energetically?'

'Energetic, sir?' said a burly corporal. 'Yes, I suppose that's the word. We really enjoy being energetic.' With that he led them over to a quiet siding where a group of Tommies were busy opening crates and causing the utmost destruction by putting in the boot and crowbar. Hardly a single aeroplane left the place in a repairable condition. An RFC pilot who had passed down the line earlier had given them expert advice on the best bits to break. The gunners among the prisoners also did certain things to the breech blocks of weapons, rendering them useless. They had never been caught by the Germans who rarely visited the siding, but on one occasion the sabotaging had been noticed by some Turkish soldiers who laughed and happily lent a hand in reducing their mutual enemy's capacity to make war! Enemy documents acquired after the war included a memo to the authorities in Berlin from the OC German Flying Corps in Palestine. In it he bitterly complained about the deplorable state in which crated machines were being received. He angrily asserted that these aeroplanes were unflyable and hoped that the packers responsible would be severely punished.

Journeying onwards, the prisoners, for no good reason that they could understand, were next tipped out at a Godforsaken hole called Alukeeshla. Cuthbert and Alfonso, as they nicknamed their two latest guards, had dragged them from a deep sleep in the middle of the night. Tempers were far from sweet. Cuthbert clumsily dropped a kitbag on Withers' badly injured arm and Fred, seeing his friend's agony, lost his cool. He drew back his size eleven boot and kicked the greasy little offender clean out of the compartment, sending him sprawling in the mud outside. Far from showing resentment, the fellow almost apologized.

They and their two guards were then led by the local gendarme, who had no idea why they were there, to a disgusting prison cell already occupied by three cringing, scarcely human scarecrows. The

POWs refused to enter. Alan, pointing to the distingushed looking Lieutenant Withers with his impressive row of medals, shouted at the policeman, 'Is this any way to treat a famous colonel?'

Given the Turk's respect for rank, and his evident terror of the giant Australian lunatic who thought nothing of kicking those who were supposed to be in authority, he guided them to what he obviously thought were superior quarters, a small second-storey room bare of furniture. At least it was unoccupied. The guards and prisoners lay side by side on the dirty floor and soon fell asleep. It was to be their home for the next ten days.

The boredom, the monotony of their existence and the sheer frustration led to inevitable quarrels. Only the mature Withers remained reasonable and exerted a calming influence. Then one of the Australians suggested each member of the party should give an account of his experience before and during the war. This worked well, especially when they listened to the numerous adventures of Alan Bott with his intriguing descriptions of well known figures he had met on his travels. Fred told them of life in Fiji and the horrors of Gallipoli, while a fellow Australian explained what it was like to rear sheep in Queensland. Withers, who had served in the Cape Mounted rifles and held both the Queen's and the King's South African decorations, had many a tale to tell of diamond mines, of Mafeking and the Vaal and the early days of Rhodesia. Even little Alfonso joined in the game. In a shattered mixture of languages he conveyed the astonishing fact that he had been in Sarajevo on the day that Archduke Franz Ferdinand had been assassinated – the event that led to the start of the First World War.

Before they were carted away to their next unknown destination Fred and Alan inscribed on one of the walls: 'In memory of some bad days and good yarns, spent and told in this dirty room of this verminous hut in this Godforsaken village.' And at the end was added one of Fred's oft shouted cries: 'To hell with the Turks!'

So in mid-May, 1918, in the early hours of the morning – it always seemed to be in the early hours of the morning – Fred and his companions were dragged off the train yet again, this time at Afium Kara Hissar in the heart of Anatolia. It was reputed to be the biggest prisoner of war camp in Turkey, yet it was not really a camp as such. It was a sombre place, a gloomy town overshadowed by a massive black rock towering 2000 feet above the squalid hovels. An ancient and ruined fortress stood on top of the cliff. It, and the prominence on which it was built, looked ready to tumble down at any time and crush the life out of the inhabitants below.

A barrier separated the street of prison houses from the rest of the town. The civilian community paid little attention to the bedraggled incomers and got on with their main occupation of producing opium.

The prison society was divided both by class and nationality. The Allied officers managed to live just above the survival level and were allowed to purchase items of food from the scruffy shops in other parts of the town. In contrast, about 200 British soldiers shut up in a Greek church received only one small loaf of bread and a bowl of thin soup per day. The Russian prisoners were virtually left to starve. Many died of cold and hunger during the winter.

It was fortunate that Fred and the others had arrived at a time when conditions were improving after the removal of a truly bestial Turkish commandant, Muslum Bey, a corrupt sadistic pervert who had been dismissed after the authorities received a secret report from a senior British officer about his unspeakable reign of terror and unchecked indulgence in sexual crimes within the camp. It was reported that he got away with little or no punishment and was last seen as a shop proprietor selling, among other things, tinned food bearing British labels, food sent from England and intended to help alleviate the hardship of those in prison.

Only the camp library offered solace and a chance to forget their squalid surroundings. Hundreds of books had been sent by various societies in England over the years. These invariably arrived in an untampered state – books printed in the English language were of no value to the Turks – unlike food parcels which were regularly pilfered.

The officers devoted many hours plotting ways of escape, while knowing in their hearts that any such project was really out of the question; the nearest coast was now more than 150 miles away. It was agreed that a transfer to Constantinople would present their only real chance of getting out of Turkey. Where there was water there were boats and ships, and boats and ships sailed to other lands offering the best opportunities of getting away.

It was like an answer to their prayers when, without explanation, Fred and his group were one day marched to the station, put on a train and sent to Constantinople – on the *European* side of the Bosporus and 1000 miles from Jerusalem. In the city they were billeted in a house in something near to luxury after what they had been forced to endure over the past months. It was only later they learned that it had once belonged to a respectable Armenian long since massacred, like thousands of his countrymen, by the tyrannical régime now ruling Turkey.

There were many nationalities living in this city of intrigue, where bribery and corruption were the currency of the time. People spoke in whispers, in corners of cafes, terrified of being overheard by ever-present spies or members of the secret police. No one was safe. In addition to the Armenian massacres there had been a savage onslaught against the Christian population, the execution of prominent Syrians and the deportation of Ottoman Greeks. At least two-thirds of the remaining population, including the Turks, were against the atrocities and corruption of Enver and Talaat who ruled the Young Turk Party. While a majority of the people were steadily sinking into a state of starvation, their German 'allies' were carting endless train loads of food produce back to the Fatherland.

Escape, escape, escape hammered inside the minds of the fliers every waking hour. Withers was taken to hospital, where, for the first time in months, his wounds were properly tended. Alan Bott was sent to hospital also, but for a different reason and to a different ward. Fearful of being transported away from Constantinople, with its greater opportunities of reaching freedom, he had feigned madness in order to get himself inside a medical institute, ready for the time when it could be used as a jumping-off spot.

After a while, when it seemed certain that they were to remain captive in the city, Alan's 'lunacy' abated and he was allowed out on Sundays with the other prisoners to attend the English church at the bottom of a winding side street near the Grand Rue de Pera. Here they made contact with the few British residents still living in Constantinople who did their best with what limited freedom they had to help in any escape plans. A Miss Whitaker even lent one

English officer, Yeats-Brown, some of her clothes so that he could move about the city disguised as a girl. Other prisoners grew beards and masqueraded as Arabs.

On occasions, accompanied by guards, Fred and the other POWs were allowed to visit a small restaurant, the Maritza, near Stanbaul station. Here a little Greek waiter, Theodore, with a talent for intrigue, served his Australian and English friends in many useful ways. For 20 piastres a time he delivered secret messages to contacts around town. Replies were delivered tucked inside the menu. Because of his hatred of Turks he proved totally trustworthy.

Alan Bott had gained enormous prestige among his captors by letting it slip that he was the second cousin of Lloyd George, the British Prime Minister! Because of his 'exalted' status he was allowed freedom to visit a number of people with whom he happened to be acquainted. One was a mysterious Mr Sykes, an English merchant operating quite freely in the town, who cashed large cheques for Bott and other officers written on dirty scraps of paper. With this 'bribe money' Alan and a fellow escapee called White managed to stow aboard a rusty old Russian steamer moored opposite the Sultan's Palace of Doluca Bagtche. They sailed out of the Bosporus, across the Black Sea to Odessa and, after many months, trekked their way to freedom.

For Fred escape was a far more difficult matter. Towering above the indigenous population the Australian, with his clean cut features and muscular body, found it quite impossible to pass as anyone but himself. Because of his physique he had become a familiar figure around the streets and bazaars of Constantinople. On several occasions he had been seen back to his quarters, after unsuccessful attempts to get away, escorted by a posse of apprehensive and respectful guards, none of whom reached above his shoulder. Often he would slip out of the back door of the Maritza while his captors were engrossed in conversation with Theodore and stroll in comparative freedom along the back lanes of the town, always accompanied by a crowd of ragged urchins looking up in wonder at this giant from another world.

With the collapse of its rotten régime, the armistice between Turkey and the Allies came a few days earlier than the general cessation of hostilities. On 30 October, 1918, Turkey ceased to be at war and Fred and all the other prisoners were repatriated. Arriving back in Australia he slowly took up the reins of a peaceful existence once more and, over the years, became an influential force in the development of his country's aviation industry.

CHAPTER FOURTEEN

# ARCHIBALD W. H. JAMES

While an undergraduate at Cambridge Archibald William Henry James had already recognized certain characteristics about himself. He had no mechanical aptitude whatsoever and he lacked any interest in aviation, a fact confirmed after enduring a short £5 flight as a passenger in a Bleriot piloted by the already famous aviator, Gustav Hamel. He had not the slightest intention of following a service career. Well endowed with worldly wealth, and with Eton and Cambridge behind him, he would enjoy an enviable independence, choosing whatever way of life took his fancy. Without doubt this was to be rooted in the countryside and largely concerned with animals, particularly horses and hounds.

Then came the war. By the end of October, 1914, 21-year-old Archibald, an early volunteer and now a subaltern, found himself in the oozing mud of Flanders among the first reinforcements of the 3rd Hussars. It saddened him to see so many magnificent horses standing in long picket lines, wretched and hock-deep in wet clinging clay.

Subsisting on a ration of bully beef and biscuit and soaked to the skin by blinding rain, the officers and men were also far from happy. Their misery was compounded when they were ordered to leave their horses behind and march up to take over trenches left vacant through shortage of infantry soldiers. These trenches were shallow, water-logged and isolated, with no connecting flanks. Dug into the side of a hill near its crest, neither James nor his troop had any idea how close the enemy was.

On the second night the temperature plunged, turning water into ice. Inadequately clothed, the Hussars froze too. No rations arrived to sustain them because, apparently, the Germans overlooked a

*211*

section of their flank to the rear making part of the supply route impassable. After three days, under cover of darkness, not having fired a shot, they were pulled out. A third of the regiment, including Archibald, suffered from trench foot, a debilitating, painful rotting of the skin caused by constant immersion in water. Later, troops were issued with protective liniment to combat this.

After a week's recovery period, the Hussars were again sent into the front line to take over another sector known as Sanctuary Wood, once covered by healthy young larch but now reduced by gunfire to gaunt fingers of scarred wood.

The ground, originally held by elderly French territorials, had become too waterlogged to dig. Consequently a parapet had been raised composed mainly of the dead bodies of those who had fallen, a grisly mound thinly covered with a layer of mud. With no protective wire in front and Germans no more than 30 yards away, Archibald, looking through a loophole in the parapet, noticed that when the enemy soldiers walked past a certain point they appeared to rise up, becoming exposed to a little below shoulder height. He guessed their trench floor to be higher at that particular section. Borrowing a rifle from one of his men, he took careful aim at the spot. He prided himself on being an excellent shot. Next time a German appeared he fired, killing him instantly. In the blink of an eye there was a return shot. An enemy sniper had spotted his protruding rifle barrel and fired back. The bullet came through the aperture and went under his armpit, grazing the skin as it went. It was the slightest of wounds but it discouraged Archibald from further sniping.

Relieved by the 16th Lancers, he and his troop returned to base camp. He immediately reported to his CO a matter that had been troubling him for the past few days, a suspicion that the enemy was sapping under their position in Sanctuary Wood. As a matter of urgency the CO relayed this information to Brigade Headquarters, but no action was taken. The following night twenty Lancers and six of their officers lost their lives. The Germans had exploded a mine in a tunnel directly under them.

Appalled by the utter futility of the land war, Archibald welcomed the arrival of a circular inviting lightweight cavalry officers to volunteer as observers in the RFC and put his name forward at once.

In spite of his previous antipathy to flying, he certainly qualified as a featherweight, having the physical characteristics of a jockey.

Granted three days leave at Christmas he had returned with four couple of hounds. With a distinguished field of finely mounted fellow cavalry officers on their first chargers, he organized hunting the hare over territory ranging almost up to the gun line. His CO, Alfred Kennedy, who ended the war as a Major-General, was a professional soldier to his fingertips. He abhorred such exhibitions of skylarking in time of war and was delighted to see the back of this upstart with his confounded hounds.

Along with two other volunteers, he was bundled off in a horse-drawn wagon to the RFC Headquarters at St Omer. The same week, in March, 1915, another young volunteer arrived – Peter Portal, later to become Air Chief Marshal and a significant influence on the air strategy of the Second World War. RFC HQ was then commanded by General Sir David Henderson who made a point of getting to know every new volunteer. His own son was later killed leading a squadron in France.

A Major Holt, CO of 16 Squadron, visiting HQ at that time, invited Archibald to join his team and drove him back in his own car. It was a fortunate coincidence that Holt and the first two pilots he flew with on 16 Squadron, Littleson and Lyn, had also been at Eton.

16 Squadron, stationed near the small market town of Merville, had only been in existence for a few weeks. Added to the original four operational units, it was the only RFC squadron to be actually formed in France. The number 16 was significant because this was the number of squadrons authorized by the British government to operate in France at that time. Trenchard, politically astute as ever, decided to start with the last and work backwards in order to hold ministers to their pledge.

There were three flights, one equipped with Voisins, one with Maurice Farmans, and one, to which Archibald was attached, C Flight, flying B.E.2cs, led by Philip Playfair who later achieved high rank in the RAF.

Officers' quarters in a small château were shared by the flyers of C Flight and one of the other flights. The remaining flight had drawn the short straw and was billeted in a nearby farmhouse. The pilots, and some of the observers, were drawn in part from other squadrons and also from a special reserve of officers posted out from England. Many of them were experienced aviators who had learned to fly before the war. Archibald found himself in a group of colourful characters who communicated in a strange language only understood by those who shared a freemasonry of the air. Inspired by this company he began to look on the business of flying in a new and more enthusiastic light.

The duties of the squadron were threefold: to carry out 'visual' reconnaissance, a worthless occupation in Archibald's opinion when those who were 'observing' barely knew what they were supposed to be looking for; to observe for artillery, an activity that was developing beyond the stage of firing Very lights or signalling to the gunners by flash light. 16 Squadron aircraft carried Sterling spark wireless sets capable of transmitting messages to the signals hut on the airfield. The RFC ground operators then relayed the information direct to the field batteries. Use of such equipment was not without its perils. On one occasion an observer began keying a message while flying directly over the hut. Without warning the aircraft blew up killing both occupants. It was surmised that a leak of petrol from the fuel system must have been ignited by a spark from the wireless set.

The third activity was to take aerial photographs of enemy installations such as artillery positions and railway junctions. Archibald emerged as the squadron's 'ace' photographer. Being so small he could crouch down in his cockpit and aim the camera through a hole in the floor, which nobody else could do. Less restricted than his bulkier companions, he found it easier in that position to make fine adjustments to the lens and had no difficulty changing the large photographic plates. These plates were developed on the squadron by an officer in his early thirties, John Moore-Brabazon, (mentioned in Chapter One) who before the war had become the first holder of a flying licence in Britain. In later life, as Lord Brabazon of Tara, he was acknowledged as one of the great names in aviation and actually had an aircraft named after him.

The squadron indulged for a short time in dropping 'flashettes' issued in bundles. These were 14-inch darts fitted with a fin to be flung over the side of the aeroplane individually when flying over enemy territory. Where they landed no one knew and it was soon conceded that the odds on them doing any damage were so slight that it was simply not worth the effort.

On the first occasion that Archibald flew as observer on a dawn patrol he failed to get further than the end of the aerodrome. In a B.E.2 piloted by Playfair they roared across the grass prior to lifting off. Towards the end of the field they breasted a hump in the ground only to be confronted by a metal plough left directly in the take-off path of squadron aircraft. They smashed into it, demolishing the undercarriage.

His first experience of aerial combat was a frustrating affair. Spotting a German machine flying at the same height as themselves he decided to take a pot shot with his rifle. Carefully setting his sights at 600 yards, a distance at which he had brought down many a stag in Scotland, he fired six shots in quick succession. He must have missed by a mile. Realization dawned only slowly among early aviators that it was essential to come within 50 yards of your enemy to stand a chance of doing him any damage, and that with something more robust than a rifle.

Equally irritating was an encounter with a Zeppelin flying sedately at 2500 feet. Archibald and his pilot were 1500 feet above the dirigible in a Maurice Farman and in an ideal position to attack. The men were well aware that this was a most desirable prize. The Victoria Cross had been awarded for the comparatively straightforward feat of shooting one down. Unfortunately for the flyers a team of British gunners on the ground decided to try their luck as well. They raised their field gun to its maximum elevation and fired. The shell came nowhere near its target but alerted the crew of the Zeppelin. Raising its nose at an acute angle the machine climbed rapidly into a layer of covering cloud and was never seen again.

There was little for the pilots and observers of 16 Squadron to do in their spare time than visit a small but convivial estaminet in the nearby town. The landlord's daughter, Marie Louise, was noted for her beauty and became immortalized in the song 'Marie Louise of Merville', a tune sung in music halls throughout Britain. Archibald enjoyed a close acquaintance with Marie during his time with the squadron and, after the war, he returned to France in an attempt to find her again, sadly without success.

The normal reconnaissance flight lasted no more than two hours, nearly half that time being spent in gaining height before crossing the lines. The longest trip Archibald undertook was at the request of the army to check on enemy supply routes west of Cambrai prior to the first battle of Festubert on 9 May, 1915. Flying with a pilot named Cunningham, Archibald had been chosen as the lightest observer on the squadron. They flew in a specially provided B.E.2a, older, but with a slightly longer range than the 'c'. He remembers envying his friend Walker in another machine when they crossed the line together at dawn flying only a few yards apart. Walker was on a regular patrol of short duration. The 'long' flight, certainly no more than 2 hours, was completed successfully although they had to land short of base to refuel. Walker, meanwhile, had suffered engine failure over the enemy lines and became a prisoner of war, remaining in captivity for 3 years until the Armistice.

During the actual battle of Festubert the troops were instructed to place white cloth strips on the ground to indicate to observers flying at 5000 feet the extent of the Allied advance. In practice all that could be seen at that height was what looked like a plethora of white strips scattered over the battlefield. Many of these were actually light-coloured planks that had lined the enemy trenches but which had been thrown hither and thither by the British bombardment. It was impossible to distinguish them from the actual markers or to make an accurate assessment of the army's progress.

Archibald developed a high regard for the strength and resilience of the early war machines. They may have looked delicate but they had an inbuilt flexibility which enabled them to withstand shocks and damage that would have brought down more modern aeroplanes. The longerons were constructed of prime ash, while the interstrutting was cut from selected spruce and the wings covered in fine Irish linen doped in cellulose lacquer.

Returning from patrol, their machine once received a direct hit from a high velocity shell which severed no less than seven flying wires. With these trailing loose in all directions and fabric flapping from wings and fuselage, they still made their way safely back to base looking more like a tattered kite than an aircraft.

While full of praise for the structure of early airframes Archibald was less enthusiastic about early aero engines. From personal experi-ence he estimated that aircrew would be let down by some form of mechanical failure during at least one flight in four. Sometimes it was nothing more than a worrying cough to be cured by mechanics on landing. At other times breakdown manifested itself in a more dramatic way as on the occasion when a complete cylinder blew out of the engine showering the pilot and himself in a thick coating of black oil. Engine failure on take-off accounted for many fatalities. Too many pilots instinctively tried to turn back if their engine cut when only a few feet above the ground, almost inevitably resulting in a disastrous crash.

With the RFC still in its infancy and those in the Corps still comparatively few, it was natural that the men who flew were quite frequently in the presence of those higher ranking officers who led the nascent force. Outstanding among these was Hugh Trenchard. Archibald, who was later to meet many great men such as Churchill, de Gaulle and others, always regarded 'Boom' as the greatest of them all.

In a way Trenchard was an enigma. Coming from a disadvantaged background the man who was to become the 'father' of the first independent airforce in the world, the Royal Air Force, rose to the highest ranks through courage, strength of personality and outstanding brain power. Yet, to the end of his days he remained a poor orator and even had difficulty expressing himself in writing. Throughout the war he was accompanied by an officer, Maurice Baring, who faithfully recorded his master's words. Often, when talking to a junior officer who had something useful to say based on his operational experience, Trenchard would turn to his assistant and boom, 'Take that down, Baring'.

Archibald formed a far less favourable impression of another leader with whom he came into close contact, Hugh Dowding, who masterminded the famous victory of the Battle of Britain in 1940. He was thoroughly disliked by the men of 16 Squadron when he took over from Tony Holt as their new CO. They found 'Stuffy' Dowding pernickety, interfering and querulous. In a matter of weeks he reduced a first class squadron to a group of disgruntled men on the verge of mutiny and was hastily removed to a post where he no longer had direct contact with operational fighting men.

It was at about this time that Archibald observed the first German gas attack. To the northern end of the Ypres Salient he and his pilot saw a yellow wall of mist moving slowly towards the Allied lines. Without a clue as to what it was they reported the strange phenomenon as soon as they landed. Within an hour a faint smell of chlorine pervaded their aerodrome, though they were stationed some 30 miles south of the front line.

In the circular that had originally inspired him to join the RFC was a promise that, after serving as an observer for three months, consideration would be given to any officer who wanted to train as a pilot. By this time Archibald was itching to take control of the machine himself, so he applied to Trenchard for permission to take a course in flying. Trenchard was reluctant to let him go and delayed his posting for a further two months, so it was midsummer, 1915, before he finally returned to England and was posted to Norwich where he took up residence in the Royal Hotel. He purchased a Model T Ford, and also arranged for two of his pre-war hunters to be sent up from his father's place in Sussex.

In between times he learned to fly on Maurice Farman Longhorns and Henri Farmans from a grass airfield equipped with a row of canvas hangars on a hill above the town. Like many other novice pilots he found both pusher machines easy to fly, especially the Longhorn, which was virtually foolproof. The Henri Farman was almost as simple to handle for as long as its unreliable Gnome engine continued to work.

Lieutenant Harvey-Kelly, mentioned in chapter 4, a celebrated pre-war and early wartime flyer, was instructing at Norwich during that period. An Irishman with a devastating sense of humour, he was acknowledged to be one of the finest pilots in the RFC and a man much admired by Trenchard. Later, when Harvey-Kelly was shot down and killed after volunteering to carry out a single-handed attack on a château housing a German divisional HQ, Archibald noted that 'Boom' who normally kept his emotions under tight control, was, on that occasion, patently distressed.

With no ground instruction and only 18 hours and 37 minutes training in the air, Archibald was awarded his wings and his flying certificate. Subsequently he concluded that many lives could have been spared if the training period had been extended. Lack of experience led to the deaths of innumerable young pilots when first posted to squadrons in France. He estimated that if a man survived the first six weeks of operational flying his chances of remaining alive increased enormously.

In November, 1915, he was posted back to France and joined 5 Squadron, then in sole occupation of the aerodrome at Abeele. This squadron was commanded by the much respected George Beck, while Archibald's flight was led by the colourful eccentric, ex-actor, Robert Loraine, (see Chapter Ten). By this time the poor man had completely lost his nerve and would sit in his cockpit on the ground, running his engine and lost in fantasies of heroic aerial dog fights.

While the other two flights flew B.E.2cs, Loraine's was equipped with the reliable twin-seat Vickers F.B.5 Monosoupape rotary pushers, now colloquially known as the Vickers Gun Bus, though Archibald never heard the nickname used until well after the war. The flight's purpose was to carry out offensive patrols and, with the Vickers' two Lewis guns, shoot down as many German aircraft as possible. It is certain that the enemy regarded these machines with considerable apprehension.

While piloting a Vickers F.B.5 over enemy lines accompanied by an experienced observer, Merlise Green, they spotted a small biplane of unknown type about 1000 feet above them. With black crosses visible on the wings, it wasted no time in coming in fast on their tail to attack. At the crucial moment Archibald threw the Vickers into a left-hand spin, intending to fire at the fighter with his upward-mounted gun. But he was completely thrown by the speed of his enemy who passed him in a flash. Then, to his astonishment, a gunner popped up from a rear cockpit in this tiny plane and opened fire at them with a slow-shooting Parabellum machine gun. At a distance of 40/50 yards his angle of fire was slightly inaccurate although his bullets were steadily chewing up the Vickers' right lower wing at only six feet from where they were sitting.

Realizing that this could not go on, Green, who was sitting in front of Archibald, opened up with his forward-firing Lewis gun. After four or five rounds the gun jammed, so he whipped off the drum, but a stripped cartridge convinced him that the fault could not be cured in the air. By great good fortune Willy Reed, a former cavalry officer on the squadron, turned up in a Bristol Scout at that very moment and, diving on the German, sent him scurrying away to the safety of his own lines.

On returning to base they put in a report on this unknown and potentially dangerous aeroplane. A couple of weeks later they encountered the same machine for a second time. On this occasion they were ready and, although Archibald only got off a few ineffective shots with his own gun, he was able to manoeuvre on to the fighter's tail very quickly, enabling Merlise to fire a brief burst into the enemy. They saw the air gunner collapse as the mystery machine went into a nose dive. It was not advisable to follow the enemy down to confirm his fate as over to the east several German aircraft were circling ominously.

The sequel to this incident was extraordinary. Over 20 years later, in 1936, Archibald James was attending the Nazi Party Rally at Nuremberg as a guest of Joachim von Ribbentrop, Hitler's foreign minister. (Before accepting the invitation Archibald, now a junior minister, had sought the advice of Anthony Eden at the Foreign Office. Eden urged him to go along and find out as much as possible about what the thugs were up to).

Dining with a group of distinguished guests he found himself seated between the two heads of the Luftwaffe, Generals Erhard Milch and Ernst Udet. The three wartime pilots had a fascinating time discussing every aspect of flying in combat and comparing the characteristics of various aircraft of that era. Then Archibald told them the story of his encounter with the mystery German biplane. The German officers were astonished. The aircraft, they said, had been named the 'Blue Mouse' a twin-seater fighter introduced with the highest possible expectations. But only two had ever been sent to the front as it had proved almost impossibly difficult to fly. One of the machines had killed both the pilot and the observer/gunner when it crashed on its own aerodrome, while the other had obviously been disposed of by Archibald and his companion. Until that moment the German officers had no idea how the second 'Blue Mouse' had met its fate.

Flying at 5000 feet, Archibald once spotted a German aircraft going in the opposite direction. Banking round to follow it he realized that its speed was slightly greater than that of the Vickers. Defying the usual practice, the enemy pilot not only flew over the trenches but continued to penetrate Allied territory, continuing his reconnaissance as far as St Omer. When he eventually swung back to the north, Archibald, who had been trailing him at a distance, turned inside him and a few shots were exchanged before the enemy machine again flew out of range. The observer in the Vickers was an officer of Italian extraction flying for the first time in action. To Archibald's surprise the young man had collapsed in a state of nerves when the firing began, but at that moment he had no time to worry about his observer; one of the German bullets had succeeded in shooting off two-thirds of a propeller blade which heralded its departure by clanging against one of the longerons supporting the tail unit, but fortunately without causing any damage. The ensuing vibration was devastating.

As explained earlier, the F.B.5s had no throttle but were controlled from a switch on the joystick by which the engine was blipped on and off. Afraid that the excessive juddering might wrench the engine away from its mountings, and very low on petrol after the long chase, he began as shallow a descent as possible at a speed just above stalling point. Then, to his consternation he saw his observer recover, look round in a wild panic and thrust his leg over the side as if to make a rapid departure. This would not have been the wisest of moves thousands of feet above the earth without a parachute, but Archibald managed to grab him and smile reassuringly. So they proceeded to descend, Archibald hanging on to his observer with one hand and blipping away with the other, until at last they landed with virtually dry tanks on the cinder-covered aerodrome. The Italian never flew again in combat but found a more suitable occupation in which he turned out to be one of the RFC's finest photographic officers.

Time came when the faithful old Vickers were replaced by F.E.2bs, two-seater pushers, with the exception of 5 Squadron which received a further quota of B.E.2cs to take the place of the one remaining flight of Vickers.

Flying one of these unfamiliar machines, Archibald, with Merlise Green as observer, was keeping a wary eye on a Belgian fighter flying on a parallel track some distance over to the right. It was known that some of their Belgian allies had a tendency to open fire and ask questions afterwards. But on this occasion it appeared that their friend was intent on continuing about his lawful business. As Archibald looked over his right shoulder he involuntarily pulled the joystick into his left groin and, as he would have done in the Vickers, kept pressure with his left foot on the rudder bar. Glancing forward, he noticed the left wing was hard down. Automatically he carried out correcting procedures as in a pusher aircraft. The result was catastrophic. The B.E.2c nosed down into a sickening and presumably irrecoverable spin. Ironically, although Archibald was by now considered a seasoned veteran in combat, his skimpy basic training had left him totally ignorant of how to recover from a spin. To the occupants of the machine it appeared as though they were hanging still in the air while the ground below, growing ominously closer by the second, was spinning round the aircraft's nose at an alarming rate. Because of the centrifugal force the men were pinned tightly into their seats. Archibald had been told by those who flew the B.E.2c regularly that it was an inherently stable aeroplane. With no other solution to hand, and praying to God that this information was correct, he took his hands and feet off the controls and left the machine to its own devices. After what seemed an eternity the spin started to diminish and at about 1200 feet the aircraft levelled out. Shaking from the experience they flew gently back to the squadron, touching down gingerly with sighs of relief.

John Hearson, their new CO, took one look at their ashen faces and asked them what was wrong. They told him that the aeroplane was a death trap and that the controls were faulty beyond belief. Calling to an experienced B.E.2c pilot he told him to take off and give the machine a thorough air test. When the pilot returned after throwing the machine all over the sky he assured them it was in tiptop condition. Turning to Archibald and Merlise, the CO ordered both men back into the aircraft. 'Take off and fly around for about ten minutes. Make sure you put it through its paces.' Archibald was convinced that this restored his nerve which had been temporarily broken.

He was much inspired by a brilliant pilot called Powell (see Chapter Ten), who was so far above average he was given the perilous task of testing out new types of aircraft in combat which were specially brought to the squadron for his assessment.

In April, 1916, Archibald was posted to 2 Squadron at Hesdigneul as a flight commander. His squadron CO was Reggie Cooper, while the wing was commanded by Colonel Beck. The squadron, also equipped with B.E.2cs, was employed in a similar rôle to the one he had originally experienced as an observer – artillery ranging, aerial photography and reconnaissance.

This was the time of rapid expansion of the RFC. Trenchard, now at the top of the organization, introduced a military hierarchy of brigades in charge of wings which, in turn, were in charge of the squadrons. As far as the flying men could tell this cumbersome bureaucracy served no useful purpose, although the more perceptive realized that it was all part of their leader's plan to build up a force equal to that of the older two services.

Protective formation flying was introduced to counter the growing superiority of the Germans in the air. It was the era of the so called 'Fokker Scourge' – the Fokker E 111 and the ultimate version the E 1V Eindecker (monoplane), with a tractor rotary engine of 160 hp. These were the world's first true fighters. Even so it was an interim design with no particular qualities, but which succeeded because it had two main advantages over RFC machines. With a top speed of only 85 mph it did have a good rate of climb, and most importantly incorporated an interrupter gear which enabled a Spandau machine gun (later two) to fire through the propeller arc. It caused particularly heavy casualties among the B.E.2c squadrons over a period of ten months from August, 1915, until June, 1916, when its reign of terror was brought to an end by the introduction of superior RFC fighters. It is extraordinary that so much trouble was caused by the Fokker Eindeckers when it is realized that no more than 425 were actually built over that whole period.

2 Squadron was ordered to fly cover for another squadron bound on a most unusual mission. At the time Zeppelin raids on London were in the ascendancy and it was thought that these monsters might be caught and destroyed while flying home across Belgium. Because of the Zeppelins' early morning return it was necessary for the two squadrons to rendezvous above Hesdigneul in the dark – a tricky operation in itself. This part of the mission was completed without mishap and what was then a considerable air fleet set off in search of its quarry. By the time they crossed the German lines dawn had broken revealing a fine cloudless day. Down below they saw a large enemy aerodrome with tiny figures busily wheeling Fokker Eindeckers out of hangers, refuelling them and preparing them for take off.

The two layers of B.E.2cs flew deeper into enemy territory for another 20 miles, but seeing nothing that resembled a Zeppelin they turned about and headed south. Coming back over the German aerodrome at 5000 feet the British flyers observed uneasily that a number of Fokkers had taken off and were climbing rapidly towards them. Archibald's squadron closed down to 200 feet above their fellow B.E.2cs for whose protection they were responsible. As they crossed the Allied lines 2 Squadron bravely turned about and dived on the Fokkers, now no more than 400 yards to the rear. To the astonishment of the British, the Germans turned tail and fled.

Archibald maintained that this was not untypical. Whereas the RFC did its regular patrolling over and beyond enemy lines, German aircraft only exceptionally crossed into Allied territory in spite of the advantage of the prevailing wind at their tails on the return flight.

In the late Spring a Bristol Scout was allocated to 2 Squadron and, as senior flight commander, Archibald was delegated to fly it. It is interesting to compare his reaction to this tiny machine with that of Donald Bremner. Bremner claimed that it was the finest machine he ever flew (see Chapter Twelve), whereas Archibald thought it was extraordinarily inefficient, while conceding it did have a reliable engine and a good rate of climb. It may have had something to do with the physical characteristics of the two men. Bremner, having difficulty even getting into the cockpit because of his bulk, seemed perfectly content once he was in place, whereas the diminutive James complained about the Lewis gun being mounted on the top plane and fired via a Bowden cable leading to a switch on the joystick. The gun was almost out of reach when it had to be tilted to replace a drum or clear a stoppage. 'It needed two hands to fight against the slipstream' he complained, 'so how were you expected to engage in combat and fly the wretched machine at the same time?'

Archibald's most exciting adventure in the Bristol Scout occurred trying to verify a theory he had held for some time. He had often argued that the average German infantryman, unlike himself who was well used to shooting partridges, would have no knowledge of how to 'lay off' his shot (shooting ahead) in order to hit a low-flying aircraft with his rifle.

While on patrol with his observer, George Pirie, (later an Air Chief Marshal) they spotted considerable German troop movements behind

224

the enemy lines. They hurried back to base and Archibald took off again at once in the Bristol Scout, hoping that this would prove the ideal opportunity to establish the truth of his theory. Crossing the German trenches at 600 feet he made out the conglomeration of enemy troops ahead and put the small biplane's nose down, increasing the speed to a respectable 90 mph. Zooming over a myriad of spiked helmets, wagons, guns and horses, he encountered no opposition whatsoever. He banked steeply and headed for home. As he approached the enemy lines from the rear he flew alongside a road on which he had noticed a gun battery in transit only a few moments before on his outward flight. The gunners had done a most efficient job. They had unlimbered their guns, turned them in his direction and fired a salvo as he flew past some 400/500 yards away to the west. It missed him by a league but he silently congratulated them on a considerable feat of artillery.

Passing back over the German trenches it was a different story, as he ran into a veritable hail of small arms fire. There was no doubt that his machine was hit several times, and as he crossed his own lines in a dive only feet above the ground his engine was emitting the nastiest of noises. He nearly made the aerodrome, but not quite, flopping down instead in an adjacent field. When they counted the bullet holes there were thirty-five, but, apart from the one that had damaged the engine, only two were in the forward area of the fuselage. All the rest were clustered around the tail section which satisfied him that his theory was more or less correct.

Such had been the racket from the German infantry in their attempt to bring him down that it convinced British troops in *their* trenches that an attack was imminent, so much so that battalions in near reserve were called to arms!

By mid-June, 1916, feverish preparations were taking place on the part of the Allies in the build-up to the Somme offensive. Archibald was called to the squadron office to be met by his CO and the commander of the wing, Colonel John Beck, who said, 'Your're a very lucky young man. Trenchard has selected you for a special duty of the highest importance. You are to be driven in my car to HQ to meet the Commander in Chief at 12 o'clock noon, precisely.'

On the wall of Trenchard's spartan office was a large map. 'As you probably know,' he said, 'a great battle is to begin on 1 July.' He thrust a pointer at the map. 'As you can see, this straight main road running from Bapaume south-west to Albert into the centre of the battle area is the key German supply route. In order to deal with this situation I am forming a special squadron of eighteen machines. Two aeroplanes will be drawn from each of the B.E.2c squadrons on the northern two army fronts that will not be involved in the battle. This special squadron will operate from an airfield near here under my direct command with no brigade or wing in between the squadron CO and myself. You will be the CO. The aircraft will fly as single-seaters carrying 112 lb bombs which will be dropped to put the road out of action. You will fly at 3500 feet to be out of range of small arms fire. That's the scheme. Its my own pet project and I've discussed it with Sir Douglas Haig and told him what I intend doing.'

Archibald remained silent and Trenchard handed him a typescript. 'I've made out an establishment and here it is. Go for a walk and study its contents. We lunch at one. Immediately afterwards we will return to my office and you can tell me if anything else is needed to make the scheme a success.'

The interview had lasted for exactly 15 minutes. Archibald took a stroll in a nearby beechwood and sat on a fallen log to read carefully through the document. After lunch he returned to face the great man. 'Well,' said Trenchard, 'what do you have to say?'

'Only this, sir. I wish to be returned to my regiment.'

'What on earth do you mean?' 'Boom' exploded.

'Well, sir, several times when we've met in the past you've cautioned me not to argue with you and I've no intention of doing so now.'

'On this occasion I order you to argue with me!' Trenchard roared.

'As you wish, sir. The reason I won't take on the assignment is because it is doomed to failure. Machines flying single-seater, *and* unescorted, will be pounced on by the Fokkers and shot down one after the other. When the first six or eight have been destroyed the rest will very sensibly jettison their bombs and make for home as quickly as they can.'

For a moment there was silence. Then Trenchard said, 'You will not return to your regiment. You will go back to your squadron.' Archibald saluted and left.

After that Trenchard appointed an officer named Dowdswell to lead the special squadron. The operation turned out exactly as Archibald had predicted – it was a total disaster.

Characteristically, Trenchard, who never referred to the matter again, called Archibald back a fortnight later and offered him a rôle in an even more curious assignment. Field-marshal Haig, like many of his senior staff, had gained experience of war mainly in the cavalry. He had confident expectations that when the battle of the Somme started the British infantry would break through creating a breach in the German lines. It was then proposed that at least a division of cavalry would pour through the gap created and fan out to the enemy's rear. Trenchard proposed that Archibald should form a unit of sixteen airmen, experienced horsemen, who would accompany the leading elements of the cavalry in their charge through the gap. They would be provided with two horse-drawn limbered wagons loaded with wireless equipment (which the mounted division did not possess) in order to report back intelligence to army GHQ about the developing situation. As an ardent horseman, Archibald accepted this mission with alacrity, but in the event no breach was made and the operation never took place – which was undoubtedly just as well for all concerned.

After the Battle of the Somme had dragged on for months of bloody, inconclusive fighting, Archibald having flown on operations far longer than most, was sent back to England and posted to Upavon as an instructor. In this unfamiliar rôle he soon became bored and restless, longing to get back to the war in France. He concluded that there were two types of RFC pilot, those who preferred to teach, and others who preferred to fight. He was no teacher.

When he was transferred to Netheravon in the same capacity he developed a high regard for the Canadian flying recruits who were beginning to arrive in some numbers. Most of them displayed a natural aptitude as pilots, more so, he thought, than the Australians, who, though equally enthusiastic and fearless, were, by and large, inclined to be somewhat clumsy when handling the delicate controls of the flying machines. He attributed this to the fact that most of the Aussies were large men with big fists! The few New Zealand and South African pilots that he came across also met with his whole-hearted approval.

To his relief, while still at Netheravon, he was given command of an independent flight to train the men in the artillery batteries of two Canadian divisions. This was an opportunity to pass on his considerable experience gained in war. He taught them the value of the clock code where the aerial observer, spotting an enemy battery and taking it as the centre, drew imaginary concentric circles on the ground below, outwards from 25 yards, 50 yards, 150 yards and so forth. Taking the north as 12 o'clock it was a simple matter to inform the battery, via morse messages to the squadron wireless hut, about where their shells were falling both in direction and distance from the German gun emplacement.

The standard of shooting varied enormously between batteries, but under reasonable circumstances the average artillery team could end up on target after no more than three corrections from the aeroplane carrying out the spotting. It became the practice for the pilot to do the ranging duties while his observer scanned the skies ready for possible attack from enemy fighters.

Explaining how both sides had developed a degree of cunning as the war had dragged on, he told his pupils of some of the ruses employed by the Germans. How, for example, the enemy often fired dummy shell flashes in an attempt to fool Allied artillery into wasting ammunition by shooting into an empty space. How careful study of photographs by an astute squadron intelligence officer would reveal the false from the true. Telltale paths worn by many feet leading into a wood invariably revealed the genuine gun site.

The standard of photography was improving all the time. He amused his pupils by showing them examples of the enormous box cameras carried in the observer's cockpit in the early days, comparing them with the smaller lighter models attached to the side of the fuselage currently in use and shooting considerably more pictures per flight.

He assured the trainees that fewer and fewer German aeroplanes were crossing the Allied lines while more and more Allied machines flew over enemy territory. Consequently, while the Germans had little up-to-date intelligence about what was going on in their opponent's areas, the RFC had detailed maps showing every yard of ground held by the enemy.

It was natural for young pilots to ask why the RFC never issued parachutes to aircrew. Archibald's answer was that it had nothing to do with any reluctance on the part of the authorities (compare with Sholto Douglas's view in Chapter 2 and experiments in Chapter 12), but that it was not a practical proposition. The packs were extremely bulky at that stage of their development and would hardly have fitted into the already cramped cockpits. The harness, too, was complicated; the web of straps could well have impeded movement during moments of crisis.

It was not surprising that the great fighter 'aces' of the period were hero-worshipped by the pupils. Both Germany and France had formed elite squadrons made up of the best pilots available, such as the 'Flying Circus' led by the famous Baron Manfred von Richthofen, the highest scoring ace of the First World War with eighty-three victories. Such squadrons were sent to operate in different battle areas according to where they were most needed.

Trenchard resisted pressure to create squadrons of this type. He believed, rightly, that the standard of the normal squadrons would fall if the more skilled pilots were creamed away, while novices, new to combat, would suffer from lack of the best examples to follow and from not having the protection that outstanding flight leaders could provide. Britain had her aces, but they were spread throughout the fighter force. Consequently the RFC had more effective squadrons than other nationalities and there were no 'second class' units. In aggregate the RFC had by far the highest number of kills by the war's end.

Archibald had an intimate knowledge of some of the aces. Above all others he admired Major J. T. B. McCudden, VC, for his sheer skill as a pilot and his intelligent approach to combat. Ironically he lost his life in a tragic flying accident over Archibald's own aerodrome.

Captain Albert Ball, VC, the shy, violin-playing loner, was in Archibald's estimation bound to get killed. In the air his personality became transformed and he charged into dog fights, no matter what the odds, with fearless disregard for his own safety.

The highest scoring British ace was Major E. Mannock, VC, with seventy-three kills. He managed to join the RFC in spite of being astigmatic in his left eye. He was an outstanding example of an unselfish leader and teacher. It was generally accepted within the RFC that his score would have been even higher if he had not, on occasion, moved aside to allow less experienced pilots to shoot down the enemy. It was on such an occasion that an artillery shell pierced his petrol tank and he was burnt alive.

The much publicized Canadian, Lieutenant-Colonel Billy Bishop, VC, was, according to James, a phoney whose 'victories', although he had started off well, later became largely a figment of his imagination. Apparently this was known in the RFC, but, because of his nationality, the truth was kept from the public in the interests of Allied accord. Bishop survived the war, married an extremely rich heiress and drank himself to death. Controversy over Bishop's wartime flying career persists to this day.

It was rare for the unsung heroes who flew in the slow, vulnerable reconnaissance and bombing aircraft to receive any public recognition for their humdrum yet dangerous work over enemy territory. Yet it was the pilots and observers who flew these machines, painstakingly gathering vital information over the years, who did so much to help in achieving final victory. Aeroplanes like the poor old B.E.2cs fell in their hundreds, providing the 'fodder' on which the German aces fed their glory.

Unexpectedly, Archibald was ordered to set up a training squadron at Yatesbury in Wiltshire. He formed the nucleus of this establishment, with ground personnel, instructors and Avro 504s all in place, but before a single pupil arrived, in June, 1917, he was promoted to Major and sent back to France to command 6 Squadron stationed at Abeele, an aerodrome considerably enlarged, with all the officers and men now living on the camp and shared between two squadrons. 6 Squadron was to work in close liaison with the 10th Army Corps whose HQ was in Abeele village itself. Feverish preparations were in hand for the forthcoming battle of Passchendaele.

Archibald's squadron had been equipped with twin-seat R.E.8s powered by an air-cooled 150 hp RAF 4a Vee-type tractor engine. These machines were an effective replacement for the 90 hp B.E.2cs. On these newer machines the positions were reversed and the observer now sat at the back giving him a much less restricted field of fire. Designed by the Royal Aircraft Factory, the emphasis was still on inherent stability, an ideal quality for bombing and reconnaissance roles, but a decided disadvantage when trying to evade the attentions of the more agile German fighters.

At first the R.E.8 gained a bad reputation among pilots because of its tendency to spin in, often with fatal results. This fault was cured by increasing the size of the fin areas. A Vickers machine gun was fitted under the left-side engine panels and synchronized with Constantinescu gear to fire through the propeller arc. A ring-mounted Lewis gun was provided for the observer. Archibald thought it was a first class machine, reliable, robust and a pleasure to fly. The R.E.8, or 'Harry Tate' in cockney rhyming slang after the well known music hall comedian, became the most widely used British two-seater on the Western Front. 4099 were built in all. In spite of being outclassed by enemy fighters, the machine served the Allied cause well, and when the war ended fifteen RAF squadrons were still flying R.E.8s.

Squadrons had grown bigger and Archibald's new command was no exception. 6 Squadron had twenty-four aeroplanes divided into three flights of eight. Under his leadership he had twenty-four pilots, twenty-four observers and two air gunners. A new development was the posting of fifty airmen under two wireless officers to the various artillery batteries at the front to ensure good communication from air to ground. The wireless officers had a tough job visiting their men at the various gun sites often under heavy enemy fire.

The Battle of Passchendaele was launched by the British on the last day of July, 1917. Haig hoped the army could achieve a major breakthrough, his initial aim being to dislodge the Germans from their dominating positions on the ridge of high ground between Westroosbeke and Broodseinde. It was a race against time to beat the rainstorms expected to break in about three weeks, but, inevitably, the rains came early making further advance impossible. Infantrymen sunk up to their thighs in mud, many drowning. Tanks waiting in reserve in the hope of exploiting the situation were rendered impotent. What had been planned as a lightning strike became bogged down. When the campaign at last came to an end in November the British-held Ypres Salient had been deepened by a mere five miles. The cost in lives was unimaginable: 300,000 British, more than 8,500 French and 260,000 Germans were killed, wounded, or, in the case of the British, disappeared into the mud without trace.

6 Squadron's duties during this campaign were to fly over the battle area at no more than 1500 feet trying to assess the British line

of advance. The infantry had been provided with flares to indicate their position to the aircraft overhead. But, understandably, the soldiers were not inclined to set them off and give their situation away to the enemy.

With Autumn came a curious ground mist which pervaded the battlefield. It was not discernible from below but rose to about 3500 feet like a brown heat haze where it smoothed off into a level upper surface stretching away to a misty horizon. It made artillery spotting impossible, a phenomenon difficult to explain to the gunners on the ground.

Fortunately, there was little interference from enemy aircraft. Allied fighters were on constant offensive patrol and did a good job keeping them at bay. Over the battleground the sky was filled with flying shells in both directions and it was a miracle that more of the many low flying machines were not brought down.

In one of Archibald's R.E.8s an observer, ranging for a howitzer battery during one of the clearer days, turned his head in time to see a shell actually coming straight for him. He yelled to the pilot to duck and the shell went straight through the fuselage just behind the observer's seat, cutting one of the longerons and a cross section. Neither man was hurt and they managed to return safely to base.

During this period Abeele aerodrome was bombed once by the enemy. It was at night and the attack was made by a single machine. The German dropped a stick of a dozen or so anti-personnel bombs. Weighing about 20 lbs, they had an eighteen-inch metal rod sticking out of the nose. As soon as this came in contact with the ground it detonated the bomb causing an outburst of lethal slivers of jagged metal. The occupants of the camp, having warning of the enemy's approach, had slipped into the slit trenches dug outside each hut. Two men above ground during the raid, a wireless officer and a cook, were both killed.

By the end of the battle Archibald's squadron had sustained fifty-four casualties – killed, captured and wounded. The aircrew of 6 Squadron had, in that short period, been wiped out and replaced. From the days back in 1915 on 16 Squadron only Playfair, his original flight commander, and himself had survived to continue flying.

6 Squadron was withdrawn from active service, reduced in num-

bers of aircraft and men, and engaged in introducing high-ranking army officers to the value of cooperation between air and ground. Demonstrations were arranged by taking them for flights behind the lines, allowing them to participate in 'combat' with the use of camera guns, and giving lectures illustrated with photographic maps.

The following year, now a Lieutenant-Colonel and a senior RFC adviser on training in France, Archibald took a day off from his administrative duties. Loading bombs onto the racks of an R.E.8, and with a mechanic in the observer's seat, he took off to fly to the Lys Salient where Ludendorff's troops had broken through the Allied lines to a depth of 40 miles. Flying up the dead straight Villa Bretonneux road, the ground below looked deserted. But he knew that every farmhouse and cottage must be occupied by German soldiers. Picking his target, a spreading farmhouse adjacent to the track, he flew up and down the route four times to make sure his bombing would be accurate. He set his bomb sight, a crude metal device attached to the outside of the pilot's cockpit. He checked the two indicators, one for height above ground, the other for direction, allowing for drift. The whole area remained deserted. There was no opposition. On the fourth run he let the bombs go. He missed his target by a good 600 yards, but, to his amazement and delight, they landed smack on top of another, bigger farmhouse further down the road. He flew home satisfied – the raid on Abeele aerodrome the previous year had been avenged.

After the war Archibald William Henry James, MC, became an important figure in his country's government, eventually retiring as Sir Archibald James to farm his many acres while continuing to enjoy the country sports that had always brought him so much pleasure.

# EPILOGUE

And so that was it. On the eleventh hour of the eleventh day of the eleventh month of 1918 hostilities ceased and 'the war to end all wars' was over.

From the early days when Archibald James had aimed his rifle at an enemy aircraft and, to his astonishment, missed almost literally by a mile the technology of killing had progressed to the development of the remarkably fast and manoeuvrable single-seat, twin-gun scout fighters such as the speedy Sopwith Camel, the S. E. 5, and Germany's latest Albatros, the fore-runners of the Spitfires and Messerschmitts of the next World War.

The tiny Royal Flying Corps of four squadrons had ventured into France at the beginning with its sixty-three underpowered aero-planes, flown and kept in the air by a mere 105 officers and 755 other ranks, none possessing any idea of the nature or scale of duties that lay ahead.

At the beginning resources were hard stretched to produce enough aircraft to replace losses, let alone build up greater numbers. To speed up the supplies the Government built National Aircraft Factories, but these, with the exception of the long-established Royal Aircraft Factory, were a failure. They ran out of control, wasting money through the gross inefficiency of an inexperienced management. Bristol Fighters, produced by private manufacturers, were turned out for £1,350, while National Factories expended more than £5,000 on building the same machine. (The same price as a Spitfire in the Second World War). An enthusiastic team at the Sopwith works constructed the excellent Sopwith Pup for £711.

Yet by the Armistice so remarkably had these early setbacks been overcome, especially the shortage of aero engines, that the Royal Air

Force stood as the greatest air force in the world with its back-up industry producing no less than 3500 aeroplanes per *month*. From a minuscule force it had grown to a total of 22,647 machines of all types, including 3,300 aircraft on first-line strength and 103 airships established in nearly 200 squadrons at home and overseas. This mighty new service was maintained by 27,333 officers, 263,837 other ranks and around 25,000 members of the Women's Royal Air Force.

Yet none of this had been attained without great sacrifice. Over the course of more than four years of war the RFC and the RNAS suffered losses of 4,579 officers and 1,587 men killed, 2,839 officers and 373 men missing or interned, mostly after being shot down, and 5,369 officers and 1,876 men wounded, also mainly in aerial combat.

Matters had grown worse before they got better. In 1916 the average flying hours of a pilot, observer or gunner before being shot down had been 295. By March, 1917, it had dropped to 92 hours. After that, with the advent of better machines and more thorough training, the operational life expectancy of aircrew gradually increased.

It had been a hard-won battle and in the coming days of peace those gains were almost thrown away. Within two years the Royal Air Force had been reduced to one tenth of its ultimate wartime strength. Voices had been raised to disband this, the first independent air force, and hive off what was left between the two older services. Only the dogged determination and far-seeing vision of Hugh Trenchard and a few others of like mind saved the Royal Air Force. To them goes the honour that enough of it remained to fight the Battle of Britain in 1940 and gain victory by a slender margin.

Having won this battle, Britain went on to build a strategic bomber force the like of which the world had never seen before. The next generation of airmen, imbued with the same spirit as those who had flown little more than two decades before, took the conflict to the door of the enemy without respite and for an even longer war.

# INDEX

*AIRCRAFT: ENGINES*
American Curtiss V8 90/160 hp. V12 250/375 hp water-cooled, 62
American Liberty motors V12 400 hp water-cooled, 94
American V8 0.X. 90 hp model, 175
Antionette 8-cylinder 24 hp water-cooled, 29
Anzani 3 cylinder 35 hp radial air-cooled, 87
Beardmore 6 cylinder in-line 160 hp water-cooled, 151
Clerget rotary 80 hp air-cooled, 163
Fiat 6 cylinder in-line 300 hp water-cooled; also produced a giant V12 700 hp water-cooled, 93
Green 6 cylinder in-line 80–100 hp water-cooled, 22, 65
Hispano-Suiza V8 180/220/300 hp water-cooled, 156
Isotta-Fraschini: 6 cylinder in-line 150 hp, 270 hp, 93
J. A. Prestwich 9 hp motorcycle engine fitted to A. V. Roe's early triplane, 30
Le Rhone Gnome monosoupape rotary: 50 hp, 31, 32, 175; 70 hp, 43, 44,45, 49, 51; 80 hp, 89, 92, 163, 165, 218; 90 hp, 182; 100 hp, 140, 143, 176; 110 hp, 155, 163, 167; 150 hp, 187, 219; 160 hp, 147; 180 hp, 167
Maybach 6 cylinder in-line. 300 hp water-cooled, German-built under licence in Italy, 68; also 250 hp x 5 in R43, 171.
Mercedes 6 cylinder in-line 260 hp D.1Va, water-cooled, 170, 171; 120 to 220 hp versions used in fighter and other aircraft.
Renault all in-line or V configuration 70 hp, 43, 44, 50, 62
Rolls Royce: Hawk 6-cylinder in-line 100 hp water-cooled, 65. All V 12s: Eagle V1 250 hp; Eagle V111 375 hp, 93, 111, 112
Eagle I 250 hp; 113, 114, 115, 128; 350 hp, 70, 128
Royal Aircraft Factory V8 90/130 hp, 51; V12 150 hp, 230. All air-cooled. (RAF engines were similar to those of Renault)
Salmson (Canton Unne) 9M radial 120 hp, 180
S.P.A. Societa Piemonese Automobili, 68, 69, 70
Sunbeam 'The Arab' V8 235 hp, 'The Maori' V12 275 hp, 111, 112
Wolseley Viper high compression in-line 200 hp, 156

*AIRCRAFT: LAND BASED*
Albatros, 53, 54, 83; D.V., 157, 158, 235
Austro-Daimler 120 hp, 38
Aviatik, 142, 143, 144, 145
Avro, 37, 45, 56, 83; Lancaster, World War II, 30, 128, 132, 171; Early Avro, 141; 504K, 155, 156, 175, 230; (Aus), 194; 504J, 163, 164, 166
Boeing B.17, World War II, 152
B.E.2, 37, 83, 147; B.E.2c, 43, 44, 45, 49, 51, 61, 83, 141, 175, 196, 197, 213, 215, 219, 221, 223, 224, 226, 230; (Australian) B.E.2e, 193, 196, 198; B.E.2a, 217
B.E.8, 45
Bleriot – early type, 45, 177, 211
'Blue Mouse' German prototype 2-seat fighter, 220
Bristol 'Bullet', 149; 'Boxkite', 175; Scout/Fighter ('Barnwell's Baby'), 176, 177, 179, 181, 182, 219, 224, 225, 235; (Aus), 196, 198
British Deperdussin, 37
Caproni Ca (Ca 3), 93; C42 triplanes, 93–96

*237*